Migrants and refugees

Migrants and Refugees

Muslim and Christian
Pakistani families
in Bristol

PATRICIA JEFFERY

Research Fellow, Department of Social Anthropology
University of Edinburgh

Cambridge University Press

Cambridge

London · New York · Melbourne

Published by the Syndics of the Cambridge University Press
The Pitt Building, Trumpington Street, Cambridge CB2 1RP
Bentley House, 200 Euston Road, London NW1 2DB
32 East 57th Street, New York, NY 10022, USA
296 Beaconsfield Parade, Middle Park, Melbourne 3206, Australia

First published 1976

Printed in Great Britain at the University Printing House, Cambridge
(Euan Phillips, University Printer)

Library of Congress Cataloguing in Publication Data
Jeffery, Patricia, 1947—
    Migrants and refugees.
    Bibliography.
    Includes index.
    1. Pakistanis in Bristol, Eng. 2. Bristol, Eng. — Foreign
population. 3. Christians in Bristol, Eng. 4. Muslims in Bristol,
Eng. I. Title.
DA690.B8J43   942.3'93'00491412   75-25428
ISBN 0 521 21070 4

Contents

'Why for one lost home mourn, when grief
Can find so many a lodging place?'

From a *ghazal* in *Bal-i-Jibril* by
Muhammad Iqbal, translated
by V.G. Kiernan

Acknowledgements

During the course of the research that led to this book, several people helped me by discussing my work with me and reading various reports which I produced. Professor Michael Banton and Dr Mick Lineton were my supervisors at Bristol and I am grateful for advice which they gave me. I also wish to thank Professor Adrian Mayer, Dr Ian Hamnett, Dr Roger Ballard, Catherine Ballard, Dr Verity Saifullah-Khan and Dr Jonathan Parry for helpful comments on my work, and Miss Sabiha Kaukeb who taught me Urdu. Special thanks are due to my husband who became engulfed in my research and was involved in my obligations to my 'kin'. He also, most conveniently, goes by the name of Jeffery, which my informants unanimously associated with *Jafri* and thus accorded me the high status of a supposed descendant of the sixth *Imam*! He has also discussed my work with me at all stages, and has (usually willingly) helped me with some of the donkey-work of proofing and correcting drafts. Finally, I am obviously greatly indebted to my informants: not only did they provide me with the information on which this book is based, but they also welcomed me into their families with a warmth I had no right to expect.

Some people might take offence at a white person writing a report of this kind: I am fully aware that the area under discussion is very sensitive and that there is considerable resentment of the snoopings of white researchers. There is little that I can do about being white, and neither I nor my informants (as far as I know) see what I was doing as snooping, so I hope that my research will not be taken in that spirit. I would like my efforts to interpret my informants and present a view of their life in this country as they see it to go some way towards overcoming those misunderstandings which contribute to racial and inter-ethnic hostility in Britain.

January 1976 P.J.

Note

In order to preserve the anonymity of my informants, I have used pseudonyms throughout. Muslims have been given Muslim names, while the Christians have been given biblical or British names. The pseudonyms of spouses begin with the same letter.

The meanings of Urdu and Arabic words are given in the text where they are first used, and also in the glossary at the end; Urdu and Arabic words have been printed in italics throughout. When the fieldwork began, Pakistan still consisted of West Pakistan and East Pakistan (now known as Bangladesh). In the text I use 'Pakistan' to refer to the old west wing which remained after the secession of Bangladesh.

As will be seen, many Pakistani migrants in Britain send money to Pakistan, so something needs to be said about exchange rates: for some years several exchange rates have operated with respect to the Pakistani rupee. British people living in Pakistan obtained about Rs. 12/- per £1 sterling, and this exchange rate probably gives the closest comparability when costs of living are compared. However, Pakistanis living abroad remitting money through banks and post offices obtained Rs. 20/- per £1 sterling (until the rupee was devalued in 1974, when the rate became about Rs. 24/-). Even more favourable rates could be obtained through black-market and extra-legal routes, sometimes over Rs. 30/- per £1 sterling. Remittances of £10 per month would thus give upwards of Rs. 200/-, a sum which is more than many families earn through work in Pakistan: this discrepancy between exchange rates and costs of living is crucial for migrants in Britain.

Introduction

Over the last fifteen years, coloured immigration into Britain has frequently been in the forefront of the news, but all too often the material on this subject has been both anchored in the present and essentially ethnocentric. This book is about a small number of Pakistani families living in Britain, but it is impossible to understand their position without a consideration of the wider context within which their actions are set.

On occasion, Britain's colonial past is referred to in discussions of the growth of hostile and unflattering racial stereotypes: the slave trade, plantation economies, and colonial rule are argued to be intimately connected with the development of numerous 'racial classifications' (usually placing the white or Aryan at the apex of the species of man) during the nineteenth century, which are still held widely by people in Britain. But the crucial structural and economic impact of colonialism on both Britain and her colonies is rarely traced out. I do not have the space (nor the expertise) to deal properly with four hundred years of European economic history. However, I consider that it is vital that international migration is seen with the backdrop of colonialism clearly in view. 'Expanding Europe' penetrated the farthest corners of the world to control markets for valued imports to its own countries, and later monopolized certain areas of the world as outlets for its own manufactures. Predatory activities of colonists, latter-day ones as well as those in previous centuries, have left a world divided between the rich and industrialized nations and the poor countries of the Third World, which are characterized by food shortages, malnourished populations, enormous rates of un- and under-employment and few jobs in manufacturing industries. Even today, the countries of the Third World are still the sources of raw materials (crops, minerals) which the industrial world processes. Most of the coloured people in Britain come from countries affected in these ways by Britain.

The Indian sub-continent is one such area, often called the Brightest Jewel in the British Crown, and not without reason. Britain profited greatly from her relationship with India: the depredations which almost bankrupted Bengal in the 1760s, the remittances of the East India Company servants, the sordid opium trade from Bengal to China, the collection of land revenues in the tradition of the Mughals, the gradual

1

destruction of a flourishing textile industry by cheaper Lancashire imports and restrictions on the export of Indian textiles to Britain, and the use of native soldiers to fight Britain's colonial wars elsewhere — all are critical (if rarely publicized) benefits which Britain brought out of India. India received the very dubious benefit of 'civilization' and the very obvious damage which comes from the siphoning-off of resources and living under foreign rule. That Britain is an industrial nation and that the countries of the Indian sub-continent have poor, basically agricultural economies are not unconnected facts of history. British control of Indian markets is one of the important factors behind the development of the industrial revolution in Britain. This control also had an important and destructive impact on manufacturing industries in India. Yet how rarely are allusions made to the irony of Indians' and Pakistanis' working in textile mills in Lancashire and Yorkshire, or in jute mills in Dundee.

The destinies of the Indian sub-continent and of Britain have long been intertwined, and we should not be surprised that Indians and Pakistanis in search of work should have looked to Britain, which was itself in search of cheap labour to man industries where wages were too unattractive to appeal to British people. Having siphoned-off natural resources, we now siphon-off man-power when we consider it to be in our interests. Until 1962, people from the Indian sub-continent could enter Britain freely, but now we are only willing to take in skilled workers (such as doctors) which their countries can ill afford to lose, and we exclude those who have little education or training, complacent about the fate to which we relegate them in their own country: unemployment and poverty. Only one of my informants, a young Christian woman, saw herself within this long-term perspective: she gleefully reported to me how she had responded to being asked why 'you people come to our country' by saying that they came to retrieve the *Koh-i-noor* diamond![1] My other informants were unaware of the wider historical and structural aspects of their migration: they saw themselves as individuals living in a poor country and unable to provide properly for their families, who tried to make the best of the chances which life presented to them. In the account which follows, I have tried to withdraw myself as much as possible, and present a picture of the world as my informants see it: that they have not been made aware of the historical implications of their migration does not make those facets of the situation irrelevant. While they do not obtrude themselves in what follows, they must be borne in mind in any analysis of international migration today.

Not only have I accused much of the writing on race relations in Britain of being apparently unaware of (or unwilling to make explicit) the historical dimensions of immigration from the New Commonwealth, but I have also suggested that much of it is ethnocentric. By this I do not mean simply that the response of British people has been hostile and even explicitly racialist in tone. Certainly a great deal of antagonism and intolerance of people physically and culturally different have evidenced themselves: the 'tradition of tolerance' which we are so proud of in Britain is in reality shallow and fraudulent. Ethnocentrism is certainly present in this form, but even in serious reports on the coloured population in Britain it is all too common to find an ethnocentrism of another sort.

By this I mean that the geographical base in Britain is assumed to be important, and there is little attempt to take seriously the links which extend outside Britain to the sending country. In what follows, I shall place a great deal of emphasis on these links, for they are important to my informants as well as having analytical relevance. Firstly, migrants are likely to retain cultural links with their place of origin. Adult migrants do not arrive in Britain *tabulae rasae*; they have been socialized in Pakistan, and they bring to Britain evaluations, perceptions, memories and predispositions which have to be borne in mind when considering their behaviour in Britain. Secondly, many of them retain important social and economic links with their place of origin. Social relationships can persist over large distances, and the obligations which kin have to one another are often expected to persist after the separation which migration brings. Moreover, as will be seen, many links which could be established in Britain are not.

In addition, many of the migrants maintain important economic links with their homes: in many Third World countries remittances from nationals overseas make a vital contribution to their economies, and many families who are unable to make a living in their own country depend on money sent from members who have gone abroad in search of work. Pakistan is one such country, and migrants in Britain often send substantial sums of money to their homes, for the use of themselves or their relatives. In answer to those who complain of the removal of earnings to Pakistan, I would suggest that the colonial past be taken into account: Britain remitted enormous sums of money from the Indian subcontinent in one form or another, and current aid and trading relationships perpetuate this drain: work is scarce in Pakistan, and the remittances of migrants overseas represent the legitimate desire of

3

people to provide a livelihood for their families. Mahbub ul Haq puts it this way:

> I argued from the experience of India and Pakistan that, when we were associated with Britain in a partnership in the nineteenth century and the British had this slight problem about financing their industrial revolution and their structural transformation, we willingly brought out our gold and our diamonds and our agricultural produce for nominal prices and told them to go ahead and not lose the opportunity for a technological breakthrough. We cheerfully stayed on as an agrarian economy and applauded the industrial strides of our partner. In the modern terminology, such a thing will be called a transfer of resources, but the world was such a happy community at that time that we never even dreamed of such terms or asked for performance audits.
>
> Mr. Polanski, unreasonable as he is, wanted to know the magnitude of the transfer and I mentioned an off-the-cuff figure of $100 million — a modest estimate for which I may be disowned by my fellow economists in the sub-continent . . . I argued that this amount could be treated as a voluntary loan, at 6% interest, which has been multiplying happily over the years so that it stands at $410 million today.[2]

Remittances from Pakistanis abroad are a mere drop in the ocean, and are a tiny contribution to redressing the balance of British imperialism in India, even though they are very important at an individual level. That they are so critical to the economy of Pakistan is a reflection of the low earning power of her resources and the small sums she can earn from the export of manufactures. The economic ties which the migrants have with their place of origin have a bearing on the way they see themselves in Britain: as will be seen, for some of them there is a considerable discrepancy between their objective class position in Britain and their subjective position. Here again, the links which go beyond Britain have to be considered, for many of them are rating themselves within the status system at home, and are hoping that they will return there when they have been able to save enough to permit them to live respectably in Pakistan. It would be inhumane to see this desire as support for a policy of repatriation, for many would be unable to survive if they were sent back, and for many the desire to return is probably no more than a useful myth. Investment of savings in Pakistan and talk of returning nevertheless have an important bearing on their life in Britain.

On all these counts, the analysis has to step outside the confines of

Britain, and include the other end of the migration: any analysis which does not incorporate the important links between both ends of the migration situation will be impoverished. All social research has problems of trying to put boundaries on the social systems which are being studied in order that the exercise may be feasible. It is critical, though, that the delimitation of the unit for study does not lead to the misconstruction of the social processes within it, and I would argue that this is a serious danger if the geographical base in Britain is assumed to be a suitable unit for the analysis of the responses of migrants and of their position in Britain.

This report is a revised and abridged version of a Ph.D. thesis submitted at Bristol University in 1973.[3] It is the result of fieldwork conducted in Bristol and Pakistan during 1970 and 1971. When I began the research, I had intended to focus on adolescent Pakistani girls, particularly with respect to their parents' wishes to maintain *purdah* in Britain and to arrange the marriages of their children. I soon realized, however, that there were few conflicts between the girls and their parents, and I was very much struck with the ways in which the migrants were able to maintain a 'Pakistani' identity. I decided to shift the concern of the research and focus much more on the ways in which certain elements of the migrants' culture can be protected and how children may be brought up in a Pakistani domestic setting in Britain. In other words, I began to focus on the social processes involved in non-assimilation and the maintenance of ethnic boundaries. I made contact with informants through informal introductions, and was fortunate to be introduced to some Christian Pakistanis, as they act as useful foils to the Muslims. I go into the details of the fieldwork in Chapter 3. As a woman, I had special advantages over a man in looking at the home-lives of my informants, and it is on these private aspects of their lives that this report concentrates. These are the parts of their lives over which they have most control in the choice of activities and associates. At the moment, the adult migrants regard their work instrumentally, but it is too early to know yet how their children will react to the opportunities presented to them in Britain.

As will be seen, the Muslim and Christian informants come from urban backgrounds, and they were not involved in agricultural work in Pakistan; thus they cannot be said to be representative of Pakistanis as a whole, and this raises problems of generalizability from this research. On the other hand, other reports on Pakistanis in Britain, and indeed on Indians too, suggest that there are several parallels with the Muslim informants, even though they come from a rather unusual background.[4] As will be seen later, the Christians stand apart from the more general picture.

1. The background: Pakistan

1.0 Introduction

A central proposition of this book is that it is not possible to understand the behaviour and aspirations of my informants in Bristol without a close consideration of their life-styles and life-chances in Pakistan. This first chapter looks at various issues concerning Pakistan which are of particular relevance to the later chapters.

1.1 Islam in the Indian sub-continent[1]

Islam has a long history in India. Muslim traders are thought to have arrived near present-day Karachi in the first century after Mohammed, and Sind was under Arab rule early in the eighth century A.D. Thereafter most Muslim influence came overland from Turkestan, Afghanistan and Persia, and much of north India was under Muslim rule for several centuries. The Mughal dynasty was the most famous and last of the immigrant Muslim dynasties. Between 1525 (when Babur invaded 'Hindustan') and 1707 (when Aurangzeb died), the Mughals were more or less supreme over north India, and for a time their kingdom stretched into the Deccan, carrying with it an Islamic influence. After 1707, Mughal power declined: Aurangzeb left seventeen potential candidates for the throne and the internecine struggles left the Mughal Empire vulnerable to the growing power of the Marathas and the Sikhs, and invasions from Afghanistan and Persia during the eighteenth century. Already, the British East India Company had a base in Calcutta and in 1698 had been granted the right to collect the Emperor's share of revenue in Calcutta and the surrounding villages. During the following century, the Company gained supremacy over the other European trading concerns and took advantage of the power vacuum in north India. In 1803, the Mughal Emperor Shah Alam was taken into British protection and a British Resident in Delhi supervised his affairs. Bahadur Shah (the last Mughal Emperor) was exiled to Burma after being used as a figurehead in the Sepoy Revolt in 1857, and after that, except in some princely states, Muslim rule was replaced by British.

By this time, many people in north India were Muslim. Some undoubtedly were the descendants of men who had come to India with the

Muslim conquerors, but there are also reports of voluntary mass conversions from Hinduism. It is not possible to assess the relative numbers coming from these two sources, as converts often took on respectable Muslim names (such as Sheikh and Ashraf) which imply immigrant origins. Islam is thought to have spread in India largely because it offered better social status, especially to the members of low castes. Today Bengal and some parts of Punjab are the areas of highest Muslim concentration, while the middle Ganges lowlands and central India have predominantly Hindu populations, despite being under Muslim rule for over five hundred years. Tayyeb suggests that Punjab and Bengal were left with 'low caste' and Muslim populations after people of 'high caste' had evacuated to the central areas which were less vulnerable to invasion. This is not a satisfactory interpretation, however, and given the dearth of historical material, it remains unclear why the Muslim and Hindu populations are distributed in the way they are in north India.[2]

During Muslim rule, reference was constantly made back to Persia and Arabia in architecture, poetry and painting as well as in religious matters, and as a result many Muslims in India retained a certain aloofness from Indian traditions. Nevertheless, Islam in India has incorporated many Indian customs through its converts, and it is distinguishable from Islam in other parts of the world.

For more detailed accounts of Islam, I refer the reader to several sources.[3] Islam arose largely as a revolt against idolatry and social injustice. Its central precept is the unity of Allah, and 'islam' means subjection to his will: a 'muslim' is one who has subjected himself to God. ('Islam' and 'Muslim' come from the same Arabic root: *s-l-m*.) God gave man many gifts, including the ability to discriminate between good and evil, but man forgot the gifts and God sent messengers or prophets to put man back on the right course. The prophethood included Abraham (*Hazrat Ibrahim*) and Christ (*Hazrat Isa*) and was ended with Mohammed, who preached that only God is worthy of worship, that all men are equal and brothers and that only the good man will be rewarded in the after-life. The Koran Sherif contains the definitive account of God's ordinances, though Jewish and early Christian writings are also revered. There are commentaries on the preachings of Mohammed, and the *hadith* (the accounts of the doings of Mohammed) are used as authority in legal decisions. Islamic law is not enforced by a church or organized priesthood. There are several schools of Islamic jurisprudence, and two major divisions to which the laity belong: Sunnis constitute about 90 per cent of the Muslims in Pakistan, while Shias

(Shiites) make up most of the remaining 10 per cent.[4] Sunnis and Shias worship at different mosques. The differences between them focus on the succession to the Caliphate in the early days of Islam: briefly, the Shias considered that the Caliphate should go to the descendants of the prophet, while the Sunnis believed that it should be awarded on merit. All my Muslim informants were Sunni.

Islam has five 'pillars'. Three are supposedly compulsory and are the confession of faith or *kalimah* (*la ilaha illallah Mohammed rasul allah*, meaning 'there is no god but Allah and Mohammed is his prophet'); *namaz* (prayer, which should be performed five times a day at specified times after the requisite ablutions) and *roza* (fasting, in particular the complete abstinence from eating, drinking, smoking, and sexual intercourse between sunrise and sunset during the month of *Ramzan*). The two remaining pillars are compulsory only for those with means and are *haj* (pilgrimage to Mecca during the month of *Zulhaj*) and *zukat* (tithes for public works and sustenance of the poor, levied at various rates for cash, gold and silver). It is important to bear in mind that Islam does not portion life into 'religious' and 'secular' aspects. Many Muslim theologians argue that Islam provides a blueprint for the organization of society and covers economic, political and family relationships just as much as it decrees how Allah should be worshipped through prayer. Thus, over and above the five central duties of Muslims, Islamic doctrine specifies desirable behaviour in other areas.

One such field relates to domestic matters, in particular to the position of men and women in an Islamic society and the importance of marriage and family life. There is spiritual equality between the sexes, and religious and secular duties are the same for men and women. At the same time, however, men and women have special aptitudes and therefore special responsibilities. The primary and essential vocation of women is motherhood, and men are suited for activity in the political and economic spheres. Stable family life is essential for the stability of society and marriage is incumbent on Muslims. Marriage is a civil contract; both parties may write terms into the contract and are required to give their consent. Marriages may be dissolved, but there are checks to prevent divorce becoming too prevalent. Either party may initiate divorce proceedings, though it is more difficult for the woman. Stable family life is crucial and several injunctions are designed to preserve it. Women are discouraged from taking on activities outside the home, so that they do not neglect their domestic duties. In public, men and women are supposed to behave in certain ways so that they are not

9

tempted into marital infidelity. People should be modest and cast their eyes down in mixed company, and the body should be well covered so that men and women do not draw attention to one another. Many commentators say that women should only leave the home when absolutely necessary, to prevent them from falling into temptation and also to facilitate the dutiful fulfilment of their womanly tasks. In Pakistan, very few women work outside the home, and girls tend to receive less schooling than boys.

Some Muslim men have more than one wife, but in fact there is a religious debate about the permissibility of polygamy for Muslims. Some theologians argue that it is permissible for a man to have up to four wives at one time. Others point to a text in the Koran to the effect that a man should only take more than one wife if he can treat the co-wives equally: they argue that this is an implicit prohibition of polygamy. In the circles I knew, polygamy was very rare (I came across only two cases): most informants considered that to take on two wives was folly, and they held very negative stereotypes about the ways in which a woman would treat her co-wife and step-children.

There are several practices in Pakistani Islam which indicate the influence of Hinduism. For instance, until the Partition of India in 1947 there were many shrines which were used jointly by Muslims and Hindus. Since 1947, those shrines in Pakistan have continued to be patronized by Muslims. Often the shrine is the grave of a holy man and Allah may be approached through the dead man for the granting of favours such as the gift of sons or recovery from illness. This practice is contrary to one of the central tenets of Islam, that God should be approached directly by a believer and not through a mediator. There also seems to be widespread belief in various beings such as ghosts and demons which can influence a person's life: again these are not part of orthodox Islam.[5]

Local custom has also influenced the organization of marriages, in particular in the giving of dowries. According to Islam, a man should give his wife a sum of money when they marry (the *mahr-i-mithl*), which he forfeits if he initiates divorce and which she must return if she divorces him. The wife brings no property to the marriage until her parents die, when she is entitled to a share of their property (though a smaller share than goes to her brother). In Pakistan, it is rare for the *mahr* to be given, though a sum may be agreed, and eventually given if the man dies before his wife or divorces her. The bride's relatives, however, are expected to donate a dowry, which should include clothing, jewellery and household effects. Marriage expenses are often considerable for the families of the brides, and are widely criticized as Hindu practice.[6]

It can be seen that Islamic pronouncements cover a wide range of activities, from the 'religious' to the domestic, but also that Islam in the Indian context has incorporated some unorthodox beliefs and practices. There are, in addition, several ways in which individual Muslims fall short of the requirements of their religion. In Pakistan, many people say the *kalimah* and the prayers, but by no means all, and few of my informants in Bristol prayed regularly, though they regard themselves as Muslims. In Pakistan, the fast during *Ramzan* is taken very seriously, and working hours are altered to make it easier to fast. But here again it is possible to avoid fasting: illness or 'fever' are sufficient reasons for failing to fast; whereas it is permissible to make up lost days later, probably only the most religious do so. In Bristol, very few informants fasted, and they usually claimed to be unwell, or that working hours made it too difficult. The payment of *zukat* is rather a problem in Pakistan, since the governmental machinery is not that of an Islamic state but has retained much of its pre-independence structures. *Zukat* can be paid individually by giving directly to the poor, but the element of compulsion is absent and many who could pay the tithe do not. Again, *haj* is another religious obligation which is not performed by all who could afford the expense: in some circles, people of limited means may save for years to go to Mecca, and achieve the honour of being *haji*, while many wealthy people are not interested in gaining religious merit.[7] Islam also forbids the consumption of intoxicants (such as alcohol) and pork, and gambling is also proscribed. Pork is virtually unobtainable in Pakistan, but many wealthy Pakistanis drink alcohol and gamble. Islamic requirements are not always strictly adhered to in connection with marriage. Parties to a marriage should be able to give their consent, but the parties often have little say and even to veto an arrangement would be frowned upon. Again, marriage is a social contract and is not indissoluble: however, divorces are rare in Pakistan, and fear of dishonour and stigma puts pressure on the parties to overcome their differences.

Islam is a religion which prescribes behaviour in many spheres of life, and in Pakistan not only has pristine Islam been overlaid with local custom but there is also variation in the 'religious' commitment of individual Pakistanis. Nevertheless, Islam is a considerable force to be reckoned with, for its impact extends beyond the narrowly 'religious' into the political sphere. Many Pakistanis who are lax in their religious duties nonetheless regard themselves as Muslims, because, for Pakistanis, Islam

and patriotism are inextricably intertwined. The ideology behind
Pakistan, continually reasserted in schools and the mass media, stresses
the importance of a nation-state for Muslims independent of Hindus.
Islam has come to have political significance, and many Muslims have
long regarded themselves as essentially different from the mass of the
Hindu population. In the next section, I look at some of the recent political consequences of this aloofness.

1.2 History of Pakistan[8]

Although there are Muslims in most parts of the Indian sub-continent,
they are not distributed evenly. It is only in the areas which became the
two wings of Pakistan in 1947 that Muslims formed the majority of the
population (apart from the Princely State of Jammu and Kashmir, which
was taken over by India). The Muslim population of India was culturally
diverse, having many cultural features such as some items of dress and
language, in common with the people of other religions living around
them. Moreover, people in different regions of India had different experiences during the British Raj. Bengal, for instance, was effectively
held by the British from about 1700 onwards, and was the site of such
extensive plunder in the 1760s that bankruptcy nearly ensued. Later,
Bengal was used as a major source of the opium used in trading with
China. Punjab, on the other hand, did not fall to the British until 1849,
after two campaigns against the Sikh rulers. Punjab and the North West
Frontier were of vital strategic importance since they were vulnerable to
invasion from central Asia, and early British administrators were often
quite explicit about the need to introduce improvements in the area so
that the local population would remain loyal to the British cause. The
land of the Indus basin is of good quality, but the growth of crops de-
pends on irrigation, as rainfall is inadequate. An extensive irrigation programme established in the late nineteenth century continued until some
twenty million acres had been added to the cultivable land. Punjab is
now one of the most productive agricultural areas in the Indian sub-
continent.[9] Yet other Muslims in India were never directly under British
rule. Kashmir, for instance, was sold by the British in 1849 to the Hindu
rajah of Jammu, and his descendants retained control for the next
century.

Thus, in the middle of the nineteenth century, the Muslim population exhibited regional differences, both in culture and in experience
of British rule. A great deal of literature discusses how and why such a

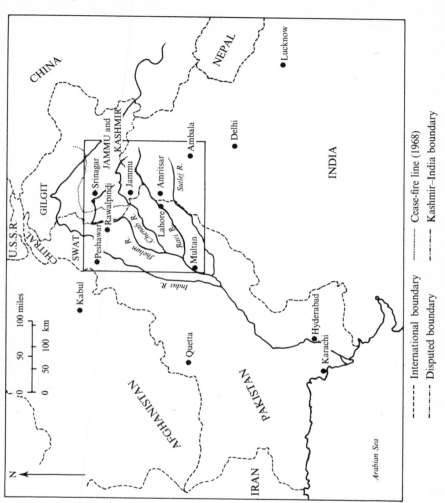

Map 1. Pakistan and north-west India

diverse population which lacked any central organization arrived in the 1940s at the point where it gave substantial backing to the demands of the Muslim League for a separate Muslim state in the Indian sub-continent. On the one hand, Tayyeb argues that one of the causes of the separation between Hindus and Muslims in British India was the favour-able treatment accorded to Hindus and others at the expense of Muslims. There does seem to be some evidence that the British adminis-tration was wary of Muslims after 1857, and Muslims were under-represented in the administrative positions open to Indians. However, Gopal considers that withdrawal on the part of Muslims was at least as important, for, by refusing to take up European education, many Muslims effectively disqualified themselves from work in the adminis-tration. Until the establishment of the Muslim Anglo-Oriental College at Aligarh in 1875 few Muslims knew English. It also seems that the British were pleased to encourage the development of a 'Muslim identity' to counterbalance the Indian National Congress, formed in 1885. It was felt that the Muslims had cause for grievances against the British, and that it was judicious to direct their hostility onto the Hindus, so that a united nationalist movement would not develop. British staff at Aligarh wrote of the dangers to Muslims of Hindu hegemony in an independent India, and this fell on fertile ground, as Muslims would inevitably be a minority. Muslims also felt threatened by the growth of several Hindu revivalist movements in the last years of the nineteenth century. In 1906 the Viceroy (Lord Minto) summoned several prominent Muslims and discussed the formation of the Muslim League and the granting of special rights to Muslims as a 'community' in India.[10]

In fact, the Muslim League soon developed an anti-British stance. The annulling of the partition of Bengal in 1912 was regarded as a sell-out to Congress, and British actions in the Middle East in the First World War resulted in the growth of the Khilafat movement. After a short alliance with Congress, a major breach developed when the Hindus began to oppose the principle of 'separate electorates'.[11] Many Muslims who had been in Congress left, among them Mohammed Ali Jinnah, who later led the Muslim League.

By the early 1930s, the stage was set for confrontation between Congress and the Muslim League. It is important to note, however, that at this time the Muslim League was pressing for separate electorates and not the partition of India: the idea of a separate Muslim state was not taken up by the League until the 'Pakistan Declaration' in Lahore in

1940. Also, during the 1930s, the Muslim League was by no means a mass political party. Its members came mainly from the professional and commercial classes whose interests would be particularly served by the preservation of special privileges for Muslims or the creation of an independent Muslim state. In the 1937 elections, Muslim League candidates did very poorly. It was not until the League had made an appeal to the masses on the basis of religion and the likely treachery of the Hindus that the basis of the Muslim League shifted: when fresh elections were held in 1946, League candidates received much more support, and it was on this basis that the claim for the creation of Pakistan was made very shortly afterwards. It is important, therefore, to be rather careful about interpreting the overt religious basis of Pakistan: appeals to the masses on the basis of religious loyalties came rather late in the day, and can be seen as cloaks for other interests.

The British Government did not approve of the demands made at the end of the war for a separate Muslim nation, and the 1946 Cabinet Mission proposed the concession of Muslim areas in the north-west and north-east which would be autonomous except in defence, finance and foreign affairs. Congress rejected the proposals, though the League accepted them, and the Viceroy withdrew the offer as he felt he could not form a government from the Muslims alone. Muslim feeling ran high, and fresh demands for a completely independent Muslim state were voiced. Meanwhile, Congress changed its mind, and was given the right to form a government. Jinnah agreed to participate, but there was lack of trust on both sides, and the Muslim demand for Pakistan was not given up. In late 1946, Attlee announced that India was to be granted independence even if Congress and the League did not agree, and Mountbatten was put in charge of the transfer of power. He concluded that Partition was inevitable.

A boundary commission was set up to establish the position of the borders between India and Pakistan. The problem for the commission was that the principle that Muslim majority areas should go to Pakistan had to be used in conjunction with other factors which were left rather vague. One factor was contiguity: a Muslim majority area would be awarded to Pakistan only if it was contiguous with other areas to be in Pakistan. Thus, many people found that they were on the wrong side of the border. In Punjab, the matter was further complicated by the position of Amritsar (the holy city of the Sikhs) and problems over the control of irrigation headwaters and canals. Partitioned Punjab was the site of the greatest panic over the boundary decisions, and there was an extensive exchange of population, with many of the refugees being slaughtered en route.

In the wake of this slaughter and distrust, a great deal of bitterness developed. It is still widely considered in Pakistan that Britain did not want India to be partitioned, and many consider that the borders were drawn up so that Pakistan would be deprived of Kashmir and of the control of irrigation headwaters, and thus would be weak. In addition to this bitterness, Pakistan had difficulties from the start. Before Partition, many men in business and administration in the areas which went to Pakistan were not Muslims, and most of them moved to India in 1947. Most of the immigrants to Pakistan were peasants, who often settled in Pakistan's cities. Much of the urban growth after 1947 is attributable to the influx of population from India.[12] Problems of accommodating these people added to the problems caused by the dearth of skilled people. Furthermore, Pakistan is not well endowed with mineral wealth: its major income came from agricultural products such as cotton (in the west wing) and jute (in the east wing), and most of the cotton and jute mills were located on the Indian side of the border.

Relations between Pakistan and India have been characterized by dispute and mutual distrust, and there has been fighting on several occasions. The first dispute arose over the use of the waters of the five rivers.[13] The boundary put the headwaters of the Sutlej and Ravi in India, while the canals fed by them lie almost entirely in Pakistan. No specification was made about the allocation of water. In March 1948, India closed off the supply of water to Pakistan from these two rivers, and in 1949 began to build new irrigation canals to be supplied by them, which would increase the area of irrigated land in East Punjab. The Ravi and Sutlej became almost dry in their courses in Pakistan, and the Pakistan Government began a programme of linking canals from the northern rivers. In 1960, the World Bank arbitrated in the dispute, and it was agreed that India should have sole use of the three southern rivers, while Pakistan should have the Chenab, Jhelum and Indus. But Pakistan still considers that it is vulnerable, as these three rivers rise in Kashmir.[14]

This is one of the roots of the Kashmir dispute. The other is that Pakistan denies the legality of the Indian occupation of Kashmir. In 1947, Muslims constituted about 75 per cent of the population of Kashmir, but Kashmir was a Princely State, and so was not allotted to either Pakistan or India. The Hindu Maharajah only decided to accede

16

to India in 1948 after the Indian Government agreed to help him against Pathan tribesmen who had invaded from the north-west. In late 1948, there was fighting between Indian and Pakistani forces. A United Nations commission recommended a cease-fire line which would give Baltistan, Gilgit and most of Poonch to Pakistan: these areas now constitute Azad Kashmir (i.e. 'Free' Kashmir). As yet, the troops have not withdrawn, and no plebiscite has been held in Kashmir, although the commission recommended it, and in Pakistan, at least, the issue is still a live one. It was one of the elements in the 1965 war between India and Pakistan.

On the internal front there were problems too. Jinnah (the first Governor General) died in 1948, and Liaquat Ali Khan (the first Prime Minister) was assassinated in 1951. The following years saw factional disputes amongst politicians lacking any mass party organization or support, and it was only in 1956 that the first Constitution of Pakistan was drawn up, *inter alia* declaring Pakistan to be an Islamic republic. Ayub Khan became President in 1958 after a military coup, sparked off by popular unrest over economic problems. He remained in power until Yahya Khan took over in early 1969, after waves of strikes and unrest among workers and students. Yahya Khan proclaimed martial law, but promised to hold the first national elections under universal franchise.

The outcome of these elections led to the separation of the east wing of Pakistan (now Bangladesh) and another war with India.[15] The Awami League won all but two of the seats in East Pakistan and had an overall majority, even though it had no seats in the West. Pakistan Peoples Party won most seats in the West, while smaller numbers of seats were won by various branches of the Muslim League and Islamic parties. Mujib-ur-Rahman argued that Awami League's absolute majority entitled it to frame the Constitution, but this was not accepted in the West, for part of Awami League's election platform had entailed the development of greater regional autonomy (though not secession). In March 1971, Awami League was outlawed, and its members declared traitors, and Mujib was taken into custody in West Pakistan. During the next nine months, Bangladesh declared independence, and Pakistan became embroiled unsuccessfully in a war on two fronts with India. Shortly after Pakistan surrendered (December 1971), Zulfikar Ali Bhutto (Chairman of Pakistan Peoples Party) became President of what had been West Pakistan. Since then he has been organizing several reforms: many high-ranking military and civil service officers were sacked, and in his onslaught on the top 'Twenty-two Families' he had made tentative steps to nationalize and put under workers' control banks and other business concerns. Schools were nationalized in 1972.[16]

At the same time, the people continue to be reminded of the aggressive designs of India. There has long been a preoccupation in public life with the dangers from India, and over the years expenditure on arms and military personnel has been very high.[17] Tariq Ali argues that Pakistani and Indian politicians since 1947 have used threats of aggression from the neighbour to divert attention away from domestic problems.[18] For various reasons (both internal and international) policies have failed to alleviate poverty, provide jobs for all, and even out the distribution of wealth in Pakistan. Indeed, there is evidence that per capita incomes for the bulk of the population have *declined* in real terms.[19] In mid 1974 inflation was running at around 30 per cent per annum. It is difficult to assess the overall effect of the loss of East Pakistan and the rise in oil prices: the prospects for some people would seem to be improved, but it is unlikely that the mass of the population will obtain any direct benefit.[20] In any case, as will be clear from the following section, prospects for the mass of the Pakistani population have been very gloomy for years, and this is the point which must be borne in mind when considering emigration to places such as Britain.

1.3 The distribution of resources in Pakistan

Here I shall focus on employment, education and the distribution of population in Pakistan, issues which provide a context within which to understand the backgrounds of my informants and their migration to Britain. Many of the figures which I have had to use are unreliable or out of date, and I use them to provide an indication of the general picture in Pakistan in the period when my informants left.

1.3.1 Employment in Pakistan

In 1951, 77 per cent of the economically active members of the population were engaged in work in the primary sector. Most workers were in agriculture, mostly producing for home consumption. Only 7 per cent of the economically active were in manufacturing, and most of this was in small-scale, relatively unmechanized cottage industry. More people were in the tertiary sector (professions, Government and private service, commerce). Most commercial activity was in the retail trade, often concerned with selling foodstuffs.[21] The balance is very much the same today: agriculture is the major occupational sector.[22]

Incomes are very unevenly distributed.[23] Ali, for instance, points to the concentration of wealth in Pakistan in the hands of a very few families.[24] The poorest workers may earn less than Rs. 100/- per month. The crucial point to bear in mind when considering incomes in Pakistan is that there are no state benefits for the major part of the population. As a result, the sickness, unemployment, old age or death of the worker mean that his family's income simply stops.[25] Many of my informants said that incomes do not enable families to save for contingencies, such as sickness (when medical treatment and medicines may have to be paid for). The sense of insecurity in this situation is an important element in migration.

The problem of low income can be circumvented by the taking up of secondary occupations after work and on rest days. Many migrant workers in cities have been sent as family representatives to supplement the family income. Often this point also applies to international migrants who remit money to relatives still in Pakistan. People who are able to save from their incomes are likely to invest in land and housing (rents from which may further supplement their incomes).

In addition to the generally low pay levels for full-time work, there is a severe problem of unemployment and under-employment. It is difficult to assess the extent of these problems in a country like Pakistan. 'Unemployment' figures are likely to be inaccurate for several reasons; for instance, people are unlikely to register as unemployed if there are no benefits in doing so. Furthermore, wage labour is a relatively small sector of the economy, and many people work in family enterprises (e.g. in tenant farming or cottage industries), in which they may only work for short hours or at specific seasons; such people often contribute cash to the family purse insufficient for their keep, but they do not appear in unemployment figures.[26] Nevertheless, Government sources are prepared to estimate that about one-fifth of the potential labour force is actively seeking work.[27] In addition, the number of people of employable age continues to increase. The Government has recognized the high rates of unemployment and under-employment and low rates of labour efficiency, and has tried to create new job opportunities. 'The Second Plan', it claimed 'succeeded in absorbing the entire increase of thirty-six lakh [3,600,000] persons in the labour force thus arresting the increase in unemployment against the background of a very high rate of population growth' (pp. 265–6). It reports that the achievement of the

19

Third Plan (if Plan estimates are reached) would 'fully absorb the addition in the labour force and will not make any impression on the backlog of unemployment' (p. 269).[28]

Another aspect of this question is the size of the labour force. The Second Plan estimated that the 'rate of labour force participation' (that is the potential labour force) in 1955–6 was 32 per cent of the total population of West Pakistan.[29] One factor behind this high dependency rate is that women make up only about 12 per cent of those registered as employed. It is widely considered shameful for women to work, and only the very poorest or professional women are likely to work. Women in rural areas often help with the agricultural work. The dependency rate is also high because of the very high proportion of the population who are children. Even so, just under 40 per cent of the boys between ten and fourteen years old are considered to be in the labour force (though this does not mean that they have work).[30] Usually, they will be from poor families in which the income has to be supplemented.

Different occupations are, of course, accorded different prestige. The least-favoured jobs are manual occupations, especially jobs like sweeping (which entail cleaning out latrines and sweeping the streets). To be a landlord is widely considered a desirable occupation. A *zamindar* may invest in land or rent-out houses. Often incomes from the holdings supplement incomes from other sources, as it is rare for ordinary people to live solely as *zamindars*. In paid employment, the professions (particularly law and medicine), Government service and the armed forces are very sought after: usually such jobs are well paid, but in addition they also give benefits which are critical in the Pakistan situation, such as job security, pension schemes and medical facilities. White-collar jobs in private concerns are less likely to have fringe benefits.

The salient features of the employment situation in Pakistan, then, are the concentration of population in the agricultural sector, the sharp contrasts between the few very wealthy families and the large numbers whose incomes do not enable them to save for hard times, and the high rates of unemployment and under-employment. These features must be seen against the backdrop of the lack of benefits for the unemployed, the sick and the old.[31]

1.3.2 Education in Pakistan

Before the arrival of the British in north India, formal education for Muslims took place in the *madrissah*, or mosque schools, which concentrated on enabling their pupils to read the major Islamic teachings. Pupils were mostly boys from the richest families; girls might be taught to read the Koran at home. Gradually the system of education through the *madrissah* was overlaid by Christian mission schools, and later by state schools and numerous private schools. Most of these schools have now been taken over by the Government. The formal organization of the education system is very similar to that in Britain: school entry age is about five, transfer to secondary school takes place at eleven, and the public examinations (Matriculation, and First Arts or First Sciences) are taken at about sixteen and eighteen respectively. There are also universities, and technical colleges for further education.

However, there is one point which has crucial consequences for how the system actually works: as yet, schooling in Pakistan is not compulsory. There are several types of people who tend to miss out; in particular, females, the poor and those in rural areas receive less and often inferior schooling.[32]

Over Pakistan as a whole, girls are less likely to be sent to school than their brothers. Many parents in Pakistan view education with considerable suspicion, and, because girls are thought to be especially vulnerable to the corruptive influences of education, many families do not send their daughters to school at all. Those girls who do go to school tend to be withdrawn sooner than their brothers, often when they reach puberty, as many families believe that girls should remain in the home, and preferably be married, after puberty. Even so, dropping out is common in all age groups, as other factors, in particular poverty, affect school attendance by girls. Myrdal reports that boys outnumber girls at the primary level by 3 : 1, by 5 : 1 at secondary level, and by 7 : 1 at college and university level.[33]

Poverty crucially relates to school attendance. Few schools provide scholarships or free education, and in addition, pupils usually have to supply their own books. On the other side, many families need the labour of children at home (or in paid employment) and cannot afford the regular absences required by full-time education. There are several consequences of this. Children of many families simply never attend school. In other families, children may be enrolled, but they drop out when the family cannot pay the fees any more, or when the child is old enough to earn his keep.[34] Also, school fees are not uniform over the whole educational system. Many schools charge fees beyond the pockets of the average family, and they are more or less monopolized by the wealthy. Mission schools are a case in point, and since they are often

'English-medium' and since higher education and many jobs require English, the pupils of these schools leave with a great advantage in the job market.

School attendance in the rural areas is lower than in urban areas. In part, this is because of poverty and suspicion of education, but it is also due to poorer facilities in country districts. There has been an increase in the absolute numbers of children seeking education, but Rauf reports that in 1968–9 there were 1,717 secondary schools in urban areas and only 3,329 in rural areas of West Pakistan.[35]

These points can be amplified by looking at literacy rates in Pakistan. Rauf quotes figures for West Pakistan[36] which highlight the contrast between urban and rural areas and between men and women:

Sex	Number of literates		% literates (aged 5 or over)	
	Urban	Rural	Urban	Rural
Male	1,931,424	2,329,162	42.2	17.5
Female	748,591	371,131	21.2	3.2
Both sexes	2,680,015	2,700,193	33.0	10.9

Myrdal's comments can sum up this section:

The school systems of the South Asian countries reflect, and in turn reinforce, the inequalities of the social structure, especially where they are most extreme. In the poorer countries . . . fewer children are enrolled in the first grade of primary school; girls, children from rural areas, and generally children from the most disadvantaged families are less well-represented. Irregular attendance, repeating, and dropping out occur most frequently among the enrolled children of these categories. Only a small percentage of all children complete primary school. Thus . . . a severe process of selection is at work, which, on the whole, excludes the less privileged population groups. This is one reason why a high proportion of those who finish primary school go on to secondary school. The drop outs in secondary school, and, later, the failures in matriculation examinations show a similar bias, and a further selection along the same lines.[37]

It is unlikely that literacy rates will increase in the next few years, since increasing investment in money terms in the educational sector is counteracted both by the increasing population of school age and by inflation.

1.3.3 Population distribution in Pakistan

The mass of the population in Pakistan lives in rural areas. In the 1961 Census, only 22.5 per cent of the population are listed as urban dwellers.[38] Secondly, those people who live in cities are mostly people who lived in rural areas until recently. Much of the rapid increase in urban population over the past two decades is attributable to immigration from rural areas. Many other urban-dwellers were refugees from India, and many of them came from rural areas. Migration from the rural areas is selective: most of the migrants are young men in search of work in the cities, and very few are women. There seems to be a tendency for residential clustering based on areas of origin, and most social mixing among migrants in towns is with kin.[39] Ties with the place of origin are usually kept up and the migrants do not necessarily become urban-based. They go home when possible and help their kin in ceremonies and times of crisis. Many worked in agriculture before migration, and they generally give economic reasons for migrating.[40]

1.4 Life-styles in Pakistan

In the previous section, I dealt briefly with some material which will be useful in the next chapter when I look at the backgrounds of my informants in Bristol. I now want to turn to life-styles in Pakistan, and the ways in which they are evaluated. I have two main reasons for this, which in some ways are contradictory. In Chapter 4, I point to the relative lack of change in the life-styles of the Muslim informants since they have been in Britain, and the following discussion provides a base-line for this continuity. In Chapter 4, I also look at those changes which *have* occurred in the life-styles of my informants, and I argue that they refer back to Pakistan, rather than being responses to the immediate social environment in Britain. Hence it is important here to look not just at the variations in life-styles in Pakistan, but also at the way Pakistanis evaluate these differences.

1.4.1 Housing in Pakistan

One of the most striking features of housing in Pakistan is the extreme contrast between the housing conditions of the poor and the very rich. The poorest people may live without shelter, or in rough hide tents, often in undesirable sites and lacking in material possessions, running water and electricity. At the other extreme are the plastered brick homes of the rich, complete with gardens and servants' quarters. They have electricity, water, modern toilet facilities, glass windows, numerous lofty rooms and expensive 'western'-style furniture. Very few people live in such opulence.

Most people in Pakistan, especially in rural areas, live in *kutcha* homes, with several rooms built around a courtyard. All the rooms are multipurpose and the flat roof is used for sleeping in the hot weather.[41] Furniture is usually sparse, and the *charpai* (beds) may be used as seats and tables during the day. Windows may have wooden shutters, but no glass. Recently, more wealthy peasants have been constructing *pukka* homes from kiln-baked bricks.[42] Generally, these homes are similar in style to the *kutcha* houses, though they may have more than one storey. The bricks are usually unplastered.

In urban areas more homes are *pukka*, though poor people continue to live in *kutcha* homes. Because space is limited, especially in long-inhabited areas, urban homes are usually several storeys high, and sometimes each storey has only one room. The roof may be the only open area and the rooms are usually multipurpose. City homes may have running water and electricity, and ceiling fans for use in hot weather. Most homes still have the traditional latrine on the roof rather than a flush toilet. Few families have space to grow vegetables, but some are able to keep a buffalo to provide them with fresh milk.

Due to the influx of population, housing is short in urban areas, and there are also problems of improving facilities as water supplies are often inadequate and public health is endangered by open drains and lack of sewage processing.[43] Poorer families live in more crowded conditions and tend to lack latrines, bathrooms, kitchens, running water and electricity. Bhatti found an average of 3.2 persons per room. M. K. H. Khan et al. found that over 96 per cent of the households surveyed had incomes under Rs. 500/-, and those with the smallest incomes were most likely to live in a single room, without latrine, running water or electricity.[44]

Much housing is owner-occupied in Pakistan. Government servants may be provided with homes, but there is little municipal provision for those unable to house themselves. Poor families may have to resort to renting a room in another family's house.

24

Much of the variation in housing conditions in Pakistan reflects differences in income. Not surprisingly, plastered brick homes with modern plumbing and so on are preferred to brick homes lacking such facilities, and *pukka* homes are an improvement on *kutcha* homes, which are very unsatisfactory in wet weather. Villagers' horizons probably only stretch to replacing their *kutcha* homes with *pukka* kiln-baked brick homes, while city-dwellers are more likely to aim for a plastered *pukka* house.

1.4.2 Diet in Pakistan

As with other aspects of life-styles in Pakistan, diet relates very closely to income. Meat is relatively expensive, so although Muslims like to eat meat, many Pakistanis are practically vegetarian.[45] Meats are ranked in a scale of preferences, with chicken highest in the list and goat and mutton somewhat less desirable. Beef and buffalo meat are cheapest and most despised, and should not be given to guests. Although fruit is plentiful, it is too expensive for many people.

Main meals usually consist of vegetable or lentil stews eaten with *chappatti* (or other forms of bread) or, less often, with rice. Dairy products such as milk and *dahi* (yoghourt) are drunk or used in cooking; tea and fruit juices are rather more expensive. Muslims are not supposed to take alcoholic drinks, but there are locally brewed beers and very expensive imported spirits.

Most food for home cooking is sold fresh. The richest families have servants to do the shopping and cooking, while many other families who have no servants try to ensure that their women do not have to shop for food in the *bazaar*, by sending the children, the men or the very old on errands. Cooked food is available from the *bazaar*, but the families I knew considered such food to be dirty and generally cooked all their own food. Poor families use sun-baked dung or charcoal as cooking-fuel, while people who are more wealthy use paraffin stoves. As yet, very few people use natural-gas stoves. Generally, the stoves are on the ground, and the women crouch at their work.

Closely associated with diet are norms of hospitality. My informants said that it is their duty as Muslims to provide food when anyone comes to their home, at whatever time of day or night. It was certainly very rare for an uninvited guest not to be given a full meal, or at least offered one: the family simply had to make do with smaller portions.

25

1.4.3 Leisure activities in Pakistan

Especially for women, most leisure is based in the home. Some have radios, and a few have television (though many of the television programmes come from abroad and so are understood fully only by the small English-speaking élite). There are numerous Urdu novels, but since the literacy rates are so low and many literate women are not allowed to read novels, novels probably count for very little in most homes. Many women spend a lot of time sewing, which is regarded as an essential skill for women, and in most families the clothes are all sewn at home. Many young women are expected to embroider the cushion covers, pillow-cases and sheets for their dowries. Visiting kin is also a common pastime, but many families do not approve of their women going far afield on their own, and visiting often has to take place when the men are also able to go.

Outside the home, most of the patrons of the various forms of entertainment are men, except in those circles which are considered to be *modern*. There are locally made Urdu and Punjabi films as well as imported films. Much less popular are the Urdu *dyrama* (plays) and the *mushayra* (poetry symposia). For the select few there remains a rich heritage of clubs from the British era, where the wealthy can drink and play billiards and take part in other sports in seclusion.

In this field, much hinges on the wealth of the family: televisions and radios are too expensive for many. But it is not simply a question of wealth, as several recreations of the wealthy (drinking, gambling, allowing women to go to clubs, etc.) are criticized by traditional people. Preferences in the sphere of entertainment are not always slavish imitations of the practices of the wealthy, as the wealthy do not always conform to the traditional notions of respectability.

1.4.4 Dress, purdah and the position of women in Pakistan

Dress is one of the most conspicuous modes of publicly signalling status and attitudes to different life-styles. Variations in dress are partly connected with differences in wealth, but it is in this context that we also come up against notions of propriety, the position of women and *purdah*.

Traditional attire in Pakistan is very similar for men and women. It consists of *shalwar* (trousers full in the leg and narrow at the ankle) with a *qemiz* or *kurta* (dress, shirt) worn loose over the *shalwar*. Women may

26

wear a *qemiz* or *kurta* of printed material, while men wear plain material. Beyond these basics, there are numerous variations which accentuate the differences between men and women. Women wear certain extra items, in particular the *duppatta*, the *burqa*, and most jewellery. Most women wear the *duppatta* (a chiffon length) or *chaddar* (shawl) which, like the *burqa*, are closely connected with womanly modesty. The *burqa* is worn only outside the home and (at least traditionally) completely covered the woman and protected her from the gaze of outsiders. Although some men may wear rings, such jewellery as bracelets, necklaces and earrings is worn only by women and girls. Women should not cut their hair, as it is considered to be their glory: it is usually tied back in a bun, or a single plait (often adorned with a *pranda* woven into it). Men should keep their hair short, and very few have beards. (Mohammed had a beard, and in Pakistan the more religious-minded are the most likely to have beards.)

Many of the other variations in dress are closely related to differences in wealth. The quality of material worn by women can range from *khaddar* (coarse cheap cotton) through fine cotton or cotton lawn to silk or satin. Jewellery too is an index of wealth. Gold is most sought-after, but poor women may have no more than coloured glass bracelets. Girls have little jewellery until they marry, and then their parents are expected to give as much as they can afford: a bride should be given earrings, nose-studs, necklaces, bracelets, rings and *tikka* (a piece attached to her hair which hangs over her forehead). These should all be gold, and may be set with gems. The thickness of the gold, the number of solid gold bracelets and so on are a very striking index of the girl's family's wealth (or perhaps pretensions to wealth). Again the *burqa* displays differences in wealth. The old-style relatively cheap *burqa* is made of a circular piece of cloth (often cotton) whose radius is the same as the woman's height. The centre is embroidered to form a cap which fits over her head, with holes worked in it so that she can see, and the rest of the *burqa* falls round her to her feet. The new-style *burqa* is more expensive and made of satin or cotton. It consists of a fitted coat and a cape to cover the head. A chiffon veil is attached to the cape and may be used to cover the face. For men, the crucial variation in dress related to wealth is the possession of a 'western' suit, since this is much more expensive than *shalwar—qemiz*. The 'western' suit is worn at work and on public occasions, but may be replaced by the more comfortable *shalwar—qemiz* at home.

There are, however, other differences in dress styles which do not relate simply to wealth, but which are closely tied in with notions of propriety and the proper position of women. In section 1.1 above I pointed to the way in which Islamic teachings influence the relations between the sexes, and justify the separation between men and women. The wearing of the *burqa* and the *duppatta* is intimately connected with a whole complex of processes labelled *purdah*. The writings of people such as Maududi[46] reflect and probably also influence the ways in which men and women in Pakistan relate to one another. Maududi argues that physiological differences between men and women necessitate different tasks in society and that sexual temptations are hard to withstand and are liable to be disruptive. In order that men and women may fulfil their tasks properly, male and female domains should be preserved which are as separate as possible. While the legitimation for such a division between the sexes is sought in Islamic teachings, it should be said that in other parts of the Indian sub-continent (and indeed outside) non-Muslims very often create similar divisions because they consider that the honour of the family resides in the modest behaviour of its women, and this idea is also an element in *purdah* in Pakistan.

The word *purdah* means curtain and veil, and people talk of women living 'in *purdah*' or 'behind the curtain'. There are several elements here, but at the most general level they relate to the creation of separate spheres of existence for men and women. On the one hand, *purdah* refers to the division of the home into separate areas (*zenana* for women and *merdana* for men), often by use of a curtain, though sometimes with a wall.[47] Further, *purdah* refers to the subtle ways in which a woman creates and maintains social distance between herself and men through the use of her *duppatta*, *chaddar* or *burqa*. Saifullah-Khan[48] points to four general rules for *purdah* observance: limited interaction between the sexes (except close kin), segregation between the sexes before or at puberty, division of labour between the sexes, and modesty of women. Although these are not always attained, Saifullah-Khan considers that the two main ways in which people try to signal *purdah* observance are the division of physical space in the home and clothing.

Through the use of these signs, families try to assert their respectability. One crucial limitation on maintaining women in *purdah* is the expense. The provision of separate quarters and the economic inactivity of women which are entailed in the most extreme form of *purdah* can be attained by very few: many women have to leave their homes to help with agricultural work, and their homes are too small to allow for separate quarters. Nonetheless, as Saifullah-Khan points out, there are

28

devices to preserve social distance between women and unrelated men (in particular the *duppatta*), and people who cannot afford full *purdah* make do with lesser forms. However, if at all possible, the women should go out rarely (they should not do the shopping, for instance) and when they go out it is desirable that they wear a *burqa*; at social gatherings (from individual visiting to weddings) men and women should be kept physically separate. One way in which a family may show that it has 'arrived' is to put its women into more strict *purdah*, and this is an important aim for many families.[49]

There are many variations in the ways in which *purdah* is observed in Pakistan. Some of these are forced on people because of their poverty and are undesired modes of behaviour which will be discarded when possible. Other variations are contextual. The *duppatta*, for instance, may be worn in several ways: in the privacy of the *zenana* it may be lightly draped over the shoulders or perched on the bun, while the woman is praying it will cover the hair, and the young woman in the presence of her father-in-law may pull it right over her head and face and bow her head in respect. This is one dimension of the subtleties of the sign system entailed in women's dress, but there is another dimension which relates to differences in commitment to traditional modes of behaviour.[50] Some people in Pakistan are considered to be *modern* (the actual word used), and there are several ways in which their dress and other modes of behaviour mark them off from other people.[51] Some women do not wear the *burqa* when they go outside; others may wear a closely fitting new-style *burqa* with the veil thrown back to expose the face: they contrast with the women who go out fully concealed by their *burqa*. Again, the use of the *duppatta* signifies approaches to traditional notions of modesty and respect. A few women have completely discarded the *duppatta*; others only wear it draped on their shoulders and do not bother to cover their heads in the presence of men. Such women may wear bell-bottom trousers instead of *shalwar*, though hardly any expose their legs. They may have dresses with short sleeves and wear their hair loose or even cut it. Few women fall into this category, and they are widely criticized for their immodesty and shamelessness. Dress for men does not have these connotations of propriety, and wearing a 'western' suit is fairly simply connected with wealth; but for women, wealth is connected with two quite distinct and contradictory modes of dress, one entailing more stringent observation of *purdah* than can be observed by the poor, and the other connected with 'modernity'. Both 'modernity' and traditional respectability require wealth. 'Modernity' is the preserve of relatively few wealthy families mostly in large urban centres. At present, most people in towns and villages aim to be traditionally respectable and do not wish their women to flout social conventions.

Differences in dress, then, reflect differences in wealth, but they are also part of a complex and subtle system of signs in which differences in the dress of women in particular link up with other aspects of behaviour and indicate different notions of propriety. One matter which is closely related to *purdah* is the mode of arranging marriages and the nature of conjugal relationships in Pakistan. 'Love-marriages' are rare and generally bring disrepute to the families involved. While films hinge on romantic attachments, in real life such relationships are uncommon. Parental opposition and the fear of ostracism, the segregation of the sexes from puberty onwards and the very restricted and clandestine contexts in which young men and women can meet, all hinder love-matches. In Pakistan, most marriages are arranged by the parents of potential spouses. Adults argue that young people are inexperienced judges of character and that matching is better done by cool-headed parents than by an infatuated young couple. Sometimes the couple may not meet until the marriage, or they may only see photographs of each other. In other cases, the couple may meet with chaperons and may be asked to approve the match. Others may be asked to select a spouse from several possibilities, while some have in effect only the power of veto. It is quite common for siblings to make a pact that their children will marry and for the children to grow up knowing this. While some parents no doubt think largely about their own interests while arranging their children's marriages, great care generally is taken to ensure that marriages will be happy. There are several reasons why arranged marriages usually succeed: young people expect that their parents will arrange their marriages and are generally prepared to trust their judgement; there is a belief that love should come after marriage (rather than before) and that it is a developing feeling which grows over the years with the birth of children; and finally, arranged marriages are generally successful because of *purdah* and the nature of conjugal relationships. In general, conjugal relationships entail considerable role segregation between the spouses: their tasks are different and are conducted in largely separate spheres. Especially in the early years of a marriage, in large families, the wife will interact more with her mother-in-law and the other women of the family than with her husband. Thus, when questions of 'compatibility' arise, consideration is taken of how the wife will fit into her husband's wider family, as well as of the relationship between husband and wife. Only among the most *modern* families do the notions of 'love-matches' and 'companionate marriage' hold much sway. Divorce is rare in Pakistan, though it is difficult to assess whether this is because of the successful arrangement of marriages or because of pressures put by relatives to avert the shame which divorce brings. My impression is that most arranged marriages are successful, and the pressure for divorce is slight.

Generally, women expect to be based in the home, to marry and have children, and to be responsible in the domestic sphere. *Purdah* and dress styles for women are intimately connected with the position of women in Pakistan, and help to preserve the virtue and modesty of women so that they can fulfil their expected roles satisfactorily. Their behaviour affects the way the whole family is regarded, and in the next pages I shall consider how different life-styles are evaluated and the bearing these evaluations have on honour and prestige.

1.4.5 Biraderi and izzet in Pakistan

So far in discussing life-styles in Pakistan I have pointed to many diversities in housing conditions, diet, entertainment and dress. I also suggested that there are differences in the evaluations made of these various life-styles. In some cases, differences in life-style reflect differences in wealth, and sometimes the life-styles of the rich are preferred: *pukka* homes with roomy quarters, electricity and running water are preferable to *kutcha* homes lacking such facilities. But the relationship between preferences and wealth is not always a simple one: while most families would like their women to have fine clothes and jewellery, many have doubts about *modern* dress styles and the propensity of *modern* women to go out unveiled.

Here, and when I turn to 'Ashrafization' and 'Westernization', I shall be looking more closely at the evaluational aspects of life-styles in Pakistan. At this point, I am primarily concerned with the question of ranking in Pakistan and the general efforts to improve position connected with the notion of *izzet*.

Muslims in the Indian sub-continent are very conscious of rank, despite the egalitarianism implicit in Islam. Some writers say that Muslims in India simply took on the ranking system of the Hindus, while others comment on ranking in early Muslim communities outside India. Whatever the origin of the importance of rank to Indian and Pakistani

Muslims, there are many parallels with the 'caste system', though the order of ranking closely follows that among Muslims elsewhere.[52] There seems to be a superimposition of the ranking categories of Muslims onto the local system.[53]

For Dumont, the principle of ranking is the central feature of the caste system, on which all the rest hinges.[54] Dumont argues that the rankings are based on an opposition between the ritually 'pure' and 'polluted'. Purity is not a stable characteristic, for carelessness may contaminate an individual so that he loses some of his purity (maybe permanently, or only temporarily in cases where he may be able to regain his purity by performing specified rituals). On the other hand, purity may be enhanced. Dumont comments:

> The opposition of pure and impure appears to us the very principle of hierarchy, to such a degree that it merges with the opposition of superior and inferior; moreover, it also governs separation . . . The preoccupation with purity leads to the getting rid of the recurrent personal impurities of organic life, to organising contact with purificatory agents and abolishing it with agents of impurity, whether social or other. The ban on certain contacts corresponds to the idea of untouchability, and all sorts of rules govern food and marriage. It must be pointed out that . . . the relative degree of a group's purity is jealously protected from contacts which would diminish it. It must also be noted that each group protects itself from the one below and not at all from the one above, and that the actual separation from the one above is the result only of the exclusiveness of the superiors.[55]

Rank is generally thought to be determined by birth, but in practice the ranking is somewhat fluid and it is sometimes possible to enhance purity by emulating people of higher rank, or to damage purity by behaving improperly.

Talk at the level of 'caste', though, is too distant from how the system works on the ground, and it is here that *biraderi* comes in. There are some discrepancies in the ways in which this term is translated, probably because it means rather different things in different parts of north India, but here I shall use it in the way in which my informants refer to *biraderi*. Perhaps the best way of translating their usage is to call *biraderi* 'connection' or 'relatives'.[56] Blunt uses the term in a way which is similar to my informants' usage. He writes: 'The *zat* is the caste as a whole; the *biraderi* is the group of caste brethren who live in a particular neighbourhood and act together for caste purposes. The *biraderi*, quantitatively considered, is a mere fraction of the *zat*; qualitatively considered, it is the *zat* in action.'[57]

My informants use the word in a similar way: they include people in the same patrilineage, and also people related through marriage (one's own marriage, the marriage of one's father, and the marriages of both parents' siblings). For my informants, *biraderi* does not have the local connotations implied by Blunt: he talks of *biraderi* councils meeting to punish offenders. Although the *biraderis* of my informants do not seem necessarily to imply a particular locality, the ability to ostracize offenders still remains.

One point which is not made clear in the literature is whether *biraderis* are completely separate from one another, or whether their membership overlaps. My informants give the impression that the boundaries between *biraderis* are not completely clear. Individuals seem to perceive their *biraderis* radiating out from them, through their relatives on both sides (patrilateral and matrilateral kin and affines): in other words, they seem to regard the *biraderi* as an ego-centred cognatic kinship network. In this case, however, it generally seems that *biraderis* are not radically different for each individual, since all my Muslim informants say that it is general in their family to marry inside the *biraderi*. Some marriages are made outside, but in general it may be said that the *biraderis* consist of people who are cognatically related and from whom it is desirable to choose spouses. Not all Muslims in the Indian sub-continent marry close kin, but my informants preferred to arrange marriages between kin (first or second cousins, for instance).[58] As a result of involuted marriage ties, their *biraderis* tend to be like groups and can be effective in controlling the actions of members, and even ostracizing offenders even if they are geographically dispersed.[59] The ability of the *biraderi* to control its members is important. A man generally finds his friends, and also the spouses for his children, inside the *biraderi*, and it is here that the question of *izzet* comes in. *Izzet* can be translated as 'prestige' or 'honour', and it is a quality possessed by individuals and *biraderis*. If a man endangers the *izzet* of his *biraderi*, punitive actions will ensue. Dumont's comment quoted above is pertinent here: *izzet* is fragile, and 'the relative degree of a group's purity is jealously protected from contacts which would diminish it'. *Izzet* is also contagious: a man is judged partly by his own behaviour, partly by the company he keeps. In addition, the way the women of the family comport themselves has great bearing on the honour of the family as a whole. *Izzet* can easily be damaged by carelessness, and constant vigilance over the behaviour of *biraderi* members turns on the preservation of *izzet*. Each individual takes care over his associates: his *izzet* will be in peril if he mixes with dishonourable people, and he aims to enhance his *izzet* by trying to cultivate links with his 'betters'. He will also try to behave honourably to his kin and others, and strive to attain a more 'respectable' *izzet*-giving life-style for his immediate family. The man who does not do this, the man who mixes with disreputables or whose life-style brings slur on his relatives, will suffer for it: he may lose his friends and he may find that his relatives will not accept his children as marriage partners.

The links which a man makes through the marriages of his children are some of the most important which he can make, and a discussion of the way marriages are arranged can illustrate the points I have been making about *izzet*. Generally, the parents of potential spouses make the arrangements. The girl's parents begin the search for a suitable husband. All the qualities and taints of candidates should be known, and several informants told me that one reason for marrying kin is that detailed and accurate knowledge can be accumulated only among kin. A stranger might cover up some shame in his family, and then bring ruin to his in-laws when the truth is revealed. Usually, caution prevails, and the search is made first among kin, and only outside the *biraderi* if no suitable match can be made inside. Several boys may be suitable inside the *biraderi* and the girl's parents approach the parents of the most eligible. The outcome is a compromise between several considerations: the girl should be married to the 'best' man available, but her parents' financial standing will set limits on this aim. They are required to provide her with a dowry, and maintain a gift-giving relationship with her in-laws over a lifetime, so they have to make a realistic assessment of how much they can afford. Conversely, they would be disgraced if they appeared to give less than they could, and their daughter would be taunted about her parents' miserliness. Family troubles like this would further harm their *izzet*. The parents of the boy will also be concerned about the implications of a match, and they will ask about the character of the girl and her close relatives. During the upbringing of a daughter, her parents must take great care that nothing occurs which might cause their proposal of marriage to be rejected. Any hint of romantic attachment on her part would probably result in such a rejection, and would also reflect badly on her younger sisters and make their marriages more difficult to arrange. In fact, the families concerned often know one another well: with the prevalence of close kin marriages, the parents of potential spouses are often siblings or close cousins to one another. Indeed, because of constraints over dowry payments, matches are very often arranged between equals, of whom close kin are the ideal, and *izzet* is simply conserved rather than enhanced. In those cases where prestigious matches come about, younger siblings may find that their own marriage chances are greatly improved (in the same way as their chances can be harmed if they have a disreputable sibling).

In these ways, then, children become enmeshed in the status concerns of their parents. So far, I have talked of parents trying to find 'suitable' husbands for their daughters, and of trying to 'enhance' rather than 'harm' their *izzet*, and so on. It must then be asked, what behaviour is 'respectable' and what behaviour will bring shame on a family? It is impossible to give a simple answer to his. One man may not want his daughters to attend school after puberty, while another will send his daughters to college in the hope that they will be able to make better marriages. Some parents want their daughters to be educated, but do not want them to pursue careers. Some marry their daughters at the onset of puberty, others when they are in their twenties. For some, religious piety is important, for others, irrelevant. The important point remains, though: the principle of striving to enhance *izzet* is the same, even though there is considerable variation in the styles in which this is attempted, and I now want to sketch-in two modes of betterment which are important in Pakistan.

1.4.6 Ashrafization and westernization in Pakistan

This section deals with processes analogous to those described by Srinivas as 'Sanskritization' and 'Westernization'.[60] I am hesitant about using the terms 'Ashrafization' and 'Westernization', partly because they are rather ugly, but more importantly because the whole issue of cultural change which is entailed here is shrouded in problems and confusions. However, I wish to retain these terms (with the provisos which I shall mention in a moment) as they are useful in discussing points which I raise in Chapter 4.

The central issue here concerns cultural changes which take place during or after social mobility, and the reference groups which are used as role models by the socially mobile. The process of 'Sanskritization' covers the changes in life-style of the upwardly socially mobile who emulate the life-styles of those regarded as orthodox Hindus (such as refraining from consuming meat and alcohol, seclusion of women, prohibiting the remarriage of widows). There are problems, however, with this formulation.

Firstly, there are a great many reference groups in the Indian sub-continent which act as role models, not just the two mentioned first by Srinivas. What is needed in any discussion of this sort of process of cultural change is detailed information about the specific contexts in which the changes are taking place. Obviously, people can only emulate what they know, and this point has several implications. Since knowledge is likely to be parochial, patterns of emulation will usually take on local colour. In addition, knowledge about a reference group in the locality will itself tend to be limited, mainly to the realm of public symbols, rather than the realm of private 'back-stage' family customs and interaction. Ignorance of the back-stage may result in inaccurate emulation, while the conspicuous elements of life-style (such as the dress of women, the size of home) are the realm in which the most accurate emulation can occur, and the realm in which the most effective claims to status can be made to the 'audience'. Thus knowledge at the local level must be considered. Furthermore, people in different areas will be faced with different groups of people who are 'worth' emulating, for the powerful (landowners, for instance) are not always 'Sanskritic' in their life-styles. So, there are many reference groups which may be imitated. In addition to this, it must be said that the content of the role models is not specified adequately. For one thing, even among the 'Sanskritic' there are considerable regional variations, and this would be true for other reference groups. In addition, the life-styles of quite distinct groups may have some similarities, even though they are distinguishable on other counts. Hospitality is a good example of this: lavish entertainment of guests requires cash, and gives power and *izzet*, and it is an important element of the life-styles of the wealthy all over India. It is not the prerogative of any one reference group: it may generally be said that people who are worth emulating will be hospitable, even though there may be many ways in which the life-styles of the hospitable differ. It therefore becomes important to try to ascertain whom the emulators think they are emulating, especially in contexts in which there are several feasible reference groups.

These same drawbacks apply to the notions of 'Ashrafization' and 'Westernization' in Pakistan. 'Ashrafization' is emulation in an Islamic mould, and Vreede-de Stuers comments on the similarities between 'Sanskritization' and 'Ashrafization'.[61] 'Westernization' in Pakistan is similar to that in India. Here I shall briefly characterize these notions, bearing in mind the problems which I delineated above.

'Ashrafization' refers back to the Koran for justification, and it entails the adoption of genteel ways and conformity to an Islamic model. The word 'Ashrafization' is derived from *ashraf* (noble), a word which comes from the Arabic root *sh-r-f*. Other words from the same root include *sherif* (honourable) and *teshrif* (dignity). An important element here is religious piety. Members of noble families should perform the requirements of a good Muslim rigorously: they should pray regularly and fast, and if possible go on *haj*, and they should be generous in their alms-giving. In addition, the men of the family should be engaged in reputable occupations, such as being landlords, or possibly professionals, and they should not be manual or minor clerical workers. The women should be in strict *purdah* and should be based in the home, concentrating on their duties there. They should be veiled if they leave their homes, but they should rarely go out. Ideally, the home will be large and provide separate quarters for the women. The women should be able to read the Koran and perform their religious tasks diligently, though some would say that a modicum of formal education is permissible. Family relationships should be sufficiently amicable for married brothers (and their wives and children) to remain in the same household as their parents and any unmarried sisters. Noble families should also be generous welcoming hosts, and they should perform the ceremonies connected with births, marriages and deaths in their family with great pomp and expense.

'Westernization' differs from 'Ashrafization' in several ways. The orientation here is towards the supposed behaviour of people in 'the West', and not towards Islamic orthodoxy. One crucial difference concerns the position of women. In 'Westernized' families, the women are permitted to have education outside the home, even after puberty, and they may be permitted to follow a career. They may not wear a *burqa* when they go out, and their dress will be *modern* in style. As with *ashraf* families, the home should be large, but there will not be the emphasis on separating the men from the women. Entertainment should be sumptuous, and alcohol may be served. The life-style of the 'Westernized' is based on the life of the British in India, and more recently on the life in the West as portrayed in films and books. The imitation is incomplete in several ways, for the nuclear family is not widely favoured, women still cover their legs, and servants are prevalent, but the important point is that *modern* families are oriented in a radically different way from the 'noble' families. For the *ashraf*, indeed, *modern* families are shocking and act as negative-role models, while the 'Westernized' despise the old-fashioned 'noble' families.[62]

Here I have only provided caricatures of these two types of reference group in Pakistan, and have not covered the subtleties and variations between different parts of the country. Karachi is reputed to be very *modern*. In other cities totally *modern* families are rare: women do not go to clubs so much, and women who are *modern* enough to choose their own husbands often persuade their parents to go through the traditional motions so that they do not appear to be making love-marriages. The important point here is not so much the *content* of the life-styles (which show many variations) but the ways in which people legitimate their life-styles: here the notions of being 'noble' or *modern* divide more clearly than the specific types of behaviour which might be entailed in 'noble' or *modern* life-styles.

There is also the question of which people legitimate their behaviour in which way. People can only emulate what they know, and in general it can be said that village people want to 'Ashrafize'. In the urban areas, it is my impression that the newly wealthy aim to become 'noble' by imitating *ashraf* families, while people from old wealthy families may sometimes move on and become *modern*.[63]

In this section I have been considering cultural changes which may occur when families manage to accumulate some wealth and wish to establish themselves as 'better' families. As I have indicated, there are problems in defining the processes of 'Ashrafization' and 'Westernization', but I would argue that these are the two main ways in which people in Pakistan explain their indulgence in certain styles of life which are feasible only for the relatively wealthy. This issue will be discussed again in Chapter 4.

1.5 Christians in Pakistan

Christians were only 1.36 per cent of the total population of West Pakistan in 1961. Nevertheless it is necessary to consider them here, as several of my informants in Bristol were Christian, and they differ in several ways from the Muslims.

1.5.1 Christianity in Pakistan

There is a long history of Christianity in the Indian sub-continent.
There were some Christians in the south from early in the Christian era,
and Portuguese and Dutch traders made some converts. For several centuries the Muslims had a monopoly of the land and sea routes to north
India and there was very little Christian influence there until the end of
the nineteenth century. A contemporary report describes a mission of
Portuguese Jesuits to the court of the Mughal Emperor Akbar in 1580,
but Akbar was only interested in listening to the debates between
Muslim, Hindu and Christian experts, on the basis of which he developed his short-lived syncretic religion *din-i-Ilahi* (religion of God). The
Jesuits returned to south India having made no contacts outside court
nor converts.[64]

The British East India Company did not permit missionary activity
in its domain until 1813. The British position was thought to be too
precarious, and the Portuguese were thought to have failed because they
tried to mix business with religion.[65] It was considered wiser to leave
the subjects as undisturbed as possible. In 1813, however, pressure from
missionary-minded people in Britain resulted in the revision of the
Company's charter. In 1833 a further revision lifted all restrictions on
the nationality and denomination of missionaries, and Christian missions
spread across north India: the C.M.S. reached Amritsar in 1852, and by
this time most of India was covered, if sparsely, by missions. High-caste
people were the focus of evangelical activity, as it was thought that
Christianity would filter down from them, but very few converts were
made until around 1870. Then there came the sudden appearance of
what are generally called 'mass movements' among outcastes and the
most depressed castes. Pickett argues that they were essentially 'caste
movements' as they encompassed only the members of single castes.[66]
Most Christians in the Indian sub-continent today are descendants of
such converts, according to Neill, and Pickett considers that as many as
90–5 per cent of the Protestants in Punjab may be the products of mass
movements there.[67] One of the best-known movements was in the area
of Sialkot; it involved the conversion of a Chuhra man, who preached
during his work as an itinerant hide-seller. By 1915 nearly all the
Chuhras of Sialkot district were Christian.[68] Inniger writes that 'wherever there is a Christian congregation in West Pakistan, even in such
remote areas as Bahawalpur and Sindh, the majority will be found to be

second- and third-generation descendants of mass-movement Christians who have moved into new areas due to economic reasons'.[69]

Christian missions often set up schools and colleges, and several writers note that the high literacy rate among Christians is largely attributable to missionary activity. Many Indian Christians feared that their reputation for culture and education would be shattered by the influx of an illiterate rabble.[70] According to the 1936 Gazetteer for Lahore District, 58.5 per cent of Christians were literate in 1901, while only 16.3 per cent were literate in 1931. In the interim, the number of Christians had risen from 7,296 to 57,097.[71] Other critics of the mass movements argued that converts were being attracted by the hope of material gain.

On the other hand, many in the churches felt that the under-privileged should be helped. Single converts often became cut off from their families when they moved into mission compounds: they became, in Neill's words, 'aliens in their own country'.[72] Mass conversion was thought to prevent such dislocation. However, in Punjab this has not always been true. At that time irrigation schemes opened up many new areas of land for cultivation, and several Christian villages were set up in the Canal Colonies. The Christians who settled there were effectively cut off from people of different religion.[73] Mustaq Ahmad reports on how Christians and Muslims living in Christian Town, Lahore, do not mix today.[74] This element of separation, with the additional possibility that converts would become westernized, is important.

As Neill points out, the overt reasons for the partitioning of India were religious: Muslims claimed that they could not exercise their special vocation in a Hindu state and demanded a state in which Islam was the determining political and social ideology and life would develop in accord with the Koran and Shariah.[75] Thus, while Christianity can be considered alien in India (as it is not an indigenous religion), it is all the more anomalous in Pakistan where Islam and patriotism are so entwined. Because of this, Neill argues that the situation of Christians is more difficult in Pakistan than in India, as their patriotism must always be in doubt.[76]

1.5.2 The position of Christians in Pakistan

There is very little information about Christians in Pakistan today. On the one hand, Government sources deny that Christians suffer any disabilities because of their religion, but all the Pakistani Christians I knew claim that there is substantial discrimination against them (for instance in finding work), and they say that they are generally insecure in Pakistan. It is hard to assess the evidence, but it may be useful to consider some material from the 1961 Census of Pakistan.[77] Even there, material about Christians is very scanty. Some tables are only for Muslims (97.17 per cent of the population of West Pakistan in 1961), while other tables combine the 'other religions'. In any case, even where separate figures appear for Christians, it is difficult to establish under- or over-representation of Christians in certain categories, as the numbers are often small. In 1961, 583,884 Christians were enumerated, of whom 40,368 men and 21,458 women were literate.[78] Almost 10.6 per cent of Christians are literate, while the literacy rate for the whole of West Pakistan was 13.6 per cent.[79] Christian women form a larger proportion of literate Christians than literate Muslim women do of literate Muslims (nearly 35 per cent as opposed to about 20 per cent).[80] Several points are worth noting about how Christians are distributed in the non-agricultural labour force, as the pattern is not always the same as for Muslims.[81] Christian nurses and midwives make up some 12 per cent of nurses and midwives in West Pakistan. Almost 3 per cent of the teachers are Christian, and there are more women Christian teachers than men. Christians made up nearly 2.4 per cent of 'physicians, surgeons, dentists and medical specialists', but something under 0.56 per cent of lawyers, judges and magistrates. The most striking figures, however, are in the category 'caretakers, cleaners and related occupations': Christians make up 59 per cent of this category, and Christian women make up a third of the Christians in the category. Christians appear to hold very little land, as Muslims hold 99.2 per cent of the land in West Pakistan.[82]

Several points can be raised about these figures. The first relates to the relatively low literacy rate, the over-abundance in the category 'caretakers, cleaners and related occupations' and the small amount of land held by Christians. It should be remembered that most Pakistani Christians are the descendants of mass-movement converts, many of whom were poor and illiterate and came from the most depressed sectors of society. The above figures may not reflect discrimination against Christians in Pakistan, but may relate more closely to the difficulties of poor converts in educating their children, and providing a route for occupational mobility for them. Nursing is spurned by Muslims, so the over-representation of Christian women in the category 'nurses and midwives' cannot be taken as an example of positive discrimination in favour of Christians. The small number of Christian lawyers, however, is likely to be more significant, as the legal profession has high prestige and there is no reason to suppose that Muslims opt out of competition for jobs in that sector.

These comments are based on my own conjectures, however, and in one sense they are not very important. What is far more significant here is the assessment made by Pakistani Christians of their position in Pakistan. The figures cited above only suggest that Christians are relatively disadvantaged in Pakistan, but they do not help in determining why this is the case. Indeed, there are opposing interpretations of the situation. Tayyeb says that Christians are more educated than Muslims and are generally city-dwellers with relatively good jobs.[83] Indeed, it may be, despite the lower literacy rates, that those Christians who are literate tend to be more educated than literate Muslims, and therefore better qualified for 'good jobs', but there is nothing in the figures which either supports or denies such a supposition. In any case, Tayyeb appears to ignore the very high proportion of people in very low-prestige jobs (such as sweeping) who are Christian.[84] Neill, on the other hand, writes that there are reports that Christians find difficulty entering Government service, that key positions are held by Muslims, and that few Christians can obtain employment in business. The general economic position of Christians in Pakistan is bad, he says. They are 'displaced persons in their own country'.[85] Neill's view comes far closer to the views of my Christian informants than does Tayyeb's: they say that a Christian in Pakistan has no chance of finding a good job, even if he has been educated at a mission school and college. Unfortunately, it is very hard to assess the validity of either viewpoint. There may, indeed, be discrimination against Christians in Pakistan, but there are other possible explanations. For instance, nepotism may be crucial: given the originally disadvantaged position of Pakistani Christians, they may have had no contacts to help them into better jobs. Or it may be that some Christians are rejected for jobs because better-qualified Muslims apply. Or, again, since Christians and high-ranking officials are few in number in Pakistan, any absence of overlap may not be statistically significant. These possibilities, including discrimination, may all occur, but the critical point is how Christians interpret the situation. In brief, while Government and Muslim sources tend to deny that Christians in Pakistan suffer discrimination, Pakistani Christians tend to be adamant: their position in Pakistan is maintained by rife religious discrimination.[86]

Besides the issue of job-chances for Christians in Pakistan, there is the wider question of general security. Here again, there is little evidence except the comments of my informants that they feel unsafe in Pakistan. After the 1965 war with India, there were some reports of 'reprisals' against Christians in Pakistan: Christians were considered to have hampered the Pakistani cause through their unpatriotic stance, and some were accused of espionage. An incident which arose during my fieldwork in Pakistan illustrates the fears of my Christian informants. In early 1971, a Pakistani living in Manchester wrote to *The Pakistan Times* complaining about a book called *The Turkish Art of Love in Pictures*, which he said had been recently published in Britain and contained insulting assertions about the Holy Prophet.[87] There were student demonstrations in protest, several churches were desecrated, and gestures against western influence were made (wine-shops were looted, 'dancing-girls' attacked, some students stopped wearing western-style clothes, and the Lahore offices of the British Council were razed). Letters to the press deplored the publication of the book and noted it as an example of foreign hostility to Pakistan and Islam, while a letter from a Christian woman implored that Christians in Pakistan should be seen as 'true Pakistanis' and that there should be no stigma attached to being Christian.[88] These sentiments were echoed by my Christian informants. Some of them in Bristol expressed fears for their relatives in Pakistan after the 1971 war with India.

These examples are rather extreme, maybe, but in everyday affairs too, the strong Islamic slant enhances the feeling of being outsiders. The working week is organized around Friday (the Muslim holy day) and national holidays are the Muslim festivals. Missionary work and the teaching of Christian doctrine in mission schools are restricted. Links with Arab countries are fostered, and *Islamiyat* and Persian are important academic subjects. Most of the political parties in Pakistan have an Islamic slant, and some are led by *ulema*; and the press constantly emphasizes the Islamic character of Pakistan. I shall explore the ramifications of these issues in the final chapter.

2. The migrants' backgrounds and their migration

2.0 Introduction

In this chapter, I look at the specific backgrounds of my informants, and at the decisions and experiences which surrounded their migration to Bristol. Through case studies and the general discussion of the migrants' backgrounds, a contrast can be drawn between them and the general picture in Pakistan and other Pakistani migrants to Britain. It will be seen that my informants are atypical in several ways. I also consider some of the complexities which surround their decisions to migrate to Britain. In the literature, Pakistani migrants to Britain are usually portrayed as 'economic migrants', who have left their home in search of work. This portrayal entails the acceptance of two types of perspective on migration, firstly, the 'push–pull' thesis, in which it is argued that the dire situation in the place of origin pushes people to leave, while the glittering attractions in the destination pull the migrants in; and secondly, a maximization model, in which it is assumed that the migrant aims for maximum economic gain through his migration. Unfortunately, both models are unsatisfactory. In particular, the former cannot explain 'circulatory migration'; that is, having portrayed gloom in the place of origin, it cannot explain why migrants return there, and this is a point of some significance for Pakistani migrants in Britain. The maximization model, through its concentration on economic factors, overlooks social and political factors which may be very important in impelling the migration, or in encouraging migrants either to return home or to remain abroad, or in affecting the ways the economic gain is used. It is in answer to these objections that Garbett and Kapferer (in their discussion of rural–urban migration in Africa) argue that the place of origin and the destination of the migrants should be seen as a single social system: 'rural–urban migration should be viewed in the total field of social and economic relationships involving both town and country'.[1] Such an approach is applicable to international migration too, and it informs the subsequent analysis. The question of how migration situations should be viewed will be pursued later, when it will be seen that various writers have found this approach useful.[2]

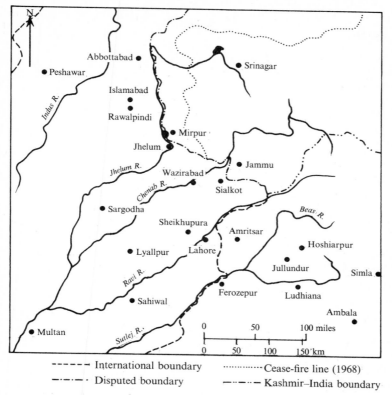

International boundary ⋯⋯⋯Cease-fire line (1968)
Disputed boundary ⎯⋯⎯⋯ Kashmir–India boundary

Mangla is on the River Jhelum, between Jhelum City and Mirpur City.
Irrigation canals are not shown.

Map 2. North Pakistan, north-west India and part of Jammu and Kashmir

2.1 Pakistani migrants in Britain

According to the 1971 Census of Great Britain, there were 169,700
people of Pakistani origin in Britain, of whom 128,000 were born in
Pakistan and 41,400 were born in Britain.[3] The following description of
the 'typical' Pakistani migrant in Britain is condensed from several
sources.[4]

One of the most striking aspects of the emigration from the Indian
sub-continent is that there are only a few, very small areas from which
people emigrate abroad. For Pakistan, two main areas are important.

Punjab is an area which saw considerable disruption at the time of Partition and has also seen pressure for land: Punjabi emigrants come from around Lyallpur (a Canal Colony town) and other areas in north Punjab such as Jhelum and Sialkot District. Other emigrants are from Mirpur, in Azad Kashmir, an area which has long been one of outmigration, where the movement of population has been accelerated by the Kashmir problem and by the construction of the Mangla Dam which has rendered many people homeless. Smaller numbers of migrants come from areas around Rawalpindi, Campbellpur and parts of the North West Frontier.[5]

People from these areas speak dialects of Punjabi, Mirpuri and Pushtoo respectively, and unless they have been to school and learnt Urdu they are unlikely to be able to communicate easily with one another. Most Pakistanis in Britain come from village backgrounds. Generally they have received little schooling and few are able to read (and speak) Urdu, and even fewer know English. The smaller numbers of Pakistanis from urban areas are more likely to know Urdu and English.[6] Some men from rural areas own land, though those who do are mainly small landholders. Most migrants were involved in agricultural work before migration though sizeable numbers were in military service. Although there are considerable cultural differences between migrants from the various areas of emigration, the literature often suggests that Islam is an important unifying factor, and Rose points out the connection between Islam and patriotism.[7] Dahya mentions the presence of some Shia Muslims in Bradford, but it is not possible to tell from the available material what the balance between Sunnis and Shias is for the whole country.[8]

The demographic features of Pakistani migrants in Britain also need to be noted. The Pakistani population is predominantly male, and many of these are men who came to Britain between the ages of twenty and forty-five. There were very few Pakistani females in Britain until the mid sixties: according to Lomas, almost 70 per cent of the Pakistani females enumerated in the 1971 Census arrived in Britain after 1967.[9] In 1971, 55,400 females of Pakistani origin were enumerated, of whom 22,900 were born in Britain.[10] Of the remaining 32,500 Pakistani females who had entered Britain, about three-quarters were over fifteen in 1971.[11] The number of adult women entering Britain as dependants peaked at 4,555 in 1967, and was just over 2,000 in 1972.[12] These women entering Britain have usually come as dependants of men already in Britain (normally their own husbands). A common pattern is

46

for the man to migrate alone. A few years later he either summons his wife and children to join him, or (if he is not already married) his relatives arrange a marriage to a girl from home who joins him in Britain. It should be pointed out, though, that the 55,400 Pakistani females are still outnumbered by 114,300 males, and since the balance between the sexes among the young children is nearly even, this discrepancy is largely accounted for by the small numbers of adult women in Britain. Lomas shows that the sex ratio is around 3 : 1 in the ages between fifteen and forty-four and over 5 : 1 for people forty-five or older.[13] One further factor which affects the sex ratio is that while a woman may be accompanied to Britain by her adolescent sons, her older daughters may be left at home, either married or left in the care of relatives. The Pakistani population in Britain still contains many 'single' men, either in the sense of bachelors or of men whose wives remain in Pakistan. The Pakistani population of Britain is not only a predominantly male one but is also a young one: this is partly because few migrants are yet aged over forty-five, and partly because, if their wives arrive in Britain, they have young children or are only at the stage of establishing their families. Of the persons of Pakistani origin born in Britain, about 75 per cent (in 1971) were under nine years old, and most of these were four or under.[14]

One further facet of the situation is the considerable mobility of the Pakistani population in Britain. In 1973, some 40,000 Pakistanis embarked from Britain, and of the 49,000 Pakistanis who entered Britain in that year, nearly 21,500 were returning from a short stay abroad. The numbers re-entering after short periods abroad was around 15,000 for each of the previous five years. These figures include women, of whom just over 3,500 embarked in 1967 and over 8,000 in 1972. In 1972, more Pakistani women embarked than entered (entry figures include dependants entering for the first time, and those entering for any other reason, including re-entry after short stays abroad), and there was also a negative balance of men entering (of about 3,500) for the first time since statistics were kept. It can be assumed that most of the embarkations are to Pakistan, as holders of Pakistani passports face immigration restrictions in many other countries.[15]

2.2 The migration to Britain

There is very little material about the antecedents to the migrants' arrival in Britain.[16] Generally, the sorts of conditions which I discussed in the previous chapter are viewed as a backdrop for the migration: the motive behind migration is often described as 'economic': in other words, the migrants are considered to be in search of a livelihood, and certainly they have tended to move to the conurbations in Britain which have labour shortages. However, as Dahya argues, this sort of explanation is not the whole story. He considers that the migration is economic, but only in the sense that the migrants have left home in order to achieve an income which can be used to improve the living-standards and status of the family still at home.[17] Remittances are used to pay off debts incurred to finance the migration, and then to improve the existing landholdings, to build a *pukka* house and to establish some sort of business.[18] In other words, the migration should not be seen simply as 'economic' (in the sense of providing for the basic biological needs of the migrant), for the economic benefits which accrue are intimately tied in with prestige at home.

The typical form of migration is 'chain migration', a point which is simply the obverse of the point made above that migrants come from a few small areas. What is implied in the term is this: relatives contribute cash for the migration of one man, who finds work in Britain; from his savings he 'sponsors' the migration of another kinsman. Subsequent savings on the part of these two enable further kinsmen to migrate, and thus the 'chain' develops. Generally, the earlier migrants help the later ones with housing and finding jobs, and thus related men from the same areas in Pakistan tend to cluster in Britain.[19] In some cases, a man may spend a few years in Britain, and when one of the people he has sponsored (a son, younger brother or nephew) is established, he may return home.

The migration from Pakistan is a recent one. Eversley and Sukdeo point out that there were very few Pakistanis in Britain in 1950.[20] Small numbers began to arrive in the 1950s, but the figure was still under 20,000 in 1960, partly because of emigration restrictions in Pakistan. The Commonwealth Immigrants Act (1962) was brought into force on 1 July 1962, and Rose quotes figures which indicate that 50,000 Pakistanis had entered Britain in the preceding eighteen months.[21] This 'beat-the-ban' rush consisted mainly of young men. During the 1960s, alterations in work-voucher controls made it more difficult for men in search of work to enter Britain, and gradually more women and children came into Britain as the dependants of men already here. The number of Pakistani dependants entering in 1967 (4,555 women and 12,664 children) was double that for 1966.[22] Nearly 70 per cent of the

48

Pakistan-born females in Britain arrived after 1967.[23] Generally, there is some time-lag between the arrival of the man and that of his dependants: partly this is a question of waiting until he is established in Britain, but there are also considerable delays in Pakistan in the issuing of entry permits to dependants.

Thus, although the Pakistani population in Britain is still largely a male one, there are now some women (and children) who have joined their husbands. Deakin sees this as an unintended consequence of the immigration controls: he suggests that a shift has taken place from the earlier male 'chain migration' (in which a man would often spend only a few years in Britain and then be replaced by a relative) towards families coming for settlement.[24] Almost certainly, immigration controls *are* closely connected with the rising numbers of Pakistani school-children in Britain, but it is possible that Deakin's assumption that the families all intend to settle in Britain is premature. Although I have little direct evidence for this, a rather different interpretation is more consistent with the present intentions of the Muslim informants. Since the introduction of immigration controls, a Pakistani man has been entitled to bring his own wife and children into Britain, and it is no longer easy (as it was before the controls) to sponsor a young male relative. Since the migrants are generally young, their wives and children are also young, and many of the children are under sixteen and entitled to enter as their fathers' dependants. Such children may only enter if accompanied by their mothers. While it may be the intention of the families to settle in Britain, several informants did tell me of women coming to Britain with their sons, but returning to Pakistan shortly afterwards, leaving the sons in Britain. Among my informants, young daughters were brought and the women have stayed in Britain, but the intention is to return to Pakistan when the girls reach adolescence, leaving the sons to work in Britain and support the family through remittances to Pakistan. In other words, for some families, the entry of women can be seen as a strategy to try to recreate the earlier situation of male-dominated chain migration within the constraints of the immigration regulations. Unfortunately, while I know from informants that this is happening (families have indeed gone home, and the language centre discussed in Chapter 3 had some boys in Britain without their mothers), the statistics conspire against any assessment of the *extent* to which this is happening. Home Office records of embarkations include women going back to Pakistan for holidays, as well as any going back permanently. In several years the embarkations have slightly exceeded the entries of women other than dependants entering for the first time. While this may lend some slight support to my argument, it is in fact impossible to assess the matter satisfactorily on the basis of the available statistics since there are far too many unknown elements.[25] Obviously, the implications of sponsoring young men (who are well-socialized Pakistanis and who do not attend school in Britain) are quite different from sponsoring young children (who have to attend school and whose commitment to being 'Pakistani' is not yet cemented), but it is important to note that parents can still insist that daughters at least return to Pakistan. The material is unfortunately scant on this, but this does seem to be another factor not discussed by Deakin.

2.3 The case studies

Here I shall present biographical details about four Pakistani men in Bristol, two Muslims and two Christians. Each informant, of course, is unique, so after the case studies I shall give a general description built up from all the informants.

Abdul is one of three Muslims who spent some time outside Pakistan before coming to Britain. He did not join anyone he knew in Britain, but several of his relatives now live in Bristol. Of these, Rashid was central in summoning their relatives. The two Christian men illustrate differences between the Muslims and the Christians in motivation for migration and in intentions about future residence. Abdul, Rashid and Matthew were all born around 1930 and had been married before they came to Britain, and Rashid and Matthew have children now in their late teens or early twenties. Emmanuel is rather younger, and he did not marry until he had been in Britain for a while.

2.3.1 Case study 1: Abdul

Abdul was born in Amritsar, the son and grandson of teachers, and had completed Matriculation shortly before Partition. With some friends, he set fire to a soap factory during the Partition disturbances (causing Rs. 100,000/- damage), and his parents immediately sent him to an uncle in Lahore. Shortly afterwards, the rest of the family moved to Lahore (by now in Pakistan). After his father's death, Abdul had to stop studying and take a clerical job to support his mother and two sisters. They bought a house, where his mother lives with one brother (who owns an electrical equipment shop). The other brother (now deceased) set up a bookshop in Karachi, where the other married sister lives. Abdul himself did not stay in Lahore long. An office friend said that conditions were better in Saudi Arabia, and in 1952 Abdul joined Arabian-American Oil Company. Although the pay was good and he was able to send money home to support his family, he did not like the dull life and he resigned after eight years.

At this stage he was married to Akhtar, who was not a relative. Her family were Kashmiris and her paternal grandfather had bought land and settled in Ferozepur (now in India). Her father was a teacher. She is twelve years younger than Abdul and so hardly remembers the flight to Lahore. She went to school in Lahore until the eighth class, when she was married. She says she did not meet Abdul until the marriage, and was very surprised to be married as she had expected to study longer, as a brother and sister had done.

Abdul found he could not settle in Lahore. While in Saudi Arabia he had heard a lot of talk about Britain. He still had enough money for the air fare, and after eight months of marriage he decided to 'take a chance' and come to Britain. He arrived on Christmas Eve 1960. He and a friend hoped to establish an import business for Pakistani goods, but could excite no interest in the various places they visited: Glasgow, Manchester, Rochdale, Newcastle and Birmingham. His friend went back home, saying that he would not stay in Britain if he had to do manual work. Abdul asked some friends in Manchester for advice: he had found the weather intolerable, and wondered if he could find a climate like the one he knew from Punjab. They told him to go to Gloucester, Bath or Bristol, but no further south as jobs would be hard to find. He was soon settled as a bus conductor in Bath.

However, his first child was about to be born, and he felt that his children should not see him as a bus conductor but should be able to say that he was 'something'. On advice from the employment exchange he did a training course in Bristol to be a fitter, and soon afterwards Akhtar joined him, in November 1961. She had been unwilling to leave Pakistan, but Abdul's brother in Karachi (who had cared for her during Abdul's absence) insisted, as he thought Abdul might not return to Pakistan. Abdul took a job with an engineering company in Bristol where he still works. Two years later they moved from Bath to Bristol so that he would have a shorter journey to work, and they bought a small house near Temple Meads Station, where they stayed for two years. Abdul's kinsmen Rashid and Javed rented a room in the house for about a year, and Rashid's sister also lived there for a while with her

51

husband and children. The house was demolished in 1966, and Abdul bought his present home. In that year, Abdul obtained a work permit for Bashir (his sister's husband) in the firm where he worked, and Bashir lived in Abdul's house. Bashir moved to Javed's house for a while and subsequently bought the house next to Javed's, which he sold when he moved to a house directly opposite Rashid's home.

Abdul and Akhtar have not been back to Pakistan. Abdul intended to, but they cannot afford to go as a family now, as they have seven children. Akhtar wanted to go when her mother was dying, but could not leave the children, and now she feels that she has no reason to go, especially as her children's education would suffer. She was very homesick at first and intended to go back soon; indeed she did not bring all her gold ornaments with her, and the jewellery came by hand (brought by Abdul's brother's daughter Jamila when she came to marry Javed, and by myself in 1971). Abdul and Akhtar think their children are too young for them to be thinking far into the future, but they think the children are unlikely to want to live in Pakistan. Abdul has considered taking British nationality so that he and Akhtar could live in Pakistan and yet easily return to Britain to visit their children.

2.3.2 Case study 2: Rashid

Rashid was born in Amritsar, the son (by a second marriage) of a teacher. Rashid was the third son, and Mumtaza (who is also in Bristol) was the only daughter and the youngest child. Their father died when the children were small, and the family had to live off rents from various properties. By 1947, Faisal (the eldest brother) was already married, and he and his wife and child fled to Lahore and set up house with Faisal's mother and siblings. In the rush, Rashid's mother mislaid some papers relating to their property in Amritsar, so they were unable to claim full compensation in Lahore; and in addition, Rashid's half-brother began to make claims on the inheritance from their father.

Rashid had completed Matriculation by 1947, but his education was interrupted. Faisal had been trained as a *hakim*[26] and Ghulam (the other brother) is a trained homeopathic doctor, though he works in Government service. Rashid had no special training and began clerical work in a private business. In 1955 (when he was about twenty-five) his mother made arrangements for his marriage: he was to make a choice from four girls, and eventually married Ruxsana after asking his relatives for advice. She is a relative (though not a close one) and was fourteen at

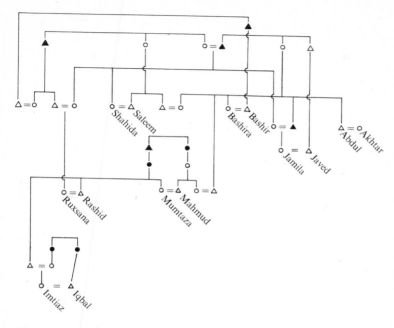

All genealogies are incomplete: only individuals necessary to show
up the links between adult migrants have been included. The following symbols
have been employed:

△   man
○   woman
▲/●   deceased
=   married

Fig. 1. Genealogy for case studies 1 and 2, Abdul and Rashid (2.3.1 and
2.3.2)

the time. She is the eldest of ten children of a Lahori man involved in
wholesale watch-strap selling; his wife is his father's sister's daughter
and was brought up in Amritsar. Ruxsana was taken away from school
when she was twelve, as her father did not want her to go out any more.
   Ruxsana and Rashid occupied one storey of the house in the old
city where Faisal and Ghulam lived with their wives, children and
mother. Their mother was unwilling to send Mumtaza away in marriage,
but the brothers said she should be married, and the match was arranged

53

with Mahmud (also a relative). About four years later, Mahmud had
gone to Britain, and Mumtaza had joined him. Rashid and his family
were concerned for Mumtaza's well-being in a strange country, and
Rashid began to think of moving to Britain, for, he explains, it is a
brother's duty to care for his sister. His brothers had more family responsibilities, and Ghulam could not easily leave his work in Government service. In addition, Rashid was not as well off as he would have
liked and friends advised him to go to Britain. His mother was against
his going and wanted Mumtaza to return to Pakistan: she was always
distressed that two of her children should live so far away. But Rashid
decided he had to leave immediately, because of impending immigration restrictions in Britain. He asked his employer to lend Rs. 1000/-,
and the employer insisted on giving him the sum towards his fare.
Rashid arrived in Britain early in 1962. Ruxsana stayed with her children in Rashid's brothers' home, living mainly off rents from houses
owned by Rashid as his inheritance. Rashid also sent money from
Britain, which enabled his second son to attend an English-medium
school, though his first son was going to an Urdu-medium school.

Rashid first joined Javed (his kinsman) in Rochdale, and then
moved to Newcastle, where Mumtaza was living. Then, for a short while
he did 'women's work' in a cotton-spinning factory in Rochdale, until
1963 when (on Abdul's advice) he moved to Bristol with Javed. They
lived in Abdul's house for a while. Rashid suggested that Mahmud move
to Bristol, which he did later that year.

Rashid's mother became seriously ill, and Rashid went back to
Pakistan overland after he had been in Bristol for less than a year. He
spent a year in Pakistan, and then returned to live in Bristol. In 1965 he
went to Pakistan for a holiday, but a travelling-companion robbed him
in Quetta, and he had to spend longer than intended in Pakistan to save
for the return journey.

Ruxsana did not want to come to Britain at first, partly because
Rashid had been able to visit Pakistan. However, the children were un-
settled and were asking where their father was; moreover, she felt she
should be with Rashid, because she felt rather cut off from the outside
world. She could not go out alone and Rashid's brothers could not
easily take her out. At first Rashid thought he would be unable to save
the air-fares for the family: he told Ruxsana she could come if they
sold their houses. Eventually, they decided to go overland, and Rashid
again went to Pakistan in 1968 to arrange passports for his family. They
had a difficult journey: one son was ill, they were robbed in Zaidan at a

Muslim shrine, and trains were cancelled and delayed. They arrived in Britain with £2, and were taken to Bristol by Mahmud. At first they rented rooms in a house belonging to an unrelated man from Calcutta, but Ruxsana was unhappy as she was the only woman and unused to mixing with men. Mahmud had recently bought a house, and Ruxsana suggested they move there, so that she would have company (and also not have to pay so much in rent). Within a year of arriving in Bristol, Ruxsana was able to move into her own home, as Rashid arranged a bank loan to buy a house a few streets away from Mahmud.

Rashid has had several jobs in Bristol. He is here for the money and not very concerned about the type of work, provided he is well paid. He has taken some jobs outside Bristol (as he considers there are few well-paid jobs for people like him in Bristol) but he likes living in Bristol as there are few 'coloureds' (i.e. West Indians) there. He is unwilling to take time off work to do a training course as he intends to return to Pakistan soon; he is content to work hard and do as much overtime as possible.

Ruxsana went to Pakistan for a holiday in late 1971, with her youngest child, a son born in Bristol, and with Rashid's niece Imtiaz (Faisal's daughter) and her two children. Ruxsana was delighted to be going home: before coming to Britain, she had been able to see her mother and sisters daily, and she missed them a great deal. Imtiaz was going to show her children to her relatives, and attend Iqbal's brother's wedding. She also intended to buy some land in Lahore, but did not because of the political situation at the time. Because of the danger, Ruxsana was summoned back to Britain by Rashid, but Imtiaz delayed as she was making arrangements for her younger brother to come to Britain. (He arrived after I had finished fieldwork, and still lives in Imtiaz's home in Bristol.)

Rashid and Ruxsana say they would go back to Pakistan permanently now if they could 'afford' to. Ultimately, they will go, as their relatives and property are there. They may go back in 1975, leaving the two eldest boys in Britain: Rashid hopes that he will have enough property in Pakistan to be able to live off the rents, with some contributions from his sons. The two girls are coming to the age when Rashid does not want them to mix with boys at school, and he wants them to go to a mission school and then women's college in Lahore. The boys left in Britain will eventually return to Lahore and support the family with a business, he hopes.

Rashid is an important focus in his family, as he has called several relatives to live in Bristol. His sister Mumtaza was first to come. Iqbal (a relative, now married to Rashid's niece Imtiaz) lived in London with his own sister until his marriage, but Rashid wanted Imtiaz to move to Bristol to be company for Ruxsana. Javed also bought a house in Bristol under Rashid's influence. For a while he lived in Manchester and left the house under Bashir's care. When he married Jamila (Abdul's brother's daughter, and also Ruxsana's mother's sister's daughter), he sold the house, and lodged with Iqbal's sister in London. London was too expensive and he later bought a house in the street next to Rashid's home. Bashir bought a house opposite Rashid's in 1971 and Rashid helped him with the paperwork involved in bringing Bashira and their children to Britain. Rashid also helped Ruxsana's mother's sister Shahida when she came to Britain in 1969 with her five children. They all lived in Rashid's house for nearly a year (paying rent, but eating together), and Rashid helped Shahida's sons to buy a house a few streets away. With the exception of Abdul, all Rashid's relatives in Bristol now live within a very close radius of his house.

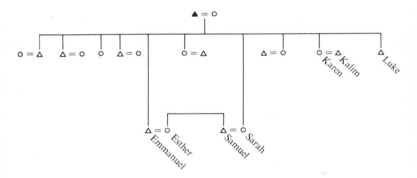

Fig. 2. Genealogy for case study 3, Emmanuel (2.3.3)

2.3.3 Case study 3: Emmanuel

Emmanuel is one of ten children of a Christian man who worked in hospitals in Rawalpindi District. Three of Emmanuel's brothers and a sister came to Britain, and have all moved on to Canada. One brother did a Ph.D. at Leeds (and married a British woman) and is a university lecturer; the other two brothers are in business in Canada (and have married Canadian women); the sister is a nurse. Emmanuel studied after

Matric, in Pakistan, and on his brothers' advice and with their help, he moved to Bradford in 1960. His brothers and sister then went to Canada, and Emmanuel met up with Robert (no relation). Robert had been advised to leave Pakistan by his father, and had lived in Tehran (with his sister) for five years before coming to Britain, where, he was told, life was better for Christians. He had no relatives or friends in Britain.

Emmanuel and Robert moved to Bristol late in 1960 because there were 'too many Muslim Pakistanis' in Bradford. They bought a small house and lived as brothers. Robert's marriage was arranged in 1963, and after going overland to collect his wife, he continued to live with Emmanuel. Emmanuel went overland to Pakistan in 1964 to collect his mother and a young brother and sister. (His father was still working and intended to come when he retired, but he died shortly afterwards.) Only three of Emmanuel's siblings (all married sisters) remain in Pakistan. Emmanuel was married in 1966 to Esther, the sister of his own sister's husband, who is a teacher. In 1968, Robert went to Pakistan with his wife and children, and returned with his parents as well. Because the original house had become crowded, Emmanuel bought a separate house, where he moved with his wife, mother, brother and sister. Robert later bought a house nearby and his parents moved to another house. The original house was rented out, until Emmanuel's sister Karen married and arranged to buy the house from Robert and Emmanuel. Robert's father was widowed in 1970 and has lived with Robert ever since.

The major reason for coming to Britain was to obtain better work, but they also point to the position of Christians in Pakistan. According to Karen, they thought they were coming to the 'Holy Land' and would no longer have difficulties. Robert and Emmanuel both trained as fitters, but Emmanuel did not do well financially, and his brothers suggested he join them in Canada. His brothers sent money for the air-fares and Emmanuel and his mother went to Canada in 1970. Emmanuel decided to settle there, and told Esther to sell the house in Bristol, and she and their daughter joined him later that year. Karen, her husband and her remaining brother live in the same house. Karen is worried that she has no control over her brother, who works very irregularly, and her brothers may sponsor him as well, in the hope that he will settle better in Canada. Karen herself would like to go to Canada, but Kalim (her husband) is not very keen to go. In 1972, she went to Canada to attend a brother's wedding.

57

Robert and his family may also leave Britain, as he considers that there are too few well-paid jobs. They have thought of going to Canada, and as they all have British passports, Australia was then also a possibility. He would not go back to Pakistan as he considers there are too many difficulties there for Christians.

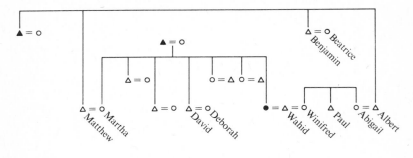

Fig. 3. Genealogy for case study 4, Matthew (2.3.4)

2.3.4 Case study 4: Matthew

Matthew is one of four sons of a pastor whose parish was near Sialkot. Matthew's eldest brother was a teacher and never left Pakistan, but his other two brothers, Benjamin and Albert, are also in Bristol. Their sisters are all married and living in Karachi. Matthew studied beyond Matric. and worked in the army in Karachi for a while. After Partition he married Martha, a Christian woman from south India who had joined her brothers in Karachi. Matthew considered that his chances as a Christian in Pakistan were poor, and though his family thought he was unwise to leave the good job he was in, he went to Tehran and became a guard at the British Embassy. His wife and children and Martha's mother and three brothers joined him there, along with the Muslim man who had made a love-match with one of Martha's sisters (who had later died in childbirth). They lived in a large house, and the children attended the Indian school (learning to read Hindi rather than Urdu).

After nearly ten years in Tehran, Matthew became concerned about their security as Christians in Iran. Then in 1961, they visited Pakistan and were horrified by the poverty. A year later, Matthew finally decided to go to Britain. He asked his two brothers in Karachi to join him in Tehran, and they went overland to Britain together. They stayed in Bradford for six months, and then moved to Bristol as they had made contact with Robert (through his sister in Tehran) and had heard that there were very few immigrants there. The three brothers bought a house and the families began to be summoned.

Matthew's household from Tehran arrived first, with the exception of one of Martha's brothers, who still lives in Tehran. Wahid also came, and in 1964 he married Albert's wife's sister Winifred from Lyallpur. In 1966, Benjamin brought his wife and children from Karachi and they set up a separate house a few streets from Matthew's home. Martha's unmarried brother married a Bristol girl in 1968, and after living in Matthew's house for a year, they moved to a house at the end of the street. Wahid and his family moved to a council house, as Winifred began to feel that she could not cope with living in a single room in Matthew's house with her small children. Martha's older brother also moved to a council house with his wife and adopted Persian daughter, and Albert moved into a house with his English 'girl-friend' and son. (His wife and two daughters still live in Pakistan.) Albert's wife's brother Paul (who is also Winifred's brother) lived in Matthew's house while doing 'A' levels. He is at London University, and when he completes his course will probably go to Pakistan to collect his mother and Albert's wife and children (whom he has been supporting) and to marry, and then he may go to Canada.

None of them plans to go to Pakistan permanently. Benjamin's wife visited Pakistan in 1971, but none of the others has been back. One of Matthew's daughters says she and her husband will never go back to Pakistan as he had bad experiences of getting work in Pakistan, and she thinks that they too may go to Canada.

2.4 The backgrounds of the informants

2.4.1 Place of origin

Most of the informants are Punjabis. Several families have lived for many generations in Pakistani Punjab, while others fled to Pakistan from eastern Punjab in 1947. This uprooting may have brought difficulties of settling and made candidates for emigration, but I have little direct evidence for this. Even the informants who came from Karachi are mainly Punjabis, since they moved to Karachi in 1947 or more recently. They speak Punjabi at home, and make marriage ties with kin in Punjab. One family from Sialkot had extensive connections in Jammu before Partition, and a Christian family from Rawalpindi has links in

Abbottabad. Martha, her siblings and Wahid are the only ones with slender links in Punjab: they moved to Karachi from Mysore.

2.4.2 City residence

All my informants came from large towns or cities, such as Sialkot (population about 150,000 in 1961), Lyallpur (about half a million), Lahore (one and a half million), and Karachi (over two million). One household comes from Jhelum and another from Wazirabad.[27] The Muslim informants who have property generally hold it in the form of houses rather than land. Some own their own homes, and others which they rent out, and a few people also own some land. One man, for instance, was allotted some land after he retired from twenty years' military service. Only the man from Jhelum holds the major part of his property in land. The Christians have no property in Pakistan.

Several families have long connections with city life.[28] Rashid was from Amritsar, Mahmud (his sister's husband) from Ludhiana and his brother's wife from Delhi, and her sister married a Lucknow man. These relatives are now scattered in various cities of Pakistan. Another family moved from Amritsar to Lahore after Partition. Matthew's father was Lahori, though his work (as a pastor) took him to villages.

2.4.3 Education

The male informants are all literate in Urdu and most knew English before coming to Britain.[29] Several were educated to Matric. or beyond. One man has an extensive vocabulary, as he used to learn English prose passages, while another man says he has only progressed since coming to Britain, as he did not like his English teacher. All the men can now converse in English, though not always fluently.

2.4.4 Occupation before migration

No family lived solely on incomes from property before migration. None of the men worked on the land: most did clerical and secretarial work. Zafar was a clerk with the Electricity Department in Lyallpur; his maternal uncle was a High Court advocate in Lahore, and three of his wife's brothers run a drapery business in Sialkot, one is a dam-keeper and another a government clerk. Saleem trained as a fitter, and worked in the Middle East before coming to Britain. Mahmud came to Britain

while still at college; his father and father's brother are retired judges.[30]
All the other men were in employment before migration, though their
incomes were not adequate for their needs and ambitions. Zafar even
thought his job in Pakistan was a good one, even though he was unable
to save any money, until he came to Britain and found what he could
earn.[31]

2.4.5 Religion

Most of my informants are Sunni Muslims, who are the majority in
Pakistan. The literature about Pakistanis in Britain does not indicate
whether they are mainly Sunni or how many are Shia, or of the various
sub-divisions of these main branches. However, some informants are
Christians. The literature does not comment on Christian Pakistanis or
Indians, but there are several settlements in Britain. I met a British
Anglican priest in Lahore who had several Christian Pakistanis in his
parish in Slough and who had taken leave to get some idea of life in
Pakistan; there are also Christian Pakistanis in Glasgow and Birmingham,
and possibly elsewhere.

2.4.6 The female informants

As I have indicated, there are still far more Pakistani men in Britain (and
in Bristol) than Pakistani women, and the very presence of my female
informants in Bristol makes their menfolk unusual. All but one of the
women are literate in Urdu, most of them having been taught at school.
Two women had private tutors at home to preserve *izzet*, and of these
one, Yasmin, trained to be a teacher and the other, Zebunnisa, made no
effort to learn and is effectively illiterate (her brothers by contrast all
speak English well). Few of the women learnt English. One of the older
Muslim women, Tahira, learnt English over thirty years ago and has
forgotten all she learnt. Her daughters learnt English but are unable to
read or converse adequately. One reason why the women do not generally know English is that English is introduced only in the higher grades
(except in English-medium schools) and many of the women were taken
away from school before they had started learning English or when they
had learnt very little: Ruxsana left school at twelve and Akhtar at fourteen. One Muslim woman stands apart from the rest as she has B.Sc.
from the University of the Punjab. Several of the Christian women are
trained teachers, but only one of them taught in Pakistan. They went to

mission schools and can all converse in English. Very few of the Muslim women had any training and none of them worked outside their homes afterwards.[32]

2.5 The migration to Britain

2.5.1 Reasons for leaving Pakistan

There is a sharp distinction between the Muslims and the Christians on their reasons for leaving Pakistan. In Chapter 1, I discussed the problems of poverty, low pay and the lack of security and state benefits in Pakistan. My Muslim informants point to these factors when they talk about leaving Pakistan: they say that, although they had jobs in Pakistan, they were unable to provide their families with long-term security there. A few pointed to the pressures in such a poor country for people in good positions to help their relatives, and they say that nepotism blocked their entry into better jobs. In such a context, the man without influential contacts has to rely on himself, and emigration is a means of alleviating his problems. Most of the Muslim men plan to stay in Britain just long enough to let them acquire enough property in Pakistan to give their families security when they go back home. A few have no definite plans to go back, but their reasons for leaving Pakistan are the same.

The Christians emphasize religion: Pakistan is an Islamic country, and, the argument runs, Christians suffer from discrimination when they apply for jobs. Several consider that Christians have no future in Pakistan, and they thought in terms of 'getting out' to escape the insecurity they saw. Theirs is a permanent exile, for (unlike the Muslims) they do not think that temporary emigration can solve their difficulties, which are religious as well as financial.

2.5.2 Reasons for coming to Britain

From the vantage point of Pakistan, several places are possible destinations. Several families have relatives in the Middle East or Denmark or North America. Some of the men in Bristol (three Muslims and several Christians) even tried out some other country before coming to Britain. Why, then, was Britain eventually chosen?

There were three main factors involved. Firstly, information filtered back to Pakistan about conditions abroad: there is a widespread feeling in Pakistan that wages are better in certain other countries and that people there can easily save from their earnings. Most of my informants mention specific people who reported about foreign parts. Britain's temperate climate compares very favourably with Middle Eastern countries, and several men said that while wages were high in the Middle East, there were no facilities for passing leisure time. A second important factor is that several (though not all) of the men had relatives living in Britain before they left Pakistan, and they joined up with them here. A few informants came to Britain rather on speculation, having no contacts to help them when they arrived here; some, but not all of them, have helped relatives to come to Britain. A final and rather negative reason for coming to Britain is that as Commonwealth citizens, Pakistanis were free to enter Britain until the introduction on 1 July 1962 of the Commonwealth Immigrants Act (and since the Act, several informants have persuaded their employers to sponsor a relative from Pakistan, several other countries (such as the U.S.A.) had immigration restrictions which effectively prevented the entry of such people as Pakistanis.

2.5.3 Financing the migration

Migrations from Pakistan seem generally to have been financed by relatives pooling savings to enable a young man in the family to leave. When he arrives at his destination, he either repays the loan or begins a chain of migration by paying for the fares of another relative. In turn each new migrant settles his debts and helps another to migrate or sends money back to his close family, so that they can improve the home or buy land or machinery. This is the sort of pattern described by Dahya.[33]

My informants appear rather different. Some managed to migrate without becoming indebted to anyone by using savings or by selling or mortgaging their own property. A few were helped by their brothers in Pakistan, and in only a few cases have relatives already in Britain helped the man to migrate. Furthermore, these migrants are much less the representatives of their wider family than the men described by Dahya: they have decided for themselves to migrate, and the benefits of the migration go to the migrant and his wife and children.[34]

The major expenses of the journey are obtaining a passport and the fare for the journey itself. Standard fees for passports are nominal, but many informants told of substantial bribes to persuade passport clerks to process their application (as much as Rs. 1000/- in some cases).

Others claimed that they managed to get their passports without extra expense only by being threatening.[35] Most informants came by air, from Karachi to Heathrow Airport. A few came by the much cheaper overland route, including the Christian men who had been living in Iran, but at the time they came the roads were poor and there was little organized traffic.[36]

2.5.4 The time of migration

All but two of the male informants arrived in Britain before the enforcement of the Commonwealth Immigrants Act (1962), and thus did not require any entry permit. Bashir was later sponsored by his wife's brother, and Tariq had been in the British army before independence and so had priority in the allocation of vouchers.[37]

Several informants say that rumours of impending immigration restrictions in Britain impelled them to migrate at the time they did: Zafar said he had been contemplating coming to Britain, and felt that he would have no chance if he left his decision any later. He arrived at 9 p.m. on 30 June 1962!

2.5.5 Migration within Britain

Only a few of the informants moved directly to Bristol. For the Christians the choice of Bristol was fairly clear-cut: they all spent some time in Bradford, but decided to move to Bristol as Bradford had too many Muslim Pakistanis, and they heard that Bristol had very few. Two Muslims seem to have arrived in Bristol by chance: Zafar (with no contacts in Britain) helped an illiterate man through British Customs who suggested that he join him in Bristol, and Abdul moved south in search of tolerable weather. Most of the other men moved to Bristol to join relatives; Saleem rarely stays in Bristol, but his wife and children joined relatives there.

This picture is probably over-rationalized, as my informants have been accounting for their own behaviour and portray themselves as men of decision. An extreme case might counteract this impression: Mahmud was still a student when he came to Britain. His elder brother in Britain was rumoured to be having an affair with an English woman, and Mahmud's father wanted this sorted out. Mahmud came (at his father's expense) supposedly for a short visit in 1960. His wife came a year later with his brother's wife, and Mahmud did not return to Pakistan until he went for a holiday in 1969.

2.5.6 The care of dependants left in Pakistan

Nearly all the men were married when they arrived in Britain, and usually there was some time-lag between the arrival of the man and of his wife and children. A few men had their marriages arranged only after they had been in Britain for a few years, but for most there arose the problem of the temporary care of their dependants in Pakistan. Usually, the woman stayed in the home of her husband's parents, remaining under the guardianship of her husband's father or brothers. A few women went to live with their own relatives.[38] Yasmin was brought up in Karachi, but moved to Jhelum when she married her father's brother's son. When Yusuf came to Britain, she returned to Karachi and lived with her widowed mother in her mother's brother's home. Bashira lived with her widowed mother and one of her married brothers and his wife and children, because Bashir is an only son and his parents are both dead. Only Shahida lived in a household alone with her children: her husband's only brother lived in Karachi (and cared for his widowed mother) while she stayed in Lahore. Otherwise, the migrants' wives all had some male relative immediately available if necessary.

2.5.7 The dependants who come to Britain

There are still relatively few Pakistani women in Britain, and it is a matter of some importance to discover why these few have left Pakistan.[39] It is often suggested (with some justification) that the position of women in Islam and the importance of *purdah* and modesty discourage Pakistani men from exposing their wives to the dangerous influences of Britain. Moreover, bringing a wife and children to Britain entails several expenditures: over and above the cost of the journey, it must be clear to the migrants that sterling in Britain buys a lot less than the sterling equivalent does in Pakistan, and the extra expenditures can only delay their anticipated return to Pakistan.[40] Men who bring their wives to Britain are not only endangering their *izzet* but are also being economically irrational. It is somewhat surprising, then, that Muslim men have brought their wives to Britain, for it would be cheaper and safer for the man to keep his dependants in Pakistan and visit them periodically. Indeed, this is what most Pakistani migrants in Britain have done.

Generally my informants say that the wife can only execute her duties by living in her husband's household. In some cases, the migrant suggested that his wife join him in Britain, in others the husband gave in to his wife's pestering. One woman could not cope with her children without her husband's taking any direct responsibility for their up-bringing. Tahira commented that a woman has two homes, her parents' before marriage and her husband's after: in some cases (like her own) her duty to her husband may mean that she follows him to places she has no desire to see. Now her husband is surrounded by a happy united family, whereas before she came to Britain, he was alone and had to do all his domestic chores. She also benefits, as her husband is available to help the children understand the difference between right and wrong. She came to Britain four years after her husband, but would have come earlier if the arrangement of passports and entry permits had not taken so long. (She had two daughters over sixteen and therefore had to per-suade officials that the girls were wholly dependant on their parents.) In general, the Muslim women say that uniting the family and having their husbands present to discipline the children were important reasons for their coming to Britain.

I suspect that another factor may operate, though this has not been made explicit by informants. In Pakistan, I was often told of relatives in Britain who set up home with British women and stopped supporting their wives and children in Pakistan. Fear of this may be behind the reasons the women give for coming to Britain, though to confess as much to me would obviously reflect badly on the woman's opinion of her husband. Some comments do lend support to this point. A young married woman in Lahore told me that her husband wants to go to Britain, but she will not allow him to go alone, because her father's brother treated his wife badly and she does not want the same to hap-pen to her. The case of Mahmud lends additional weight to this point: he came to check up on his brother, and after he had lived with his brother for about a year, he asked his father to send Mumtaza to Britain. His father said that his brother had been in Britain longer, and there was still the problem over the English girl-friend, so the two women came to Britain together. Mahmud's father (who is explicitly worried about the corrupting effect of life in Britain) wants Mumtaza to return to Pakistan with her daughters: Mumtaza says she will not leave Mahmud in Britain alone. A further factor may be the one mentioned above (2.2) that bringing the whole family to Britain enables the man to ensure that he can be replaced by his son when he wants to return to Pakistan; again, informants are not explicit on this, but several of them do intend to return to Pakistan with their wives and daughters, leaving sons in Britain to help support the family.

The Christians are in a different position with respect to bringing dependants to Britain. The wife and family of the migrant try to move to Britain as soon as possible. Furthermore, while the Muslim men have only brought their wives and children, and helped other male relatives to migrate in some cases, the Christians have often brought aged relatives and younger siblings of both sexes to Britain. I shall go into the reasons for this in the final chapter.[41]

Having made the decision to come to Britain, several methods were used by informants to bring their families. Some men went to Pakistan overland, organized the passports and papers and then brought the family to Britain. This is cheap but time-consuming, and means that the migrant has no earnings in Britain for some time. More often male relatives in Pakistan helped the woman and children with the paperwork and the migrant's relatives flew to Britain. Often the process of arranging entry permits was harrowing: several women told of nightmare experiences at the British High Commission when their terrified small children were taken aside and made to recite all the names and addresses of their grandparents, parents and siblings (in order, it was supposed, that entry permits would not be given on false pretences). Yasmin told of numerous journeys from Sialkot to Rawalpindi because her eldest daughter is slightly darker than her siblings: a Pakistani official at the High Commission noted this, and the family was involved in considerable expense and lengthy correspondence with Yusuf in Bristol before officials were satisfied that she really was his daughter.[42]

2.6 Conclusion

It is important to appreciate that the arrival in Bristol of the migrant's dependants is not the end-point of the story. Several of the Christians have either already gone to Canada, or intend to do so. The Muslims say they do not plan to stay in Bristol but intend to return to Pakistan. In fact, during the fieldwork two families returned to Pakistan; in both cases there was an adolescent daughter who was to be married, and in one case the girl's father wanted to contract a second marriage as he had only one daughter from his first marriage. In addition, several migrants or their wives have spent holidays in Pakistan, often of several months' duration. One family moved to join relatives elsewhere in Britain, and soon afterwards began to talk of going back to Pakistan permanently. The situation, then, is very fluid, for people are leaving Bristol as well as arriving there.

In this chapter, I have been looking at the decisions of my informants to leave Pakistan and come to Britain, and their plans for their families. Although economic factors are important, they are complemented by social and political factors in the decisions to migrate, to live in Bristol and to move on (back to Pakistan or to some other country). The Christians, for instance, refer to their special position in Pakistan, and several migrants have moved to Bristol to join relatives there. In the final three chapters, I concentrate on aspects of the 'total field of economic and social relationships'[43] in which the informants are involved in Bristol, and consider the ways in which the ties back home and the incapsulation of the Muslims constrains their present activities and affects their decisions about the future. In the final chapter, I consider the different involvements of the Christians and Muslims in this total field of relationships, and the implications of these differences.

3. Pakistanis in Bristol

3.0 Introduction

Bristol's growth has been closely linked with overseas trade, much of it with places now in the Commonwealth: wealth came in from the slave trade, and contemporary interests in tobacco, sherry and chocolate point up this connection. Perhaps surprisingly, then, Bristol was not characterized by a large coloured quarter before the Second World War, as such ports as Cardiff and Liverpool had been.[1] The central residential zone of the city has experienced an exodus of locals to the suburbs, leaving an area of decaying and cheap houses which has attracted people from outside Bristol. At first, these were mainly Irish and Europeans, but during the late 1950s and the 1960s increasing numbers of people from the New Commonwealth have moved to Bristol, largely into the now very heterogeneous central area of St Pauls. Some have moved into the adjacent areas of Easton (to the east) and Montpelier (to the north), and others to Totterdown and Bedminster to the south of the city centre.

Even so, Bristol's coloured population is small when compared with other cities in Britain. According to the 1971 Census, the total population of Bristol County Borough was 426,655, of whom 21,490 people were born outside the United Kingdom but are normally resident in Britain. Of these, 8,775 were born in the New Commonwealth: 3,620 in Jamaica (and far fewer in the other parts of the Caribbean), 1,535 in India and 855 in Pakistan. Of the Pakistanis, 565 were male, 315 of them married; there were 290 Pakistani females, but only 180 of them married.[2] This ties in with Richmond's finding that in 1965 half the Indo-Pakistani households consisted of 'single' men and only a quarter had children present.[3] The 'Pakistani' population enumerated in 1971 includes some Bengali Muslims. Most of the people from what used to be West Pakistan come from Mirpur (and have generally not brought their wives to Britain) and from villages in Punjab. There are also some Punjabis from cities, some of whom have brought their wives and children to Britain, and it is from this sector of the population that my informants come.

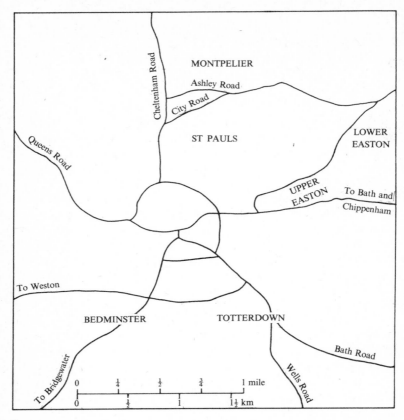

Map 3. Sketch map of central Bristol, showing major roads and the areas where my informants live

3.1 The sources of the informants and the fieldwork

Since my informants are unrepresentative of the Pakistani population in Bristol, it is important to consider the ways in which I gained entry: my methods have, after all, affected the nature of the sample. There were several reasons for deciding at the outset that it would not be satisfactory to draw up a random sample of Pakistani families in Bristol. Firstly, I felt that personal introductions would give better entry in view of the rather touchy situation at the time (late 1969) and the likely fears of potential informants: my suspicion was later borne out, and I did indeed

find personal recommendations the most satisfactory way of making
contacts. In any case, there would have been the insuperable practical
problem of drawing up a random sample: in view of the pattern of migration (described in Chapter 2) the 1961 Census was out of date, and
the 1966 10 per cent Sample Census[4] (which did not break down the
figures for New Commonwealth residents of Bristol County Borough by
nationality) was also of little use, since I was interested in locating
Pakistani women, and very few were in Britain by 1966. So the Census
material could not indicate the number of Pakistanis in Bristol; furthermore, the situation is very fluid and the voting register would have been
unable to provide a random sample: not only are Pakistanis rather less
likely than the native population to be registered to vote, but also the
population is a very mobile one. The most up-to-date figures which I
could obtain were for the numbers of Pakistani children in Bristol
schools (144 in 1969),[5] but even these would have needed care in interpretation, since some of the boys (particularly adolescents) were
living alone with their fathers, and some married women did not yet
have children of school age. The prospects for drawing up a satisfactory
sample of Pakistani families were slight, and even if I had been successful, the sample would have been out of date by the end of fieldwork
two years later.

As it transpired, there were distinct advantages in not trying to draw
a random sample. However, the practical problems were uppermost in
my mind at the beginning, and I decided to rely on personal contacts.[6]
My informants can be attributed to three sources. From January 1970,
I began to attend the Language Centre at Hannah More School.[7] The
six Pakistani girls had their classes separately from the boys. At half-
term, I visited the girls in their homes and explained my interest in
learning about their life in Britain. I was warmly welcomed and my contacts with these families radiated out through their networks. They were
all from urban backgrounds and mixed with kin, and so this route did
not provide access to any rural families. The president of the Pakistani
Association also introduced me to a family which had been in Britain
since the 1950s (the adolescent daughter was born in Britain). I was also
introduced to a Sikh girl who feared her parents' response if she had
anything to do with me: she put me in touch with two Christian women,
and through them I made contact with the Christian Pakistanis in
Bristol, but with no more Muslims, except two lapsed Muslim men married to Christian women. By spring 1970 I had established contact with
some twenty Muslim households and some ten Christian households

71

(the numbers varied since people moved in and out of Bristol during the fieldwork period), containing about seventy adults and adolescents.

There were two main reasons for not developing many more new links. On the occasions when I tried to make contact by myself, I met with rebuff, while contacts made through informants flourished, so I decided to make the most of the contacts I had. Furthermore, it was difficult to cope even with the informants I had, without endangering the rapport I had established: visits often took several hours or even a whole day, and many informants put great store on my visit and asked if I was angry if I did not visit them frequently. Thus, I decided to develop broader relationships with these relatively few people.

As a woman, I had obvious advantages: the women and girls were happy to meet me, even if they could not speak English, while the men would treat me as an 'honorary male'. The converse would not have happened for a male researcher. The major problem was language: only the men and the Christian women speak English, and my contacts with the Muslim women and newly arrived girls could plainly not proceed until I learnt Urdu. I had already established that the families were from urban backgrounds and that the Muslims, at least, maintained strong links with their kin at home. A stay in Pakistan was the best way to solve the language problem, and from November 1970 to April 1971 I was based in Lahore: I had regular Urdu lessons and made contact with as many of the migrants' relatives as possible.[8] Naturally my facility in Urdu is rather limited, and while I can generally use leads gleaned from informants talking to one another, my most important information has come from situations where I have been more able to control the pace of conversation.

On returning to Bristol, I re-established contact with informants there. My informants (especially the women) were pleased that they could now speak Urdu with me, and that I was sufficiently interested in their country to have gone there. The women became more relaxed: I was considered to have 'become Pakistani', a person who knew their ways and brought news from the homeland. During the final seven months of fieldwork in Bristol I gained the most valuable information from my informants there; at this time, I had problems of 'over-rapport', as I was unable to be a 'good kinswoman' to all my informants at once. Generally, I met them in their own homes: some men disapproved of their wives or daughters going out to visit, and all emphasized the importance of traditional hospitality. Several families put me into the position of 'married daughter of the household', and thereby precluded reciprocal hospitality.[9] With several people usually milling around, it was generally impossible for conversations to be other than informal: often when I had a particular issue in mind conversation would be diverted onto the latest wedding in the family, a letter from home or an impending visit to Pakistan, and in any case my informants were just as curious about me and British people in general as I was about them (and often their questions and assumptions would suggest new lines of enquiry for me).

In discussing a random sample of Pakistani families in Bristol, I commented that there were in fact advantages in not having drawn one up, though these only became apparent later on. As the research proceeded, the whole issue of the 'unit for analysis' (which I discuss in Chapter 5) became more important, and in the light of that, taking a random sample of Pakistani families in Bristol would have been an irrelevant activity: the ways in which the families are linked and the connections which are maintained outside Britain would not have shown up. By following up the threads in my informants' networks I was able to look at the connections between individuals, and employ the connections to cross-check information or learn how they evaluated one another's actions. Furthermore, by my maintaining contact with families over two years, rather than using single formal interviews with informants, trust could be built up, and chance comments gave me new leads to follow up. Since leaving Bristol, I have maintained contact with some of the families and I have also visited some of the migrants' relatives in Pakistan again.

3.2 The occupations of the informants

The men have come to Britain largely in search of work, and most of them are employed as unskilled labourers in various factories and construction sites in and near Bristol. A few have had training, for instance as fitters, and they have skilled jobs; Tariq is a Post Office sorter, Mahmud a bus conductor, and Iqbal has a supervisory post at a smelting works in Avonmouth. Only two of the men are wholly self-employed: now that Javed's clothing stall at a local market is established he finds he no longer needs to take paid employment; Kalim used to work in Avonmouth, but now devotes his time to a car repair business he had been building up in his spare time.

Most of the men have been in several jobs since they came to Britain, and even in several types of work. Zafar used to be a bus conductor, but changed his job after a passenger insulted him and told him to go back to his own country. Yusuf also used to be a bus conductor, but decided he would get better pay in factory work. Rashid has worked in factories and also on several construction sites around Bristol. In general, it can be said that the men have had a radical change in their work since coming to Britain; while bus conductors or Post Office sorters require knowledge of English, most of the men are in work which requires no such special skill, and only a few of them have had any training for a trade.

The net household incomes show considerable variation, from about £20 to about £50 per week.[10] Zafar (with five children) earns about £22 and his children are entitled to free school lunches. At the other end of the scale, Tariq reckons that his household has over £50, as he brings home about £30 and each of his three working daughters brings home £10. Iqbal's gross pay is nearly £40 (in his supervisory job) for which he does not need to work overtime. Most of the men earn less than this, and they often have to work overtime or on night shifts in order to do so. Several of the men increase the family income by taking in lodgers or doing part-time work, mainly at weekends. Yusuf used to work on a stall at a Sunday market and was paid £5; then he became a partner in one of the film clubs and takes a share of the profits, along with two other informants. The two self-employed men have allowed their previously part-time work to become their major sources of income. The other Muslim men without second jobs usually take overtime when it is available: Mahmud has a basic pay of under £20 working on the buses, but he makes this up by working two or three hours of overtime each day. Rashid and Zafar used to work on night shifts but both found that this was unsatisfactory after their families arrived. Only one Muslim man, Abdul, refuses to take overtime, and he derides the Pakistanis who spend their lives working and cannot enjoy their family lives.

While most of the Muslim men work in the company of other Pakistanis, the Christians generally avoid Pakistanis. A factory at Yate, the smelting works at Avonmouth and a power-station construction site have concentrations of Pakistani workers; on the other hand, a few of the Muslim men do work in factories, or factory sections, in which there are no other Pakistanis. Since the focus of the fieldwork has not been on relationships at work, I have no direct information about the extent and quality of mixing between work-mates. However, many of the Muslim men do not eat in works canteens and my impression is that there is little contact with British work-mates. Certainly, outside work, the Muslims do not mix socially with British work-mates, in their homes, pubs or clubs, and they do not often mix with other Pakistanis who are not kin.[11] The Christian men mix rather more with British people, but even so, not often with work-mates outside the work context. The men are usually union members, but largely because their places of work are union shops, and they are not involved in union work.

3.3 Pakistani institutions in Bristol

There are two mosques in Bristol, one in an old church in Totterdown run by Sunni Pakistanis,[12] and one in a house in Montpelier run by Ahmadiyyas. My informants have little to do with either: few attend even the festivals. The men appear to have been more involved in mosque affairs before being joined by their wives, and some keep up their contributions to the purse, although they rarely attend. However, the children are generally much more involved: both mosques hold Koran reading classes daily, before or after school for about an hour. Young children and adolescent boys make up most of the classes: several informants no longer send their daughters to the classes. A few families have never sent their children to the classes but teach them at home, or have a private teacher. Until mid 1971, the Christians held monthly Urdu services at the Y.M.C.A. with the help of a Pakistani pastor from London. Since his death, they have no special facilities, but they attend local churches.

Several organizations help with problems such as completing income tax forms and the paperwork entailed in bringing families to Britain. One of my informants is involved with the Pakistani Association, and he spends several evenings each week helping illiterate Pakistanis who come to the Association's offices. He told me that the Association was largely set up to compete with a wealthy man who charged fees for writing letters: the Association charges only the cost of postage and stationery and is putting the other man out of business. None of my informants has used the services of the Association.

There are several Pakistani and Indian grocery shops in Bristol, selling spices, oriental vegetables, and in the case of Pakistani shops, *halaal* meat. There are also drapers and a travel agency. Most are in St Pauls and Totterdown. My informants buy foodstuffs at the grocery shops, but generally buy other household goods at local supermarkets, and cloth at the Sunday market.

There are two film clubs, one run by Indians, the other by Pakistanis, which show films on Sundays, usually Indian films as these are regarded as superior to Pakistani ones. Most of my informants have seen films at the clubs, but very few go frequently. My impression is that only a hard core of single men attends regularly. My informants often said that they could not afford to take the whole family every week. The cinema programmes are posted in local Pakistani and Indian shops, and several informants are on the mailing-lists.

3.4 The schooling of the children in Bristol

Most of the migrants' children are still attending school in Bristol. Children born in Britain, or who entered Britain when of primary-school age were directly allocated to schools. Baptist Mills School in St Pauls took most of the secondary-school-age children and provided special lessons for those with language difficulties, but in 1968 the school became a primary school, and older children were dispersed: the dispersal was overseen by the Education Committee, who wanted an even spread of immigrant children in the city's schools. The language problems of new arrivals were to be dealt with at a special centre at Hannah More School: most of these children are from India and Pakistan, though a few Chinese and Cypriot children have also attended. Until the children have a basic knowledge of English, they attend the centre full-time, and then gradually increase their attendance at the secondary school to which they have been allocated. When set up, the centre had 24 boys, but by 1970 there were two full-time classes of over 20 boys and a class for 6 Punjabi Pakistani girls and a Cypriot girl which met twice a week. By 1971, most of these girls attended their secondary school full-time. When my fieldwork finished there were enough new arrivals to warrant a full-time class for girls.

In January 1969, the Education Department reckoned that there were 144 Pakistani children (57 of secondary age) and 178 Indian children (61 of secondary age) in Bristol schools.[13] Separate figures for girls and boys were not kept, though few of the secondary-age children were girls: this corresponds with findings elsewhere in Britain and with the lack of need for a class for girls at the Language Centre until 1970. Teachers at the Language Centre said that several boys were living with their fathers in Bristol, while their mothers were in Pakistan. It is likely that village Pakistanis are opposed to bringing their adolescent daughters to Britain, but lack of contact prevents checking my suspicion. Among my informants (from urban backgrounds) adolescent daughters were not generally left behind in Pakistan but even by the end of the period of fieldwork, no village girls had passed through the Language Centre, though many of the boys came from villages.

Several parents (particularly Muslims but also some Christians) are concerned that a number of secondary schools are co-educational and that they have little choice about which school their children attend. They are especially concerned about their daughters, but say there is little to be done; several families are thinking of returning to Pakistan (as some have already done) with their adolescent daughters to avoid having them educated with boys. Muslim parents are also worried about school lunches, for they want the children not only to avoid eating pork but also any meat which is not *halaal*. The children at the Language Centre have lunch there, but eat no meat. Teachers at the Centre told of the humiliation these adolescent children experienced when they first arrived, when their inability to cope with British cutlery was exposed in full view of the much younger British children who attended a junior school in the same premises. The Pakistani children themselves commented on the unpalatability of the food. On one occasion the Pakistani children boycotted the lunches as they were worried that the puddings had been cooked in 'pig-fat' and for several days they refused to take any food at the school. Children at other schools usually take packed lunches or go home for lunch. Apart from the special language teaching, the girls have lessons in traditional Indian embroidery and sewing, but there is no formal teaching in Urdu or Hindi, and religious instruction takes place only at home or in the mosques. As with the question of men mixing with work-mates, I have no direct information about how Pakistani children mix with one another and with British children (and children of other nationalities). The Christian children have more contact outside school with British children, and often criticize Pakistani children for sticking together. The difference is certainly in part related to facility in English, as most of the secondary-age Muslim children still find it easier to speak Punjabi than English, while the Christians are all fluent in English. However, it is not simply this, for the Muslim children rarely visit the homes of other Pakistani school-friends (unless they are kin): this is especially true for the girls, though even the boys are normally at home outside school hours and go out only to the mosque or with the rest of their families. Few of the parents have much contact with their children's school, or have met the teachers. Thus, as in the work sphere, it seems that in the educational sphere, at least at present, very few inter-ethnic relationships have developed, and those which have are largely restricted to the school context.

3.5 The women informants

Each woman has come to Britain as the dependant of a man already here, usually her own husband, though in one Muslim family adult unmarried daughters have also come. Among the Christians, three women came as dependants of their children, and one as the dependant of her brother. None has come in her own right, by obtaining a work voucher in Pakistan.

Very few of the women work outside the home. Of the married women, one Muslim works in a laboratory of a chocolate factory (the woman with the B.Sc.), and two Christians work, Ruth in a laundry (since 1971 when her youngest child began nursery school and she felt bored at home) and Karen running the shop attached to her house. Winifred would like to work. Tariq's three eldest daughters (all unmarried) work together in a bakery; this is because they have several younger siblings and the oldest brother is still in Pakistan.

The men consider that it is shameful for their wives to work: Winifred is prevented from working by Wahid, and Robert put up a great deal of opposition when Ruth wanted to work. Generally, though, this is only one factor, for several women have young children and consider that they should devote themselves to domestic duties. The men all learnt to cook before being joined by their wives, but now they do not contribute to household work, unless their wives are in hospital or on holiday in Pakistan. In Pakistan, the pattern would have been rather different: most households contained more than one adult woman, or at least were near to relatives' homes, and in times of crisis other women (and not the husband) would take over the household work. In Pakistan, several informants pointed out, domestic chores could be shared, and the work redistributed when anyone was ill or away, but in Britain, they have to cope single-handed, as each household generally eats and cooks separately, and this makes it difficult for one woman to help another. Sometimes, though, they may help one another out, by cooking or shopping, especially if the woman has gone to Pakistan and has left her husband to care for some of the children.

There is another difference between Pakistan and Britain, for the women now do some of the family shopping, whereas they used to shop in the *bazaar* only rarely. Most are helped by their children after school.

Generally, the women are more completely responsible for the stocking and organization of their homes than they were in Pakistan, and many of them (especially those with several children) spend much more time alone at home doing housework than in Pakistan. Most manage to make time to visit relatives (or friends) during the day or after their husbands and children are at home, and this is their major recreation. Although there are English classes for Indian and Pakistani women, none of my informants attends now (as they consider that they do not benefit much and have plenty to do at home). Most of the women are based in their homes and orient their lives to their domestic work and their relatives.

3.6 The informants' housing conditions and life-styles

While all the informants live in those areas of the city in which most of the Commonwealth citizens live, none lives in a road with more than three Pakistani households. The early-twentieth-century houses are all terraced, and most have two storeys (a few have three) each with two main rooms, and all have internal bathrooms, some of which have been built onto the back of the house recently. Only three households are in rented property, all of it 'patched' property in Totterdown owned by the Council. All the rest of the families live in homes which they are buying or have already paid for: the prices were around £1500 in 1968, but were over £2000 and sometimes nearer £3000 by 1971.

As can be seen from the previous chapter, it was quite common for migrants to share their homes with relatives until they were able to buy their own homes: now almost all the households consist of nuclear families, that is, just the migrant with his wife and children. Sometimes, some of the children have not come to Britain: Tariq's son was in Abu Dhabi when his mother came to Britain and he now lives in Pakistan; Mahmud's eldest daughter lived with her grandparents in Lahore for several years, but she has now rejoined her family in Bristol; in two other cases, adolescent daughters were married before their mothers came to Britain. In most cases, however, the migrant has brought all his children to Britain. Only one Muslim family is not nuclear: Saleem works outside Bristol, and his wife and children live together in a house which his sons bought, with his help. Three Christians, Emmanuel, Robert and Martha, have brought aged relatives to live in their households; Matthew's married son lives in the same house, and in another case Luke lives with his married sister Karen. In a few cases, family income is being supplemented by the taking in of lodgers, but the lodgers do not eat with their landlords and there is little contact between them. Emmanuel had West Indian lodgers, and a British prostitute lodged with Robert (though he refused to let her practise in his house). Zafar has a British family living in his house, and several other Muslim men have had lodgers in the interim between buying their houses and the arrival of their wives.

In 3.2 I indicated that even after overtime and supplementary jobs, the net household incomes show considerable variation. Despite this, the life-styles of the families vary little. The houses themselves are very similar, and they have been furnished in similar ways; all the houses have a television, a tape recorder (to tape film songs or messages for relatives) and a refrigerator, and several households own a car. Most are also buying their own homes. Richmond found that the housing conditions of coloured people in general in Bristol did not vary in relation to occupational status, as they did for white people: generally, they were living in rather poor housing, despite variations in income.[14] However, Richmond's interpretation of how this has come about is not sufficiently substantiated to be acceptable. He writes, 'It can be asserted with confidence that the poorer living conditions experienced by coloured immigrants in the Bristol survey area are not due to demographic or economic factors, but were almost certainly due to discrimination against them because of their race or national origin.'[15] While I would not deny that discrimination exists, it is necessary to consider another possibility which makes more sense of my findings among Pakistanis, and might be applicable to Indians and West Indians too.[16]

I would argue that it is essential to establish what is done with the net household income. For British people, it can fairly safely be assumed that this sum is effectively the spending money at the disposal of the family, but at least for my Muslim informants another factor has to be taken into account (one which Richmond himself mentions, pp. 93–4, but which he subsequently omits), that is, the amount of money which ceases to be at the family's disposal in Britain because it is sent out of the country. In addition, my informants like to visit Pakistan, and this entails considerable expense. I shall elaborate on some of the implications of this in later chapters, but it is vital here to bear in mind that newly arrived migrants may dispose of their incomes differently from British people of the same objective class position, and that spending patterns have an impact on living conditions in Britain. For my informants, differences in income related largely to differences in amounts sent to Pakistan and hardly to differences in life-styles in

Britain. Tariq, for instance has a wife and eight children to support in Bristol, but he also supports a son and his widowed sister in Pakistan. Other families have sent money to buy land or a new house in Pakistan, or to help brothers support their parents. The effective incomes which the informants leave at their disposal in Britain vary only slightly, though take-home pay ranged from about £20 to over £50 per week. Richmond also points out that coloured people generally pay for their homes faster than British people (and often at much higher rates of interest): while this means that they pay out more each week for their homes, my informants (some of whom had short-term bank loans) considered that it was best to complete the payments, so that they would actually own their houses within a couple of years. Here again cultural differences are important, and it is important to bear in mind that property ownership is a very important element of status in India and Pakistan. This is a point also made by Dahya.[17] Moreover, my informants were not interested in moving to the suburbs: they saw the benefits of living near relatives and could see little point in spending more on their houses, as this would reduce the sums available to invest in Pakistan. In sum, it is vital to consider the extent to which the housing conditions of coloured people in Bristol are affected by discrimination on the grounds of colour, and how much they are the result of options taken by the migrants themselves. For the Muslim Pakistani informants, a great deal hinged on their own decisions.

4. Ethnic separation and cultural change

4.0 Introduction

In this and the final chapters, I look more closely at the lives of my informants in Bristol: with whom they mix and do not mix, and why; attitudes to Britain; and responses to migration. In this chapter, I am concerned with the changes and the continuities in behaviour and attitudes of the Muslim informants.

Pakistanis in Britain are often described as 'non-assimilating', and this is true for the Muslim informants. The question, then, needs to be asked, given the geographical contiguity of British people, how is it possible for Pakistanis to cling to many of their 'old' ways and fail to adopt British life-styles and values? I look at this issue in terms of boundary maintenance, and consider the social boundaries which Pakistanis erect which effectively insulate certain areas of life and protect them from modification. However, the migrants' behaviour has changed in certain respects, and I also consider the question of how to interpret such changes. It is vital to be clear whether such changes should be called 'assimilation' or whether they are more appropriately viewed in a different light.

4.1 Assimilation and boundary maintenance

An issue of concern to writers considering the ways in which immigrants adapt to life in their new homes is the nature of 'assimilation'. Total assimilation can be said to have occurred when two processes have taken place: when the immigrants have completely sloughed off their old culture and taken on that of the host society; and when they have become involved in all types of social relationships with members of the host society. Recent writings point out, however, that the process of assimilation is not only complex but is by no means inevitable.

Gordon considers that there are two major dimensions to assimilation, the structural and the cultural.[1] Cultural assimilation entails the adoption of the values and behaviour of the 'host society', while structural assimilation involves the development of primary group relationships (i.e. kinship or intimate friendship links) with members of the host society. What has happened in the United States, Gordon argues, is that cultural assimilation has occurred, but large-scale structural assimilation has not: American society is characterized by structural pluralism and not cultural pluralism, with Protestants, Catholics, Jews and Blacks being the major discernible groupings, within which people tend to marry and find their close associates. Greeley considers that Gordon has overdone the element of cultural similarity between these structurally separate groupings and argues that there are cultural differences (especially in the realm of kinship norms) even among groups which have been in the United States for several generations.[2] This seems to make sense, for it would be difficult to see why groups would remain separate unless differences existed or were believed to exist which prevent people from developing friendships outside the ethnic group. With this proviso, Gordon's attempt to break the process of assimilation into its elements is useful, since it points to the complexity of the process and to the fact that it is possible for distinct groups to remain so over considerable periods of time: after all, the Blacks in the U.S. have yet to become assimilated, after three hundred years in America.

Assimilation is complex, and in addition discussions of it frequently beg the question of just what it is that the immigrant is supposed to assimilate into. In the British context, as Patterson and Allen each point out, it has often been presumed that Britain is homogeneous and that 'the British way of life' can easily be described. They both argue that this is not so, and that recently there has been more recognition of the complexities and cultural diversities of British society.[3] How, then, is it possible to talk in any simple fashion about assimilation? Britain is divided by regional differences, class, education and religion. While there may be a basic level of agreement, there is also a wide range of issues on which British people disagree, or at least put a different emphasis. Moreover, these differences cover many aspects of social life, such as family life and leisure pursuits, career ambitions and political orientations. Given this diversity, how can the process of 'anglicization' be delineated in terms of the cultural traits which it might imply?

In fact, my informants are not inclined to 'assimilate' in any case, and they also tend to perceive 'British culture' as monolithic and react to it as if it were. Furthermore, to focus on the cultural aspects in this way is unsatisfactory, for as Barth points out, objective cultural differences and similarities are not necessarily congruent with the way social relationships are patterned: he prefers to concentrate on structural features in order to delineate the boundaries between ethnic groups. His particular concern is with the social (or structural) processes which enable distinct ethnic groups to co-exist through time, even when they occupy the same territory and when their members have social relationships not only within the ethnic group but also with members of the other group.[4] Barth discusses the 'boundary maintaining mechanisms' which organize relationships between people in different ethnic groups. His focus is on the *structural* aspects of the situation, that is with the way in which social relationships are patterned and the nature of the relationships involved. He explicitly rejects the idea that ethnic groups can be adequately defined in cultural terms (I shall discuss his reasons below), and argues that the proper way to demarcate an ethnic group is to look at the way different types of social relationships are patterned.

This point rests on a distinction between single-stranded and multiplex relationships. All relationships are not the same: some are transactional (as between employer and employee or shopkeeper and shopper), others are concerned with education, others with power distribution and patronage, others with religion. In other words, the 'content' of social relationships may differ. Furthermore, some relationships may entail only one content, while others may have several strands: this is the difference between single-stranded and multiplex relationships. In a situation in which ethnic groups co-exist, Barth argues that single-stranded and multiplex relationships are not randomly distributed. Multiplex relationships are concentrated inside the ethnic group (not all members of the ethnic group necessarily have multiplex relationships with one another — it may be too large or there may be restrictions on the free mixing of the women — but there is the potential for the development of such relationships inside the ethnic boundary). On the other hand, relationships between members of different ethnic groups are single-stranded: they are limited to certain specified realms of activity, as for instance the relationship between a white employer and the immigrant worker, and they do not carry over into other activities and become multiplex.

This patterning of social relationships hinges on a system of signals, whereby people broadcast their membership of one or another ethnic group by the use of 'diacritical signs': these may be dress, hair-style, language, religious allegiance (all aspects of culture which the individual can change if he wants to change his ethnicity) and physical features, such as skin colour, hair texture or things like initiation scars (which cannot be altered at will). When people meet, these signs indicate their ethnicity to one another and imply allegiance to different basic value orientations which demarcate the groups in question. On the basis of these signs, a relationship may develop, either as a single-stranded one (between members of different ethnic groups), or into one which may end up covering many aspects of social life (such as religion, family life, leisure activities).

The critical focus of investigation from this point of view becomes the ethnic *boundary* that defines the group, and not the cultural stuff which it encloses. The boundaries to which we refer are of course social boundaries, though they may have territorial counterparts. If the group maintains its identity when members interact with others, this entails criteria for determining membership and ways of signalling membership and exclusion. Ethnic groups are not merely or necessarily based on the occupation of exclusive territories; and the different ways in which they are maintained, not only by a once-and-for-all recruitment but by continual expression and validation, need to be analysed.

What is more, the ethnic boundary canalizes social life — it entails a frequently quite complex organization of behaviour and social relations. The identification of another person as a fellow member of an ethnic group implies a sharing of criteria for evaluation and judgement. It thus entails the assumption that the two are fundamentally 'playing the same game', and this means that there is between them the potential for diversification and expansion of their social relationship to cover eventually all different sectors and domains of activity. On the other hand, a dichotomization of others as strangers, as members of another ethnic group, implies a recognition of limitations on shared understandings, differences in criteria for judgement of value and performance, and a restriction of interaction to sectors of assumed common understanding and mutual interest.[5]

Ethnic groups may persist even when there are relationships between people in different groups, since there are also rules for the conduct of inter-ethnic relationships: certain sorts of contact are permissible in sectors which are allowed to 'articulate', while other contacts are not permissible and enable certain types of activity to be 'insulated' inside the ethnic group. These insulated sectors Barth calls the 'backstage' for the ethnic group: they are largely irrelevant to non-members and are protected from 'confrontation and modification'.

85

> Entailed in ethnic boundary maintenance are also situations of social contact between persons of different cultures . . . Yet where persons of different culture interact, one would expect these differences to be reduced . . . Thus the persistence of ethnic groups in contact implies not only criteria and signals for identification, but also the structuring of interaction which allows the persistence of cultural differences. The organizational feature which . . . must be general for all inter-ethnic relations is a systematic set of rules governing inter-ethnic encounters . . . If people agree about these prescriptions, their agreement on codes and values need not extend beyond that which is relevant to the social situations in which they interact. Stable inter-ethnic relations pre-suppose such a structuring of interaction: a set of prescriptions governing situations of contact, and allowing for articulation in some sectors or domains of activity, and a set of proscriptions on social situations preventing inter-ethnic interaction in other sectors, and thus insulating parts of cultures from confrontation and modification.[6]

In other words, signals of ethnicity indicate what sort of social relationships are appropriate or inappropriate for the actors concerned, and the resulting patterning of social relationships means that some sectors of activity can be insulated from outsiders and be the locus of cultural differences between co-existing ethnic groups. A mapping of social relationships will locate the boundaries between ethnic groups by contrasting between those areas characterized by dense networks of multiplex relationships (concerned largely with the insulated sectors of activity) and those areas characterized by single-stranded relationships, which may involve only certain members of the groups with people outside in a limited range of activities.

In focusing on the way in which social relationships are patterned in situations of contact between ethnic groups, Barth makes an explicit departure from the commonly held view that ethnic groups can be adequately defined in terms of the culture which they contain. For Barth, ethnic groups are definable only by the way in which relationships are patterned, and he denies that cultural content is a useful way of demarcating groups. He has several reasons for this position. For one thing, two ethnic groups may look remarkably similar to an outsider: he could draw up a cultural inventory and establish that they share many cultural traits (e.g. language, items of dress). However such an activity may prove totally irrelevant to the actors and thus to the way in which members of the different groups interact, for (to them) the similarities may be rendered unimportant by just a few differences which they may latch onto and treat as critical ethnic markers. To them the differences may be substantial, and this perception has important implications for the way in which relationships develop. For instance, it would be possible to draw up cultural inventories for Punjabi Muslims and Punjabi Sikhs, and establish that in language, dress, diet, notions of *izzet*, the giving of dowries to daughters when they marry and so forth there are many similarities between Sikhs and Muslims. However, to them, differences in religious allegiance (and the political allegiances implied by religious differences in this context) are the crucial element which demarcates them from one another, and these differences are echoed in subtle differences in dress, language (for instance the forms of greeting) and diet. In other words, actors may ignore certain similarities and make much of a few differences. Conversely, they may ignore differences which are quite obvious and stress such similarities as they find. Rischin indicates that differences between Jews of German origin and Yiddish-speaking Jews of East European origin were buried in this way in New York.[7] In general, a cultural inventory would not help in predicting which items in the inventories will be considered relevant ethnic markers to the actors involved. Another way of putting this is to say that social phenomena are very complex, and that the ways in which various cultural traits are distributed among people do not necessarily coincide with the boundaries of ethnic groups or with one another. While there may be a myth that an ethnic group contains a totally distinctive culture, empirically this is rare: ethnic groups living near to one another often have a lot in common and can only be distinguished by the few markers which are accorded special relevance by the actors.

Furthermore, ethnic groups living side by side over considerable periods of time may use the same names and operate ethnic boundaries between their groups, and yet their cultural contents may change radically. At the level of national groups, the confrontations between the English and the Scots or the English and the French have long histories, but English culture has not remained static, any more than the Scottish or French cultures have, even though the dichotomization English—Scottish persists and may even become sharper. This same principle may operate on a much smaller scale. Again, over time, ethnic groups may become (in terms of their cultural inventories) more similar, but if certain markers persist and are used (e.g. skin colour or religion), then the demarcation will continue and the relationships between people will be organized around the *assumption* of 'basic differences' (of which colour

or religion are simply the most conspicuous). Moreover, not only may
the culture contained within an ethnic group change, but so too may
the items which are used as markers or signals to indicate ethnic group
membership. If cultural traits in themselves are regarded as basic to
ethnicity, it becomes a problem to explain how ethnic groups remain
separated through time given the changes in cultural content. Barth
looks at the matter from the other side: specific cultural traits are fluid
and flexible and in his view are not capable in themselves of demarcating
ethnic groups over time. The continuity consists in the persisting dichotomization between members and outsiders (and the patterning of relationships which relates to this dichotomization) and *not* in the cultures
contained by the ethnic groups and used as ethnic markers by them.

It is very common for ethnic group members to believe that they are
inherently different from outsiders, and that these differences result
from biologically heritable traits. This is particularly true of 'racial'
groups, but it is true also of groups between which it would be impossible to delineate any cluster of genetic differences and whose differences are those brought about by different processes of socialization. It
is often felt that ethnic groups can gain members only by the birth of
children to adult members, and lose them only through the deaths of
members. While this is probably true in most cases, individuals *may*
change their ethnicity and become incorporated into another group.
When an ethnic group vanishes, it is not simply the case that all the
members have died out: often more important is the drain of members
who have become incorporated into another ethnic group and have
managed to cross the ethnic boundary and take on the ethnicity of
another group. Such a process would be complete 'assimilation'. The
balance of such defections need not be all in one direction, though, and
Barth argues that it is quite possible for there to be a 'flow of personnel'
in both directions between ethnic groups and yet for the groups to remain. What is required are means of incorporating new members (by
educating them into the group's culture — the way in which religious
converts are dealt with is a good model of this), and for individuals to
have incentives to defect, such as the belief that they will do better in
the other group. If individuals find incentives to defect in both directions then two groups may persist, even though individuals change their
allegiances.

Barth has laid out a way of looking at inter-ethnic relationships
which is based on structural and not cultural matters. He concentrates
on the way in which different types of social relationships are patterned

in situations in which there is inter-ethnic contact, and he argues that cultural traits are too flexible to be used as defining points of ethnic groups. The culture contained within ethnic groups may change, and also objectively not be completely different from the cultures contained by neighbouring groups, and furthermore individuals may move across the ethnic boundaries and join another ethnic group. Yet the ethnic groups concerned may persist and live side by side over time, provided that there are rules for the conduct of inter-ethnic relationships. It should be pointed out that while this is an important contribution to the understanding of inter-ethnic relationships and the ways in which social factors help in the maintenance of cultural differences, Barth deals only cursorily with the factor of power: 'agreement' over the rules for inter-ethnic contact may conceal what is merely compliance on the part of a weaker partner who would really like to be accepted by members of the stronger group. However, as will be clear, this particular drawback to Barth's analysis is not crucial for my Muslim informants (though it is for the Christians) since they wish to maintain their separation from British people, and do not want to be merged with them.

In the next part of this chapter, I shall look at the boundary-maintaining mechanisms which are operated by the Muslim informants in Bristol, by considering the ways in which social relationships are patterned and the reasons behind such patterning. At the outset I should make it clear that boundaries are erected by both sides and that there are ways in which British people keep contacts with Pakistanis to a minimum and do not let Pakistani people penetrate the private 'insulated' sectors of their lives. Rejection by neighbours, discrimination by estate agents and in council housing may be important mechanisms for exclusion. However, my informants very rarely talked of these factors, and I have only been looking at the situation from their side, and considering the ways in which the Muslims have created boundaries to exclude the British (and others too). Some of these boundaries have been consciously constructed, while others reflect lack of language skills and so forth, and yet others are inevitable if the migrant properly fulfils his commitments inside the ethnic fold.

4.1.1 Structural aspects of boundary maintenance

This section considers the involvement of the Muslim informants in various spheres of activity, and those areas in which Pakistani institutions duplicate parallel British ones.

The most important sectors in British society which are not duplicated by Pakistani ones are the work and educational spheres. Only very few Pakistani men in Bristol obtain their incomes solely from work within the ethnic group (e.g. the *molwi* ('priest') and to a certain extent the shopkeepers). While some of my informants supplement their incomes through work patronized by Pakistanis (for instance those involved in the film society) all have been forced outside the ethnic fold in their search for work. The children, too, are perforce involved in British institutions; there are no full-time schools for Pakistani children staffed only by Pakistanis, though many of them do attend part-time religious instruction organized by the mosques. They all have to attend schools which are under the auspices of the Bristol Education Department. These two sectors, then, are the sites of 'articulation' between ethnic groups. As I indicated in the previous chapter, I have no direct information about the nature of the relationships the Pakistani men and children have at work and school. The men appear to mix very little with their British work-mates, even while at work: several take lunches to work with them, and particularly those who work in 'Pakistani gangs' have little need or opportunity to develop skills in English and to mix with British workers. Outside work there is no mixing with British work-mates. Similarly, the children do not mix with British children outside school; and bearing in mind that several of the children speak very poor English, I suspect that a lot of what happens in class simply washes over their heads. Considerable caution should be exercised in interpreting the nature and extent of influence on some of the men and children which their involvement in these 'articulating' sectors entails. Certainly, such relationships as they develop with British people in these contexts are single-stranded, but it appears that at least some of the men and children are very peripheral in these sectors and can hardly be said to have anything which merits the name 'relationship' with British people.

In other sectors, there may be duplication of institutions, and dual movement. My informants use Pakistani and British shops, as they often say that Pakistani shops are expensive for some items and they prefer to go to supermarkets. The relationships with British people which this entails are fleeting and single-stranded. However, they do patronize Pakistani shops for certain critical items, especially spices, *chappatti* flour (which they buy in 70-lb sacks) and *halaal* meat. One family has an arrangement with a farmer who sells them several chickens each week, which they distribute to their relatives; but most informants obtain their *halaal* meat from Pakistani traders who have made arrangements to kill the animals in the required fashion. Further duplication occurs in the field of communications, in which informants often use both sets. There are several Urdu newspapers, and some families take British and Urdu papers; the British ones are read by the men. Other families take only the Urdu papers, such as *Mashriq* (East), *Asia*, and *Daily Jang* (War), which, although they are printed in Britain, focus on events in India and Pakistan and matters relating to Pakistanis in Britain, as well as major world issues. The B.B.C. also has a television and radio programme for Indians and Pakistanis. *Nai Zindagi, Naya Jeevan* (New Life, New Livelihood) is shown on Sunday and Wednesday, and varies in form, having song requests, discussions, film reports and interviews. This is only one of several programmes which informants watch, as they often take an interest in documentary films and news programmes, though the women especially cannot understand much. They do not listen to the radio, except for their own programme, *Apna hi Ghar Samajhiye* (Make Yourself at Home), on Sunday morning: this is main-ly a record request programme, but also deals with issues such as the effect of E.E.C. membership on Indians and Pakistanis in Britain, how to trace relatives feared lost in Bangladesh, and hopes that registrars of marriages could be persuaded to work on Sundays (since the religious ceremonies often take place on Sunday, but a civil ceremony is also re-quired). The radio and television programmes are often taped by inform-ants so that they can have more of their own music on tap. Yasmin even confesses to watching both showings of the television programme, be-cause she feels so starved of her own culture. They do not listen to the overseas Indian and Pakistani services often, although several did during the 1971 war. During the 1965 war, the B.B.C. incorrectly reported that India had captured Lahore and its credibility took a serious jolt, since the Pakistanis consider that this was a piece of Indian propaganda swallowed whole by the British. In general, on issues relating to Pakistan they place their faith on the Urdu press and radio. They accuse the British press and television of mis-reporting casualties during the war, and I was told that the refugee camps in Bengal (during the Bangladesh crisis) were in fact filled by starving Biharis whom Mrs Gandhi was unable to feed and that she was playing on world sympathy.

While use of British communications does not entail inter-ethnic re-lationships, it is an important way in which informants learn about life in Britain. As will be seen in the next section, they have come to Britain with rather negative attitudes towards British moral standards. Tele-vision is a major way in which they get their impressions of British people, especially for the women who are not involved in inter-ethnic relationships at school or work, and what they see does little to encourage them to revise their judgements. While they do not trust news reporting about Pakistan, they are prepared to accept that plays and films accurately portray the moral depravity which they had expected.

These are the major areas in which there is contact between Pakistanis and British domains of activity, and it can be seen that much of this contact is fleeting and superficial; it is also limited to the spheres in question. Other sectors are represented in the Pakistani and British domains, though my informants remain inside the Pakistani fold, or 'incapsulated' in spheres which are 'insulated' from inter-ethnic contact.[8] These are 'private' spheres of activity, in which there is greatest room for personal choice to operate, in other words, friendship, leisure activities, religion and kinship.

Very few of the Muslim informants have male relatives who have married British women (and none have female relatives who have married non-Pakistanis), and such unions are discouraged. One man had an English girl-friend before his wife and children came to Bristol, and he now lives outside Bristol with this woman. His relatives are very critical. Another man (whom I have not met) married a British woman and stopped supporting his wife and children in Pakistan, and his brother was compelled to support them. Parvez's girl-friend was still living in his house when his wife arrived, but his wife insisted that the woman remove herself forthwith. Not only is disapproval voiced, but the men who behave in this way are often pushed out of the Pakistani camp. Simultaneous membership of the Pakistani and British camps is not considered feasible, and the man has the choice of being pushed out (and not necessarily being accepted by British people) or of persuading his British wife to 'become Pakistani'. In one such case the woman lived in Mumtaza's house before the marriage, was taught to read the Koran and recite the prayers and to cook Pakistani food; she now wears *shalwar–qemiz* and is regarded as very *sherif* by her Pakistani in-laws because she has learnt to be Pakistani. It could almost be said that such a strategy removes the problem of 'mixed' marriages (for the Pakistanis), as both spouses are 'Pakistani', one by ascription and one by achievement, and the children will also be Pakistani. As Barth points out, there may be defections on both sides of the boundary, though the basic separation between the groups remains.[9]

Outside work and school, there is very little contact between the informants and British people: work- and school-mates do not exchange visits. (I have met British children only twice in my informants' homes.) My position was obviously anomalous, but this was usually circumvented by putting me into a kinship position (such as married daughter of the house, or sometimes younger brother's wife), and I was expected to know and conform to Pakistani ways. They were specially pleased when I wore a *duppatta*, and I was expected to attend religious and other family functions with my husband. One of Tahira's daughters told the tale of a British man who shared a flat somewhere in Britain with three Punjabis; after a time, he spoke fluent Punjabi, and the Punjabis knew no English. This went down very well with the rest of the family, and her mother commented that Pakistanis would always try to gain converts rather than learn other people's ways themselves. Apart from a couple of students (whom I introduced to teach some of the children English), we were the only British people to visit my informants' homes, and there was considerable effort to make us into 'Pakistanis', who could be assumed to be 'playing the same game', by telling us the right ways to behave.

Contacts outside the home are also limited: apart from Kalim and Wahid (both married to Christian women), none of my Muslim informants drink alcohol or go to pubs and British restaurants. A couple of men said they did drink before their wives came to Britain, but they no longer do so. British food is regarded as tasteless, and in any case the meat is not *halaal*; but my informants do not eat in Pakistani restaurants either, because of a disliking for *bazaari* food and a preference for eating in privacy.[10] In addition, my informants do not go dancing or to see British or American films. Entertainment outside the home consists of visiting other Pakistanis, seeing Indian or Pakistani films at one of the clubs or going on family outings to the seaside and historic places. Several families find the expense of the films (50—75p for adults, depending on the cost of hiring the film) too great to make this a regular outing. Yusuf told me that he joined the film club partnership so that he could take his family to the films free. Obviously, religious practices involve the Muslim informants in no inter-ethnic contacts, though, as I described in the previous chapter, the adults in fact have little contact with the mosques, and visits are mostly at festival times, while some of the children attend the daily lessons.[11]

In general, the private sectors of kinship, friendship, leisure and religion do not entail inter-ethnic relationships, while the articulating sectors of work and school entail single-stranded relationships between my informants and British people. In a similar way, the informants are also set apart from other nationalities. Contact with West Indians is as limited as with British people, though some of the Indian and Pakistani shops stock vegetables, fruit and spices used by West Indians. There is some more contact with Indians (though this is again rather fleeting and does not extend into the home) through sharing of shops and attendance by some Pakistanis at the Indian film club.[12] In some respects this lack of contact is rather surprising, but it is a good example of the point raised by Barth, that it is not possible to predict which cultural items will be used to mark groups off from one another. Pakistanis and Indians in Bristol share many cultural traits, especially those from Punjab, for their language, dress and diet are very similar. However, religious and political differences are the most significant factors for the actors, despite all the similarities which could be enumerated, and only one family has contact with an Indian family, who come from Amritsar, the Pakistani man's hometown.[13] There are, then, several sectors of activity in which the Muslims are insulated from contact with British people, as well as people of other nationalities, and these are the private and domestic spheres.

4.1.2 Cultural aspects of boundary maintenance

The roots of the insulation of certain spheres of activity can be located largely in a number of cultural factors. I shall consider the spheres in which articulation occurs in 4.2.

4.1.2.1 Evaluations

One of the most important reasons behind the lack of contact between Pakistani people and other nationalities is the way in which they evaluate their own and other peoples' cultures. They are aware of different cultures, but for the adults, at least, it is not true that they are in a position to choose between them, because of the differential values placed on the different cultures which they see around them.

People in Pakistan have ideas about an undifferentiated 'British way of life' which is not substantially different from the views held by informants in Bristol. Colonial history and the behaviour of the British in India, the showing of British and American films, and reports from Pakistanis in Britain mean that people in Pakistan have a clear (if often erroneous) view of British culture. Thus the migrants come to Britain with ideas about British morality, which do little to encourage them to strike up contacts with British people, especially intimate contacts.[14] Many opinions formed in Pakistan are not tested by direct contact, and television plays and films tend to confirm existing opinions. While notions about Britain as Eldorado tend to evaporate fairly quickly (once it is realised that wages may be higher, but expenses are also greater), ideas on British morals are not subjected to the test and are little modified.

In brief, they disparage British morals on several grounds. Many critical attitudes appear with respect to family matters, such as divorce, illegitimacy and duties of parents and children to one another. Rashid told me that the divorce rate in Britain is 75 per cent (i.e. there are seventy-five divorces for every hundred marriages which occur in any year), and many other marriages are unhappy; but in Pakistan, no more than one marriage in a million is unhappy. The fragility of the marital bond was a common concern among the Muslims and was seen as an important index of British morality, since it was coupled with infidelity. Another concern focused on premarital sexual relationships and illegitimate births. The dangers of allowing young people to have friends of the opposite sex were a common point of conversation. Shahida (who did not meet her husband before they married) commented that British people are lucky to be able to meet their future spouses, but that the Pakistani system does preclude all the evils of illegitimacy. Yasmin considers that it is only right to let her children meet their future spouses since they have to spend their lives together, but under no circumstances will they meet alone. After Mumtaza had a baby in hospital, she was also very worried about 'making babies' before marriage, for she was in a ward with four women, two of whom were unmarried. The attitude to British women who marry Pakistanis sheds an interesting light on this issue: Zafar considers that all British women who marry Pakistanis are 'rubbish', and several informants argued that such women completely 'spoil' the Pakistani man. British women are seen as sirens who lure the men and as a perpetual threat to the moral welfare of Pakistanis in Britain. Mumtaza told of the opposition in the family when a relative wanted to marry a British girl: relatives in Pakistan wanted the man to marry one of their daughters and Mumtaza told him he would be spoilt, but now she is reconciled as the woman has shown herself to be *sherif*. In general, British people are to be feared, for the freedom of intercourse between men and women in Britain is in sharp contrast to the behaviour entailed by *purdah* practices, and confirms their assumption of 'loose behaviour'.

Criticism is also made of the ways in which parents and children ful-

fil their duties to one another. British parents do not do enough for
their children. Sons should be provided with a place to live, and Rashid
(among several) says that he will not return to Pakistan until he has a
house for each of his three sons. A daughter should be provided with a
dowry which enables her to set up her home and to dress well, even if
her parents and brothers have to make a considerable sacrifice to do so:
it is the duty of parents to do the best for their children and give them a
good start in life. British parents do not think in this way, and similarly,
children do not care for their parents: as soon as they are adult the children leave home and parents have to fend for themselves in their old
age. Informants were horrified by what they saw on television of homes
for old people, and argued that just as parents should care properly for
their children, in due course the sons should ensure that their parents
live a dignified and happy old age with their family, as they do in
Pakistan.[15]

Religion is another issue on which criticisms are made about Britain.
It is not, it should be pointed out, that my informants tackled (or even
seemed aware of) widespread lack of interest in religion; rather they
concentrated on making several basic criticisms of Christianity in comparison with Islam. One of the most common points is that the alterations and translations of the Bible mean that it can no longer be taken
as the authoritative word of God. The Holy Koran is still used in the
Arabic in which it was revealed to Mohammed by Allah, and it has not
suffered any textual amendments. Again, while Christ is accepted as a
prophet of Allah, it is regarded as blasphemous to consider that he is
the son of God. Several informants pointed out that the Old Testament
forbids the eating of pork, yet Christians persist in disobeying the injunctions of their religion. Others criticized the idolatrous elements in
Christianity. The one saving grace for Christianity is that it is a religion
of 'The Book'.[16]

Informants also take exception to the leisure activities of the British.
On religious grounds, dancing is considered wicked, especially when
men and women are in close contact, and they disapprove of drinking
alcohol. Several men disliked the way in which British girls are allowed
freedom to visit, and said that it brings disrepute. Tariq told me that
girls do not visit in Pakistan, and this was why he would not let his
daughters come to my home. Parvez (who had had an English girl-
friend) would not let his daughter visit other people, and disapproved of
the freedom given to Yasmin's daughter. Yasmin has since restricted her

daughter's movements, and the daughter is in full agreement, as she says
that people (i.e. other Pakistanis) only gossip and make trouble. British
and American films are considered far too explicit on sexual matters,
and Ruxsana said that she is too embarrassed to watch them when they
are shown on television. She does not understand how British people
can bear to look at them.

But British people are not the only ones to be subjected to critical
scrutiny. West Indians come in for particular criticism. Not only are
they noisy, and their family morality no better than the British, but
they have dark skins. In India and Pakistan fairness of complexion
(coupled with black hair and brown eyes) is very important, especially
for girls.[17] One woman said that the first question asked when a child is
born is if it is a boy; if it is a girl, the relatives want to know if she is
fair. When marriages are being arranged, one of the questions asked is if
the girl is 'fair'. A brand of cosmetics available in Pakistan called Tibet
Snow includes white powders and whitening creams, highlighting an
important concern with skin colour in Pakistan. People with dark skins
are considered to be rather primitive, and many Punjabis deride Bengalis,
who tend to be darker in complexion.[18] These notions about skin-colour
are carried over to Britain, and West Indians are an obvious target for
disdain. Rashid does not like Birmingham as there are too many 'black
people' there, and several informants who had once lived in St Pauls
commented that the area they lived in now was much better as there
were few West Indians. Yasmin's daughter says that she prefers Karachi
to Bristol because there are no West Indians. During a display of
Gujarati dancing at a *mela* ('harmonious assembly') in Bristol, one of
Saleem's sons commented that one of the women dancing looked 'like a
gorilla . . . or a West Indian'. A couple of homes had West Indian lodgers,
but they were unpopular and there was little contact between landlord
and lodger.

In relation to Sikhs in Bristol, my informants made criticisms which
were standard in Pakistan. Despite many points in common with
Punjabis from India, my informants would stress the points of difference, in particular religion. Ideally Islam is free of idolatrous activity
and the word of Allah has been preserved from contamination and
change. It is also monotheistic. This cannot be said of Hinduism and
Sikhism, my informants consider; one woman put it graphically: 'these
Hindus just see a pretty stone and they go out and worship it'. Sikhism
is contaminated by idolatry and polytheism, and moreover its holy

book, the *Guru Granth Sahib*, is a hotch-potch of ideas from many sources and cannot be taken as the authoritative word of God. At least Christianity is a religion of 'The Book', but Sikhism is beyond the pale.

These, then, are some of the ways in which my Muslim informants criticized and set themselves apart from people around them. From the other angle, there were also several matters on which they clung to their old ways. At several points above, I have indicated how they would comment unfavourably on other ethnic groups, and argue that their own ways were self-evidently superior: issues surrounding family morality and religion are particular cases in point which entailed very strong moral feelings. Dress is another matter on which they feel strongly. As I commented in the first chapter (1.4.4), the connotations of dress for men are not bound up with notions of morality and modesty, but for women they are. In Bristol, the men and boys rarely wear Punjabi dress, whereas before they would have worn *shalwar–qemiz* at home or to go to the mosque; at most they might wear an embroidered waistcoat, and some of them had satin suits made up in Pakistan for their young sons to wear on their birthdays. However, the women and girls have hardly changed their dress, except that none wears the *burqa*. All of them keep their legs covered, either by wearing the traditional *shalwar–qemiz* or a trouser suit, and they wear a *sari* on special occasions. While some of the women no longer wear the *duppatta* in the home, they all keep their heads covered when they go out, either by a *duppatta* or by a headscarf. There is a strong aversion to mini-skirts, which serve to confirm my informants' fears for the morals of British women: such women are bound to be 'loose' since they are so immodest in the ways in which they display their bodies to the world. While a few of the girls may wear trousers with a pullover or blouse at home, this is not common and it is considered rather indecent not to keep the hips well camouflaged by a dress. The girls all wear trousers under their school tunics. My informants feel that the way their women dress leaves their modesty and decency in no doubt.

In the field of entertainment, Indian and Pakistani films are still the most popular. Their themes are usually romantic (though I was once taken to a stirring film about the independence movement called *Shahid* (Martyr)). While the films often hinge on young couples trying to persuade their parents to let them marry, they are generally regarded as harmless entertainment, as they contain no risqué scenes. Those informants who go rarely say that they cannot afford to go more frequently; Abdul, however, tries to go often as only his eldest child was born in

Pakistan and he sees the films as a good way of teaching his children about Pakistan.

In the realm of diet, little change has been made. Apart from some use of breakfast cereals, the families continue to eat Pakistani food, with main meals consisting of a meat or vegetable stew (*salen*) or lentils (*dahl*) eaten with *chappatti* or rice. Some changes are due to the unavailability of some fruits and vegetables, and cold drinks have been replaced by tea, but otherwise there is little notable change. While diet does not entail moral judgements (except in the realm of eating pork and meat which is not *halaal*), nevertheless the Muslims have no desire to change their ways. Indeed, their major sentiment is pity for the British who have such a colourless diet and only know how to boil vegetables in salted water. No doubt, this is information obtained from their children who have had to take school lunches, and it was a matter of such importance that many of their relatives in Pakistan would ask me concernedly if it was really true that British food was so tasteless. Concern for the source of meat is the crucial factor behind many of the children eating their lunch at home, but there is also a marked distaste for British food and no inclination to be subjected to it.

In brief, the Muslim informants find fault with a great many aspects of life in Britain, while they regard their own ways as natural, proper and superior. These opinions lie behind the lack of effort to extend their contacts with British people (and those of other nationalities too) beyond the sphere of the school or the work-place.

4.1.2.2 Social skills

Although my informants consciously set themselves apart, there are other factors over which they have less control. Language is one such factor. In Pakistan none of the families spoke English, and while most of the men learnt English at school they say this does not enable them to communicate easily. None of the men is at home speaking English, even after several years in Britain, and they quickly lapse into Punjabi. Since several of the men work alongside other Pakistanis and have little contact with British people even at work, they do not have much chance to improve what English they know. Usually, both parents speak Punjabi or Urdu to their children, while the children may incorporate English in their conversations. In only one family does the father speak English to his children, and it is quite obvious that his wife is cut off from conversation.

Of the older women, Tahira and Akhtar learnt some English, but they have forgotten what they learnt. Hamida, the woman with the university degree, is the only one fluent in English. The language barrier is much stronger for the women as a whole, and several of them regret that they cannot even respond when their neighbours greet them. Although Tahira's eldest daughter did learn English at school, she can only understand the gist of television programmes without her father's help, and says that she does not like being in Britain as she cannot talk to anyone outside her family. She and two sisters have very little contact with British people, even though they go out to work: they work on the same machine and take lunch together, and after three years in Britain could not converse in English.

In fact it is very easy for the women to 'get by' without knowing English. Pakistani shops and familiarity with English counting mean that shopping is not difficult.[19] Pakistani broadcasts, newspapers and films give little impetus to learning English. The present attitude to the English classes for Pakistani women is summed up by Yasmin, who considers that the women only go to gossip (in Punjabi) and the children make such a noise that no one can concentrate; in any case, she forgets what she learns between one lesson and the next. She would like to learn English, but her children will only speak Urdu with her, and without practice she is unable to string the words she does know into sentences. A woman who came to Britain in the 1950s cannot converse in English, even though her son has an English wife. While I had learnt more Urdu in the short time in Pakistan than they had English in several years in Britain, several women said this was only to be expected. After all, the whole tone of their upbringing had been to make them dependant on their husbands, and they had not been encouraged to brazen it out in the way that British women might try to. So, not only have few of the women ever been formally taught English, but they have little necessity or encouragement to learn, and this is an important boundary between them and their British neighbours.

One further factor behind the lack of impetus to learn English returns to the questions discussed in 4.1.2.1. The migrants arrive in Britain believing that there is a basic discord between their values and those of British people, or in Barth's phraseology, they consider that they are not 'playing the same game' as British people. Barth argues that when people consider that they are strangers to one another, they will accept that there are limits to their shared understandings and interaction will be limited to certain restricted sectors in which there is as-

100

sumed to be some understanding. My informants consider that there are many matters on which there is little in the way of shared understandings with British people, and that amicable relations can only cover a few limited matters. Their opinions about British values and behaviour (in the realm of family morality and religion) inhibit the development of more rounded relationships with British people, and most of them do not see their lack of English as a handicap on the social front. In addition, the women are unused to mixing socially with men who are not kin, and they appeared awkward on those occasions when they had to; but here again, their lack of skill (as with lack of English) does not encourage them to learn, for they disapprove of the way British men and women are so free and easy with one another, and they do not think that the ability to relax in mixed company is one which should be cultivated.[20]

It may be said, then, that the migrants do lack certain interactive skills which they would need to develop before easy relationships with British people would be feasible. On the other hand, however, given their judgements of British people, they have little desire to develop such relationships and little incentive to learn the skills in question.

4.1.2.3 Social and economic constraints

In the next chapter, I shall be looking more fully at the relationships which *are* maintained by the informants, so here I shall only comment briefly on the constraints within which they act. It is important to bear in mind that migration does not necessarily detach the migrant from his family ties and obligations to kin in Pakistan. Kin at home may care for the migrants' property, while the migrants are expected to spend money on visiting Pakistan and taking presents to relatives there. The migrants also allocate money for investment in Pakistan, for a new family house, for instance. People who try to escape these constraints are treated with disfavour by their relatives, in Britain as well as in Pakistan. Migrants should also fulfil obligations to kin in Britain.

It is not just a question of social pressures keeping migrants in line, though these are certainly present. Although the migrants are aware of a different way of life, they are not in any dilemma, because of the way in which they evaluate their own ways and those of the British. To them, it is only natural that they should maintain links with their kin, and these constraints are not burdens unwillingly taken up. However, the constraints do canalize the way they spend their money and choose their friends, just as their aspirations for the future make their behaviour in Britain fall into certain patterns.[21] As a result of kinship obligations and expenditure patterns, they have little time to mix with British people, and no desire to spend their money on British leisure pursuits. Not only are the boundaries maintained by negative evaluations of British people, but they are also a consequence of the 'natural' behaviour of the migrants.

Finally, I want to come back to the point made by Barth about the possibility that individuals may leave one ethnic group and join another. Obviously, some Pakistani men have tried to become 'British', but my own informants have not. Barth argues that individuals must have incentives for defection (or incentives not to defect) and one such incentive is how the individual perceives his success in his own group and his likely success in another group. There are dangers of circularity, but interestingly, the Muslim men anticipate that they will be more successful than they were before when they return to Pakistan, and (given their evaluation of British culture) they are not interested in trying to be successful in the British camp, irrespective of whether they think they could be successful defectors. The probable ostracism which would ensue if they were to defect adds further weight to their intentions to remain 'Pakistani'. This is just one more factor which weighs in the same direction as the other matters which I have been discussing in this section: all of them are consistent with the patterning of social relationships described in 4.1.1, of very restricted and superficial contacts with British people.

4.2 Accommodation

In the previous section, I stressed the insulation of certain 'private' sectors of activity, and the retention of old ways and values by the Muslim informants. However, there have been some changes in their behaviour, and in this and the next section of the chapter I want to consider how to interpret such changes as there have been. Most of the information on behavioural changes comes from my own assessment of the backgrounds of the informants in Pakistan and their lives in Bristol, though informants have also corroborated my assessments.

4.2.1 Behavioural accommodation

Here, the focus is on those aspects of behaviour which have changed in order that the migrants may 'accommodate' to the demands made on them. Broadly, substantial changes in behaviour have occurred only in those spheres in which the migrants have no choice but to change: in Barth's terminology, the changes take place in those sectors of activity which are not insulated by boundary-maintaining mechanisms. For my informants these articulating sectors include the work and school situations.

Desai writes about the participation of Indian migrants in the work situation:

> Participation is, of course inevitable; the host society provides the jobs and the Indian immigrants come to earn money. There are two possible forms which the resulting integration can take. The first is 'assimilation', in which the immigrants come to share the attitudes, behaviour and values of the social group within the host society with which they identify themselves. The second is 'accommodation', in which the immigrants accept the relationships available to them and act on them with some degree of conformity, but do not share the bulk of attitudes and values which are part of the host society. Assimilative participation extends far beyond the work-situation; accommodative participation tends to be restricted to it . . .
>
> The culture of their own society and that of the host society differ considerably. Total participation would require from the immigrants varied and extensive cultural change. In fact most of them only accept those cultural changes which are a minimum condition for making money.[22]

These observations are similar to my own. There are not enough Pakistani businesses to employ all the Pakistani men in Bristol inside the ethnic group, and most of the men seek work outside. Similarly, the children of school age have to attend Bristol schools. Apart from the few women in paid employment, these two articulating sectors impinge only indirectly on the women, through the constraints imposed on their menfolk and children.

As I indicated in 4.1.1, involvement of the men in the British work sphere does not necessarily entail extensive social contacts with British people even in the work context itself. Nevertheless, there are adjustments to be made by the men when they go to work. The major change is in the type of work which the men do: in Pakistan most were engaged in some sort of clerical work, but on arrival in Britain they found that such jobs pay poorly in Britain, and several in any case were not very

103

proficient in English. Zafar (an Electricity Department clerk in Pakistan) first worked in Britain with a building contractor: 'I'd never had to work so hard in Pakistan. It's O.K. for these village-types, they're used to it — but I was a clerk before.' Abdul came to Britain with a friend, who returned to Pakistan when he discovered he would have to take manual work. Abdul had been a clerk and expected to do clerical work in Britain, but his first job was as a bus conductor. In Pakistan, bus conductors are not highly regarded, and he soon decided to have some training, as a fitter. Manual work is despised in Pakistan, and several informants had to swallow their pride when they came to Britain in order to obtain work. They say they are prepared to do it, as it is the only way to earn better pay.

Tariq's three daughters are an illustration of the sort of accommodation which has to occur. In Pakistan they would not work, but they have to help their father support their family in Britain as well as a brother and widowed aunt in Pakistan. They work in a bakery, and shortly before I went to Pakistan one of them impressed on me that I should tell their aunt that they work in a clothing factory: people in Pakistan think of dirty *bazaar* cooks who wipe the sweat from their brows with hands that knead the dough, and their aunt would be ashamed to think of them working like that, whereas she would not mind so much to think of them using their sewing skills.

Another adjustment is in working hours. Several of the men work or have worked on shifts, since such work is usually better paid. Others work only in the daytime, but for all of them, it is important that the British working week does not revolve around Friday, the Muslim holy day. In Pakistan, most schools and offices close on Sunday, but they are also closed on Friday at noon, so that workers can attend the *juma* prayers. The mosques in Bristol hold these prayers too, but my informants generally cannot attend because of work. They are also unable to make the enjoined prayers; while not all of them prayed regularly in Pakistan, most did during *Ramzan* (the month of fasting), when work hours in Pakistan enable workers to fast, pray and read the Koran during the day. In Britain, most of the men do not fast, since it is not worth fasting if the prayers cannot be said. Zafar considers himself unusually lucky, since his foreman lets him pray at work, and lets him off work one afternoon at the end of *Ramzan* to buy presents for his children for the *eid* (festival) which marks the end of the fast.

The women are affected by working hours in Britain, for in Pakistan shops operate long after office hours, and the men do most of the shopping, especially shopping in the *bazaar* for food, which many families do not allow their women to do. In Britain, it is much harder for the women to avoid shopping, though they send children shopping, or their husbands to the Pakistani shops which remain open in the evening, and take advantage of the delivery services offered by the Pakistani shops.

Education is highly valued by the Muslim parents, and they say that schooling is better in Britain than Pakistan; they also do not face the expense of school fees, which can prevent children from attending school in Pakistan. Most want their daughters to be well educated. However, they are worried about co-education, particularly for their daughters: they fear that the girls will be corrupted by mixing with boys, and even if the girls are not affected, their marriage chances will be damaged as people believe that girls inevitably become contaminated by contact with boys. The recently arrived girls express considerable anxiety about having to go to school with boys, and Yasmin (whose eldest daughter is fourteen) said, 'Now she is bigger, we do not send her to the mosque school any more, as the boys tease her. She has private lessons to learn the Koran. But we can't stop sending her to school – we have no choice in the matter.' Rashid intends to circumvent this problem by returning to Pakistan with his two daughters; Ruxsana commented, 'We can't afford to go back yet, but we shall when the boys are old enough to fend for themselves – then we shall go back with the girls and the baby. The girls are getting bigger now, and you know what the *mohalla* (surroundings, atmosphere) is like here. We couldn't let the girls go through college here – we want them to train as doctors in Lahore.' It was this sort of worry over co-education for girls which resulted in the formation of the Bradford Moslem Parents Association which centred on the refusal of one father to send his daughter to a mixed school and his prosecution for this. As I write this, the Pakistan Education Minister has just announced on a visit to London that the Pakistan Government intends to establish two schools in Britain for Pakistani children in order to 'help families facing cultural problems in children's schooling'.[23]

4.2.2 Accommodation in evaluations

Behavioural accommodation occurs in the work and education sectors, and here I want to consider the nature of these changes. Philip Mayer's discussion of urbanization is very pertinent here.[24]

Mayer considers that urbanization is more profound than 'the mere change of abode', and that the person who stays in town for a long time will not necessarily become fully 'urbanized'. Mayer divides the urbanization process into two aspects (which do not necessarily go hand in hand), the structural aspect (which entails becoming 'town-rooted' in social relationships rather than remaining largely 'country-rooted'), and the cultural aspect (which relates to the adoption or internalization of urban values). His study of Xhosa migrants in East London focuses on those aspects of life in which the migrants have choice about their associates (the 'private' sectors), and the commitment of migrants to behaviour which is imposed on all urban dwellers. He points out (p. 6) that 'the question of values is important, for in many situations people might conform outwardly, but still remain inwardly determined to revert to pre-urban patterns when opportunity arises'. This point is crucial in considering the 'accommodation' of the Muslim informants in Bristol: they have changed their behaviour in some ways, but do these changes imply commitment to the new behaviour, and changes in evaluation?

Briefly, the changes described above entail paying lip-service to behaviour imposed on the informants, and given the choice, my informants would not behave in these ways. The men were compelled to accept manual work when they came to Britain, but they do not like their jobs.[25] They retain their evaluations of different types of work, and are only prepared to accept the jobs they are in because they pay well: the pay overrides the disadvantages of the work. The men generally want to return to Pakistan and invest their savings, so that the family may be more respectably supported: the lowly job in Britain is accepted temporarily (it is hoped) as it permits the fairly rapid fulfilment of these dreams. None of the men wants to do manual work: they look forward to a time when they run a business (photographic, electrical, drapery) or are landlords in Pakistan.

Again, parents disapprove of girls being educated with boys. Ruxsana plans to escape this by taking her daughters back to Pakistan and sending them to single-sex schools and colleges. Mumtaza does not send her daughters to the mosque school (she teaches them herself), and when they are older she will go back permanently to Pakistan with her husband. She does not want them to be 'spoilt' by living in Britain, and will send them to mission schools in Pakistan where their inability to read Urdu will not be a disadvantage. Yasmin, on the other hand, says her family cannot afford to return to Pakistan yet and they will have to put up with the problems of co-education.

I would argue, then, that the observable adaptive behaviour of my informants should not be assumed to be undertaken willingly. It is probable that they will drop these new modes of behaviour when they can. This view contrasts with that of others. For instance Patterson[26] at one time considered that 'accommodation' is 'an early phase of the adaptation and acceptance in which migrants and local people achieve a minimum *modus vivendi*' and that, given time, mere outward conformity to the host society's basic norms would be converted into commitment. Later, however, she suggests that cultural diversities may persist,[27] and this is more in accord with Mayer's view. Among my informants several have been in Britain for more than ten years, and retain 'Pakistani' views on co-education and the status of different types of work, and they would return to Pakistan any day if they could 'afford' to. I would argue then, that the accommodative behaviour of my informants is not accompanied by commitment to it: it is regarded as inevitable, as forced on them, and is accepted as a temporary inconvenience. Values are extremely resilient, and my informants would like to discard a lot of adaptive behaviour if the opportunity presented itself.

4.3 Anglicization, Ashrafization and Westernization

In Chapter 1 (1.4.6) I discussed how different life-styles are evaluated in Pakistan, and considered two modes of emulation, Ashrafization (based on Islamic respectability) and Westernization (based on the supposed behaviour of people in the 'West'). Here I want to consider another set of behavioural changes among my informants, which unlike 'accommodative' changes are not forced on them. Here again, values are resilient, and the changes to be discussed here are eagerly adopted by my informants, for they represent life-styles to which my informants aspired in Pakistan but were unable to attain. This is where Ashrafization and Westernization come in again.

It is often assumed that changes in behaviour among migrants can in some direct way be seen as adaptations to the immediate environment. However, there are aspects of my informants' behaviour which can be readily understood only if the focus is shifted to Pakistan. There are two reasons why this is a fruitful approach. I have shown above that the Muslims are fairly successful in insulating those spheres of life in which they particularly dislike British ways, and so it is unlikely that they would want to become 'anglicized': they would not want to 'emulate' ways which they consider *inferior* to their own. The boundaries which insulate the 'private' sectors are connected with their evaluations. Barth argues that insulation prevents comparison of one's own ways with those of 'the others' based on accurate knowledge rather than stereotypes. Thus, if the Muslims wished to imitate British ways, the imitation would probably be inaccurate. As it happens, neither do they have the information for accurate imitation, nor are they inclined (on the basis of the information which they have) to ape the British.

Furthermore, the Muslims say they will return home one day and it is important to consider how their plans affect their assessment and adaptation of themselves in relation to Pakistan. It is not at all certain that they are so oriented to British values that they adapt their behaviour in accord with them: in many ways, their eyes are more firmly focused on Pakistan than on Britain. The matter is complex, though, as 'anglicization' has elements in common with 'Westernization'. However, I shall argue that 'anglicization' is not the appropriate way to characterize what is happening.

My informants consider that they have achieved upward social mobility (if only slight) since their migration. They also say that relatives in Pakistan expect this, and that they plan to return to Pakistan. This then, raises the question of what is the audience to which the informants are addressing themselves and what are the modes of behaviour and symbols which they use to make claims of status? I wish to argue here that much of the behaviour of the Muslims in Bristol is congruent with their newly acquired status in Pakistan, and that they are rating themselves in the status system of Pakistan: the people at home are the relevant judges of their having 'arrived' (or not), while their British neighbours (who are operating in a different system of status symbols) are irrelevant, and indeed probably do not understand the system of symbols which my informants are using. Dahya's discussions of Pakistani migrants[28] point to the same concern among his informants: they are preoccupied with their status at home, they want to improve the position of the family, and they send money back home for the family to use in ways which enhance their position *at home*: they may replace the *kutcha* home with a *pukka* one, or buy land, or establish a business which relatives can run. There are several parallels with my informants, for it is clear that they, too, believe that they are only in Britain for a short time, and they often mention what they will do when they go home. Their ambitions are rather different in detail from those of Dahya's informants, but they are equally comprehensible within the status system in Pakistan. Ultimately they will live in new *pukka* homes in the new colonies of their home cities, whereas before they came to

Britain, they lived in *pukka* homes in the older areas of town. They will have servants, so that their wives will not have to shop and cook any more, they will have fine clothes and furniture, and they will provide their daughters with good education and large dowries. The differences in detail in the plans of Dahya's informants and of mine simply point up the contextual variations in the expectations held of the *England-returned*. Dahya's informants were sometimes made painfully aware that people at home had expectations of how the returned migrant would behave: he was expected to dress well, to have plenty of money and not to be too worried if shopkeepers and *rickshaw-wallahs* charged him more than they charged non-migrants. My own informants also appreci-ated that people at home believed Britain to be the place where every-one makes a fortune, and they wanted to live up to the expectations that once they return they will be in a position to distribute largesse to their relatives and indulge in life-styles which were beyond their means before they came to Britain.[29]

The behaviour of the Muslim informants in Bristol looks 'upper class' in terms of Pakistan: in their diet, leisure activities and dress, it can be seen that they are relating back to Pakistan. Several informants have decorated the outside of their homes in styles which are strikingly rem-iniscent of those to be seen in some areas in Pakistan: especially in the new colonies, *pukka* houses are plastered and painted, often with the reliefs picked out in contrasting colours, and in Bristol the plaster reliefs over the front door and the sitting-room window have often been painted in this way. Inside, the houses are also distinctively Pakistani, though again reminiscent of homes in the new areas: all the families now have a formal sitting-room (whereas before, they usually used sitting-rooms as bedrooms as well), and, as far as space permits, they furnish them like the much more spacious rooms to be found in the homes of the wealthy in Pakistan: chairs and settees are placed rather formally round the walls, and are decorated with embroidered cushions, often the traditional fat sausage-shaped cushions covered in satin. Orna-ments and especially pictures of the *Ka'ba* in Mecca and mosques and quotations from the Koran all enhance the atmosphere of Pakistan.

There has been little change in the diets of my informants since coming to Britain, but what there has been reflects their greater ability to attain their ideals: in particular, chicken (the most favoured meat) is frequently on the menu, whereas it was an item reserved for special oc-casions in Pakistan. Moreover, ideals of hospitality are also more easily accomplished: now they can afford more lavish entertainment and

109

improve their *izzet* thereby. In the next chapter, I shall consider the social networks of the informants, but for the moment it suffices to point out that they are very circumspect about making contacts with other Pakistanis whose reputation would damage their own *izzet*; and they restrict their contacts to people whose qualities are known, in other words their own kin if possible.

Dress and fashion are other matters which can also be better understood by shifting the focus back to Pakistan. When the following points occurred to me during fieldwork, I was very conscious that the changes in dress styles in some cases might simply appear to entail adaptation to the situation in Britain. However, informants' comments and consideration of details of dress made it clear that they were following Pakistani fashion, and a recent paper by Saifullah-Khan about Mirpuris in Bradford adds strength to my argument.[30] Saifullah-Khan points out that in Pakistan strict *purdah* can only be observed by the most wealthy and that considerable prestige can be maintained through the ability of a family to keep its women in *purdah*. Her informants in Bradford were unable to keep their women in strict *purdah* at home (though the women would be modest when outside and would cover their heads with a *chaddar*), but now in Bradford, the wives of the migrants are living in much stricter *purdah* than they previously experienced. In my terms, they can be said to be Ashrafizing. She points out that the women observe *purdah* in front of Pakistani men, who are part of the one social system (in this context, British men are in effect no more than part of the natural environment); few of the women have economic cause to go out of their homes, whereas before they probably helped with agricultural work; the migrants intend to return home and they maintain close ties with their places of origin; they do not wish to harm their *izzet* and indeed through property-owning and *purdah*-observance in Bradford, they are using traditional 'status symbols' to announce their success to the world.

For my own informants the situation is somewhat different, but the same process is at work. The women were all accustomed to being almost completely restricted to their homes in Pakistan, and wearing a *burqa* when they went outside. In Bristol, they are shifting somewhat away from this to a more *modern* approach to dress, and this is why it might appear that they are becoming 'British' in their dress-styles. Close consideration of the details and their own interpretation of what they are doing indicates that the process is analogous to that described by Saifullah-Khan. In Pakistan, 'silky' material, especially if embroidered

110

with silver or gold thread, is highly valued and should be worn for special occasions. In Bristol, the women wear such shiny materials at family parties, and some wear them when they go out shopping and visiting their relatives, and even around the house. They patronize a Pakistani man in Bristol who embroiders cloth with gold and silver thread in the traditional styles. Again, all the women and girls keep their legs covered, usually by *shalwar* or by the narrower *churidar-pyjama*: the width of these items closely follows fashions in Pakistan and India. A few years ago, the *shalwar* were very baggy and were loose at the ankle, then they became narrower, and more recently they have become looser again. The style of *sari* blouse also echoes changes back home: the old-style *choli* with sleeves to the elbow covered the body to the waist, but recently it has become much shorter and some women even wear sleeveless *choli*. Bell-bottom trousers are still regarded as rather avant-garde in Pakistan, and are rarely seen in the old city areas. Some of the women in Bristol wear bell-bottoms occasionally, and they are amused that what they consider to be Pakistani fashion has become so popular in Britain in the form of the trouser suit. For them, at any rate, the direction of influence is from Pakistan, although from the outside it might be taken as an index of 'Anglicization'.

Another realm of change relates to the *burqa* and the *duppatta*. None of the women wears the *burqa* in Britain. Indeed, as one man commented, wearing the *burqa* in Britain would be the surest way of attracting attention and defeating the object of the garment. Yasmin first moved to an area of Bristol where no Pakistanis were living and did not wear the *burqa*, but she would have liked to wear a *burqa* after they moved to St Pauls as there were so many Pakistani men around, but she did not. In some respects, this appears to be conformity to British standards, and some informants did find it difficult to adjust to going outside unveiled. However, there is another element, which can also be seen in the way the *duppatta* is used. It is an item used in Pakistan in the home, and women usually cover their heads in the presence of men or while praying. Some women in Bristol still use the *duppatta* like this, but several have either completely discarded it or only wear it draped over the shoulders. This is taken as a symbol of modernity in Pakistan. The women should not be thought to have discarded their old habits completely, and they all wear a head-scarf or *duppatta* over their heads when they go out, but there is a slight relaxing of requirements towards what I designated above as 'Westernization'.

This is particularly evident when the women told me about what

111

they intended to do or had done when on holiday in Pakistan. Before Ruxsana went to Pakistan in 1971 I asked if she intended to wear a *burqa* when she was in Lahore, as I knew that her father was considered rather old-fashioned in the family connection. (She had told me that her father 'closed' everything to her when she was twelve and her mother had — to her chagrin — bought her an old-style *burqa* so that people would believe she was an old woman.) Ruxsana was in fact rather anxious, for she did not want to wear a *burqa*, and did not know how her father would react: but after all, she said, people in Karachi and Gulberg (a new Lahore suburb) do not wear the *burqa* and her father would have to change with the times and get used to her without one. She eventually solved the problem by staying in the home of Rashid's second brother, so her father could do nothing: ironically this man is not *modern* but he considers the *burqa* to be unnecessary since there is nothing in Islam which decrees that the *burqa* should be worn. (His daughters do not wear the *burqa*, but he has yet to persuade his wife to go out unveiled.) Ruxsana was accompanied by Imtiaz, Rashid's other brother's daughter, who also did not wear a *burqa* when she stayed at her parents' home or with relatives in other parts of Pakistan. Similarly, Tariq's eldest daughter (who was going back to be married) intended that she would not wear a *burqa*, though she had done before coming to Britain. While I was in Lahore, I met a young woman related to informants in Bristol who lives in London, and she also said that she had intended not to wear a *burqa* when she came for her holiday, but she capitulated under the 'dirty eyes' of Pakistani men, and borrowed an old-style *burqa* from her mother for the duration of her stay so that she would no longer be tormented by taunts and staring of men in the old city. Other women whom I met in Lahore who had returned for a holiday did not wear a *burqa*, and always appeared immaculately dressed in embroidered suits and their gold jewellery, even when making informal visits to relatives.

The men have also changed their styles of dress somewhat. They rarely wear Punjabi clothes in Bristol, but this does not mean that they have simply taken over British modes of dress. In Pakistan, informal 'western' clothes are rare, and men who can afford 'western' clothes wear a full 'western'-style suit, even on occasions when in Britain sportswear would be more common. In Bristol, the men all have suits, and they wear them practically all the time when they are not at work, and not just when they are going out or spending an informal evening with friends. Here, given the symbolism of the 'western' suit for Pakistani men, they can be seen to be making an important claim about their respectability and position, and the tone in which they do this is strongly reminiscent of Pakistan.

The question of dress is complex for men and women alike, since the sorts of changes which have occurred give the appearance of following British fashions. However, when the details are scrutinized, and the styles and contexts in which items are worn are considered in conjunction with informants' comments, it is necessary to look back to Pakistan and ask how they perceive their positions there, now and in the future. Just as Saifullah-Khan's informants in Bradford are concerned about their *izzet* and position in Pakistan, so too are mine, though theirs is a rather different position.

Further weight can be added to this by a brief consideration of two other questions, ambitions for their children and family size. On the first, the parents do not want their sons to do manual work. While they would like to be able to return to Pakistan and live at least partly off rents from properties bought there, it is generally hoped that the sons will be able to establish some sort of business, or (if their schooling has not been too interrupted by migrating) that they should train as doctors or lawyers, the two most respected professions in Pakistan. Several families want their daughters to train as doctors (a profession in which there are many opportunities for women in women's hospitals), but they want to avoid having the daughters become too 'independent' (and therefore hard to get married) by taking them to Pakistan for training.

While attitudes to family size are not conspicuous symbols of changes in status since migration, the comments of several informants on their need to keep the family small indicate their preoccupation with how they will cope when they go back to Pakistan. Ruxsana, for instance, said that she had been sterilized after her fifth child (and third son) was born because when the family returns to Pakistan, the three youngest (the two girls and the baby) will be attending school, and Rashid will have to provide fees to send them to mission schools and college in Lahore: with any more children they might find the burden too much. Rashid's sister, Mumtaza, has seven daughters; she disapproves of having many children as none can be given proper attention, but she and Rashid are desperate for a son. When they go back to Pakistan, they will have to marry the daughters, and what would they do in their old age without a son to care for them, and to help provide dowries for his sisters? Yasmin was also concerned about the size of her family: she has four daughters and one son and Yusuf does not want her to be sterilized as he wants another son; but she feels her family has not been well endowed with sons and Allah has decided what her luck will be, and she is convinced that any more children would be daughters. She argues that they have to think of the future, and bear in mind that the more daughters they have the less there will be to provide each one with a dowry: if they do not give generous dowries their *izzet* will suffer, because people will ask how it is that they have been to such a rich country and yet come home so poor. While they all agreed when I commented that it is harder to cope with a large family in Britain, they stressed their hopes for the future and pointed to the undesirable consequences of having a large family when they return to Pakistan.

All these elements lend support to my contention that it is Pakistan and not Britain which is the status arena with which the Muslim informants in Bristol are primarily concerned. They are preoccupied with their plans for the future in Pakistan and are interested in how they will be able to live up to the expectations of relatives back home. Much of their behaviour in Britain is congruent with their new status in Pakistan; they hold very much the same ideas about respectability as they did in Pakistan, but are now more able to live up to them. This argument has a bearing on some of the assumptions which are commonly made about Pakistani migrants in Britain, in particular about the relevance of their 'objective class position'. In terms of their earnings and position in the economic structure most of the informants would unquestionably be placed rather low down in the British class structure; their position in the housing sector and the fact that they all vote for Labour Party candidates might add force to this view. However, their 'objective class position' is not a matter of great importance to the Muslim migrants. I suggested in the previous chapter that their position in the housing market is considerably affected by the ways in which they choose to allocate their incomes: several could have bought more expensive homes in Bristol, but decided to buy cheap houses and plough any surplus back in Pakistan. Commitment to the Labour Party was not because of particular policies of the party; informants did not feel that the major parties differed markedly in terms of policy, but at least the Labour Party does not have Enoch Powell, they said. They do not like the sorts of jobs they have had to do in Britain, but they say that they are prepared to accept them, as such acceptance is merely temporary, and their children will (they hope) do better once they go back to Pakistan. Because of these factors, I am not happy with a recent paper by Krausz.[31] He is discussing social mobility among immigrants in Britain and rightly

114

suggests that a great many factors are involved, including discrimination and the economic and political conditions of the receiving country (p. 283). However, he has omitted one which seems crucial to me and highly relevant to my Muslim informants, and that is whether the migrants actually *want* to be mobile in Britain. Krausz mentions achievement-motivation and suggests that lack of it may be one factor behind lack of mobility among migrants; I would contend that my informants are not lacking in achievement-motivation (indeed they are probably entertaining ambitions which will prove to be unattainable), but the point at issue is *where* the migrants want to take advantage of the achievements for which they are striving. For the Muslim informants, Pakistan is where they focus their attentions and their ambitions: they are operating in a status system outside Britain which uses a set of status symbols different from those used by British people. The sort of ethnocentrism of which Krausz's analysis is only one example ignores the very important aspects of the situation which transcend Britain's boundaries, and thus cannot accommodate the ways in which these migrants visualize their situation in Britain.

4.4 Summary

In this chapter I have been considering why total assimilation is not inevitable and looking at the social factors which enable cultural differences to persist. In this, Barth's analysis is particularly important when he points to the ways in which certain spheres of activity may 'articulate', or be the locus of inter-ethnic relationships, while other facets are 'insulated' and protected from confrontation with the culture of the other group. I suggested that the articulating spheres are the sites of accommodative changes in behaviour forced on the informants, while changes in the insulated sectors indicate the necessity of incorporating Pakistan into the analysis. Here we are beginning to bring in the question of what social unit it is most appropriate to use for studies of migrants; this will be considered in more detail in the two final chapters.

5. The networks of the Muslim informants

5.0 Introduction

In this chapter, I employ the term 'network' to elucidate the relationships amongst the Muslim informants in Bristol. It will be seen that evaluations about other Pakistanis carry over from Pakistan and that the situation in Bristol itself is very fragmented; in addition, many links with Pakistan are retained. There is little concern to establish new links in Bristol, and they expect that obligations to kin in Pakistan will be fulfilled.

These points have important implications for the way in which the situation of the migrants should be viewed. In many ways, my concerns parallel those of P. Mayer, Philpott, Manners, and Garbett and Kapferer.[1] In their various contexts, they are all interested in how to delineate the most suitable unit for the analysis of migration situations. Since migrants often retain important social links with their homes and also carry over many evaluations into their new abodes, it is important to bring both ends of the migration situation into view. Mayer is interested in 'in-town' and 'extra-town' ties, especially in those private spheres where migrants are able to choose their associates, their behaviour and their values. Many 'Red' Xhosa were characterized by the maintenance of ties with kin back home and by the retention of 'traditional' values. Philpott (in his earlier publication) concentrates on the way the expectations of non-migrating kin constrain the activities and choices of the migrants. Both of them employ the notion of 'network' to help straddle the geographical distances involved. Manners addresses himself explicitly to the problem of delineating the unit of analysis in anthropological fieldwork, and considers how the anthropologist can cope with the reality of non-isolation. In Caribbean studies, the village or island in which the research is conducted is often treated as a closed system. Manners argues that this is not satisfactory, and he examines the critical importance of remittances from migrants overseas in the economies of many Caribbean islands. The economic linkages outside the islands are clearly real, even if dispersed geographically, and should not be ignored. Similarly, Philpott points out that many families in Montserrat depend

116

for their livelihood on remittances from their relatives abroad. Garbett and Kapferer argue that differences in the behaviour of migrants in their new homes can be linked to differences in the way they are involved in the total set of relationships which span the place of origin and the new home. This also has relevance for my informants, since the position of the Christians is different from that of the Muslims and the necessity of including Pakistan in the interpretation will again be apparent.

There are, then, several ways in which the cultural backgrounds of the migrants and their continuing ties with people at home may influence their behaviour in their new homes. Use of the notion of 'network' is useful here, since it helps to overcome the tendency to assume that geographical boundaries coincide with social ones, and that the new homes of migrants are adequate units for comprehending their behaviour and attitudes there.

5.1 The literature on social networks

Barnes is usually considered to be the first to use the term 'network' to refer to the configuration of kinship, friendship and neighbourhood ties.[2] An individual's network consists of the set of friends and relatives of which he perceives himself to be the centre, and it may be visualized as points (representing individuals) joined by lines (representing the relationships between them). The network's mesh may vary between two extremes: all the people known to Ego know one another, and none of them knows any other. Bott used the terms 'close-knit' and 'loose-knit' to describe the variations which she found in the 'connectedness' of the networks of her informants.[3] 'Connectedness' she defines as 'the extent to which people known by a family know and meet one another independently of the family' (p. 59); this question of 'knit' has been of central importance in subsequent discussions of network analysis, but no satisfactory way of measuring and comparing the connectedness of different networks has been developed. Barnes considers that the confusion over the term is such that 'connectedness' should be replaced by 'density', which he defines as the actual number of links as a percentage of the total possible links in the area under consideration.[4]

Density is an important aspect of networks, and will be used in this analysis. Barnes also uses the term 'cluster' to refer to a set of people the density of whose linkages approaches 100 per cent.[5] In a network, there may be areas marked by high density (the clusters) surrounded by areas of much lower density; some people in the clusters may be more crucial to the cluster than others, who are 'peripheral' rather than 'core' members.

Mitchell's commentary on social networks is particularly important since he makes a distinction between 'morphological criteria' and 'interactional criteria': the former relate to the patterning of links in a network, and the latter to the properties or characteristics of the links.[6] Among the morphological criteria he considers that 'reachability' is the most important, though hard to measure satisfactorily: it has two aspects, the proportion of people in Ego's network whom he can reach at all through any number of links, and the number of intermediaries required to put any two people into contact. As will be seen below, my informants are involved in dense clusters, in which the 'reachability' is very high, and between which there are few links.

The interactional criteria are important for my analysis. Mitchell discusses several of these criteria. The basis on which people are linked he calls the 'content', and two individuals may be linked by a multiplex relationship in which there are several contents involved. Links may vary in their 'directedness': some may be reciprocal, others 'oriented'. In multiplex relationships, one content may be in one direction and another in the opposite. Links also vary in 'durability': some may remain for a lifetime and others may only be fleeting; ties may be discarded and others built up. The observer may see only a few links activated at any one time, but the actor may have in his mind many latent links which he can call on if need be. I have tried to take account of this dynamic aspect of networks, but in the short time available I could obviously not look properly at shifts in personnel and I had to rely on informants' accounts of the changes in their networks. The extent to which actors are prepared to meet the obligations entailed in links is called 'intensity' by Mitchell. Intense links are often (though not necessarily) multiplex, and they need not be face-to-face relationships. Mitchell refers explicitly to links with people at home maintained by migrants in which both sides continue to honour obligations. Mitchell considers that frequency of contact is not a significant criterion, since it does not relate in any necessary fashion to factors such as durability and intensity, which, like content and directedness, are far more significant and informative issues to consider.

From Barnes's simple formulation of points linked by lines, we have come a considerable distance: now the nature of the links and not just their patterning has to be considered, and in the present context it is important also to look at the dynamic aspects of networks, since the situation is very fluid.

5.2 The networks of the Muslims

For ease of presentation, I shall divide this portion of the chapter into two parts, dealing with ties in Bristol and ties outside Bristol, but it should not be thought that there is any discontinuity in practice between these two facets of the informants' networks.

5.2.1 The networks in Bristol

The situation in Bristol may be summarized as follows: there is a tendency for relationships to be conducted amongst kin, and not among non-kin, and many potential relationships do not exist at all. Relationships within the kin-based 'clusters' tend to be multiplex and the women are largely incapsulated inside these clusters. The men and children are also involved in these clusters, but additionally have relationships at work and school which are usually single-stranded. Relationships inside the clusters tend to be multiplex, intense and durable, while relationships outside the clusters tend to be transient, lacking in obligations and not entailing visiting.

Before going on to describe the networks of the informants, there are a couple of points to be made. Bott has written an extended reconsideration of her book for its second edition, and there she raises the question of geographical mobility.[7] She predicts that people who have had close-knit networks will find that these break down when they move: certainly a lot of evidence supports this. It is interesting, though, that for my Muslim informants this has not been the case: the time available to me did not enable me to consider this issue adequately, but it was clear that informants were building up new close-knit networks based on people already linked in some way who add new strands to their relationships.

Secondly, it should be noted that in this context, 'kin' refers to cognatic kin. In some senses, kinship in Pakistan can be regarded as 'patrilineal' (e.g. with reference to common residence and inheritance of immovable property), but in many contexts cognatic kinship is important, especially in the realm of friendship and when marriages are being arranged. *'Biraderi'* is a term in common use among Pakistanis,[8] perhaps especially so in Britain, where important agnatic kin may be absent. Complete *biraderis* do not, of course, migrate, and some of the ties in evidence in Bristol were latent in Pakistan. Close relatives have been re-placed since migration by others in the *biraderi* who were distant in Pakistan (geographically rather than genealogically). The strand of 'kin-ship' is an important foundation from which to build relationships with more strands in them, and create new dense kin-based networks and so overcome the problems of geographical mobility. Kinship in Pakistan is a dominant idiom for conducting social relationships (of friendship and mutual aid, for instance), and most people have real kin to fill these positions. In Britain, replacements often have to be found, maybe other kin, or maybe people who are totally unrelated but who are put into some kinship position, such as 'brother' or 'sister'. Fictive kin are dif-ferentiated from real kin by the distinction between *seha bhai/sehih behn* (true brother/sister) and *bana hua bhai/bani hui behn* (made brother/sister), and are rarely accorded equal status with real kin: sev-eral Muslim informants have 'made kin' in Bristol.

In dealing with the clustering of kin we shall be taken back to boundary-maintenance again: processes similar to those discussed in the previous chapter influence the choice of associates in Bristol. Contacts with people who are considered 'unrespectable' are restricted: they try not to mix too much with villagers (who are thought likely to gossip), kin who do not live up to their relatives' expectations, and people whose families are involved in some scandal.

One cluster of informants consisted of seven households: there were two pairs of siblings (in both cases a brother and a sister), and the other households were connected to these four and to one another by more distant links, though by no means necessarily in the male line. In fact, the situation here is quite complex, since it is the custom in this family for close kin to marry and so the genealogical links between these house-holds can all be traced through more than one route. In Chapter 2 (2.3), I have already indicated something of the backgrounds of these families and the way in which Abdul and then Rashid drew their relatives to Bristol to provide company for their wives. Abdul is now marginal but the men and women of the rest of the families form a very dense cluster. They visit one another, and their children play together, and some of the younger men regularly play cards together. This reciprocal hospi-tality takes place without extensive mixing outside the cluster. There are only two unrelated families who very occasionally visit members of this cluster. One is a Sikh family from Amritsar whom I have met a couple of times at Rashid's home: they do not visit any of the other members of his *biraderi*, and indeed when this family attended a birthday party at Rashid's home they were almost completely ignored. The other exception is Hamida (from Lahore) whose mother was Mumtaza's school teacher: Hamida and Hanif occasionally visit only Mumtaza and Rashid. Visiting among these relatives takes place at any time without special invitation: I was never at one of the homes of the *biraderi* without someone dropping in for at least a chat and a cup of tea, whether in the morning, afternoon or evening. Residential clustering has facilitated this. In 2.3 I described how some of the families housed relatives for a while before they moved out into their own homes. Rashid and Javed both lodged for a while with Abdul, and later, when Ruxsana had arrived, Rashid was even prepared to live in Mahmud's house in order that Ruxsana and Mumtaza might be company for one another.[9]

All the families (except Abdul's) now live within about five minutes' walk of each other. Bashir's first house was in St Pauls, but he sold that to move to a house opposite Rashid's. Iqbal lived in London until his marriage (his sister lives in London), but he moved to Bristol at Rashid's instigation so that Imtiaz would be company for Ruxsana and Mumtaza and he reckons that it is worthwhile keeping his wife happy! His first house was rather distant from his relatives (i.e. about fifteen minutes' walk), and when he sold it (to raise capital to invest in Pakistan) he bought another house much nearer his relatives; he feels that his situation has much improved as they visit him more often now. The amount of visiting which goes on varies, since some of the women have no children at home during the day, while Mumtaza, for instance, has two at home all day and one who attends nursery school only in the morning. She says that the housework generated by her seven daughters means that she has little spare time, although the older girls are able to help around the house. By contrast, all Shahida's children are over the age of ten and she has a lot of free time in the day. The men do no housework, but their visiting is obviously constrained by their work.

Although this cluster is very dense, the personnel in it are different from those who would be in a close-knit network in Pakistan. In Pakistan, genealogically close kin should be socially the most close, especially if they live nearby. Links between siblings are retained even over considerable geographical distances, but other links often become tenuous: visiting or exchange of letters may be infrequent, and the kinship links may only be activated when marriages are being arranged and suitable candidates are being listed. The members of this *biraderi* come from various cities in Pakistan (some of them moved from India in 1947) and in the ordinary course of events several of them in Bristol would not normally have met in Pakistan let alone be close friends. Ruxsana and Jamila (whose mothers are sisters) lived in Lahore and Karachi respectively and hardly knew one another before coming to Britain, but now they meet almost daily. Unless their links were re-inforced through marriage (of their children for instance) they would not normally have become close in Pakistan. A consideration of the marriages which have been arranged in this *biraderi* indicates that it is not uncommon for links dispersed in Pakistan through geographical mo-bility to be re-cemented in subsequent generations by marriages: Jamila from Karachi was married to Javed from Lahore, and Imtiaz from Lahore (originally Amritsar) married Iqbal from Multan. Similar links are common among the relatives still in Pakistan. The migrants in Bristol are not yet at the stage of marrying their children, but they have re-inforced their links with rather distant kin since migrating: the distant kin are on the spot, and closer kin are not, and single-stranded ties through genealogy alone have now become many-stranded.

This change of personnel in the migrants' networks has had an im-pact on the way these individuals interact. In Pakistan, special respect is accorded to parents, older siblings and their spouses and brothers (by their sisters): for most of these migrants, these people are absent. The people in Bristol are in much the same age group and do not stand in relation to one another in such a way that traditional deference behav-iour would be expected (apart from the respect a wife gives her hus-band). There is, in fact, much more relaxed interaction between these relatives, and this is most noticeable between the men and the women. In Pakistan, close relatives of both sexes in this *biraderi* mixed fairly freely, but this was not so common among distant relatives. Now, for instance, Iqbal visits Mumtaza when she is alone: he says that he con-siders her a 'sister', since her marriage was first arranged with his elder brother (it was called off when Mumtaza's mother did not want her to move away to Multan). Iqbal and Bashir both visit Ruxsana when she is alone. The other men also visit the women of the *biraderi* occasionally when they are alone, though they do not regard themselves as quite so close. The important point is that such visiting would be frowned upon in Pakistan and would carry insinuations of improper liaisons, but it is quite suitable in Bristol: Iqbal even does some of the shopping for Mumtaza if Mahmud's shifts are inconvenient. Ruxsana is quite explicit about the way in which she has changed since coming to Britain: she mixes more freely with kin (especially the men) and attributes this to the particular kin in Bristol. In Lahore, she used to keep herself well shrouded by her *duppatta* in the presence of Rashid's two brothers (who are both his elders), and she dared hardly speak to them. If they were in Bristol, she would continue in this way. When she first arrived in Britain she was very shy, and when men came to see Rashid she would make the tea and then hide herself away in the kitchen. Now she mixes quite freely with her male relatives, and she says this is because none of them is in such a superior position that she needs to perform elaborate deference behaviour in order to keep *izzet* with them. The migrants are also aware of the isolation which would ensue if some of the restraints on the mixing between men and women who are not very close kin had not been lifted, and the relationships between the particular personnel involved enable this to happen without shame descending on the families.

Hospitality and the exchange of visits are one element of the relationships, but the members of the *biraderi* also help one another in various ways. The women sometimes help each other with shopping and cooking, especially if one is ill or if preparations are being made for a family party. The men offer a wider range of help. Rashid bought his sister Mumtaza a refrigerator before his own household had one, and when Mumtaza was expecting a baby she and her children were all housed in Rashid's home so that someone would be at hand even if Mahmud were at work. Rashid also cared for their children when Mumtaza went to Pakistan for a holiday, as Mumtaza herself had helped Rashid out when Ruxsana was in Pakistan and had left him with four children to care for. One time while Rashid was unemployed he took over the task of organizing a new passport for Mumtaza's eldest daughter so that she could come to Britain again. Bashir looked after Javed's house while he was in Manchester and collected the rents from the tenants, and he also helped Rashid to redecorate his house. When he visited Pakistan in 1971 he took a case-load of presents from various relatives for their kin in Pakistan. Bashir also has a car, and he often takes his relatives on outings in the summer. Rashid helped him with documents concerning the purchase of his house and bringing his wife and children to Britain. While Imtiaz and Ruxsana were in Pakistan at the same time, Iqbal and Rashid often cooked jointly and Rashid helped Iqbal to move into his new house. Iqbal is the only one to own a telephone and his relatives sometimes use it: Bashir even telephoned Saleem's brother (who is married to Bashira's sister) in Karachi to convey details of his arrival in

Pakistan to his family. Rashid helped Saleem's sons to find work and he and Javed prevented them from buying a damp house in the nick of time and gave them advice on which house they should buy. This just gives a taste of the many and varied jobs, some small, some more important, that these relatives are able to do for one another in Bristol.

These people are fortunate indeed, for they have kin to keep them company, help them out and generally cushion the effects of living in a strange country. They know that they are lucky to have the chance to be so energetically involved with their relatives. Other informants who have no kin in Bristol lament their bad luck. Some have friends, but they can never be the same as real relatives, as they are not so dependable and may be only fair-weather friends. Tariq has relatives in London, but none in Bristol, and Tahira has become friendly with Zebunnisa, who also has kin in London but none in Bristol. Both families come from Sialkot. Zafar and Tariq met one another in Bristol before they were joined by their wives and this was how their wives first met. It was only at this stage that it was discovered that Tahira used to patronize the cloth shop belonging to Zebunnisa's brothers in Sialkot, and their friendship grew out of this contact. These two families are also very friendly with another family from Sialkot; again the men had been friendly before they were joined by their wives and children. The families live close to one another and the women and children in particular visit regularly; Zebunnisa helped Tariq's daughters with the housework when Tahira was in London buying goods for her eldest daughter's dowry. However, these relationships cannot compensate properly for the lack of real kin. Tahira is under no illusions about her relationships with her 'made' sisters: if she had relatives in Bristol she would not see her fictive kin at all, for her duties to her real kin would take up all her time. She would probably never have met Zebunnisa if any real kin had been in Bristol when she arrived. Zebunnisa herself does not like living in Bristol (despite her friendship with Tahira) as she has no real relatives nearer than London.

Yasmin is less fortunate than these two women, for she only has relatives in London, and her friendship with Parveen was severed because Parveen began to spread a rumour that Yusuf had an English 'wife'. Even when Parvez visited Yusuf to apologize for his wife's 'madness', Yasmin refused to take heed, and she is now almost completely isolated, apart from a few nodding acquaintances and occasional contact with the wife of a man who runs the film club with Yusuf. Parvez (who himself had an English 'girl-friend' when his wife arrived) took Parveen back to Pakistan after she had been less than three years here: she was miserable and lethargic all the time she was in Britain, and Parvez sent her back home when their daughter was to be married.[10] Parveen's only extensive contact has been with a woman of the same caste (but not a relative) who lived in the top storey of her home in Bristol, but this family returned to Pakistan in order that the daughter be married and the husband contract a second marriage. After this happened, Parveen became very isolated.

In general, those who do not have kin in Bristol regret this and have to turn to non-kin as rather unsatisfactory substitutes. It is recognized that kin have first claims on their relatives, and those who have kin are too busy to develop links with people who are not related: fictive kinship is regarded as a last-ditch attempt to develop multiplex ties of mutual aid and company and is an inadequate substitute for real kinship, but the best available for some.

It must not be thought, though, that even kinship ties always run smoothly. Kin sometimes fail to live up to the expectations held of them, and their relatives may try to bring them back in line. If all else fails, ostracism may be tried, which both puts pressure on the deviant to conform and (if he fails to fall in) also protects the *izzet* of his relatives, who can claim that even if he is a scoundrel at least they have had the good sense to rid themselves of him. The cases of two men are instructive, since their breach of kinship obligations sheds light on those obligations, and indicates how kin try to deal with troublesome relatives. What follows is certainly not an account of 'what actually happened' (though I think it is fairly close to that), since it is based on their relatives' justifications for excluding these men from their activities: needless to say the men themselves have not broadcast their misdemeanours to me and I had no right to stir up more trouble by probing.

One of these men came to Britain in 1961 after a few years in the Middle East. In 1969 he went overland to Pakistan to collect his wife and children. His wife moved to Bristol, while he continued to run a restaurant with two of his sons. With his help and contributions from his sons, his wife was able to buy a house within a year, but he still does not live regularly in Bristol. His relatives criticize him on several points, and would rather not meet him on the occasions when he is in Bristol. One point against him is that he has an English 'girl-friend' (some relatives say that he has married her according to Muslim custom). He did not tell his family about her until he went to collect them, and although they said he must choose, he continues to live with her. His relatives in

Bristol are sorry for his wife, and since they do not consider her in any way responsible they include her in their social activities and help her out in dealings with British officials, as she cannot read English. Her husband still sends money sometimes, but her relatives realize that that could stop at any time. He is also condemned for the way he treats his aged mother, who lives in Karachi with his brother. He rarely writes and did not go to Karachi when he went to collect his wife: his mother is very worried about him, and even sent a letter by hand with a relative on holiday in Pakistan, but he never replied. It was his wife who wrote in response to a similar message conveyed by me. He is also in trouble over his children: some relatives consider that he has damaged his children's education by leaving their coming so late that the younger ones will not catch up at school and the eldest was taken away from college. In addition, two of the boys entered Britain when they were over sixteen, and after they had over-stayed the six-month period they found themselves in trouble with the immigration authorities. They have since benefited from the amnesty, but their father was roundly criticized at the time: firstly, their mother depended very heavily on them because he did not do his duty by her, and secondly it was felt that the boys would have no chance of finding good jobs if they had to go back to Pakistan, as they had not had enough time to build up savings. The final bone of contention with this man is over the marriage of his sons: one relative asserted that he had brought them to Britain for two reasons, to free him from the duty of supporting his wife, and to make them *modern* so that they could make 'good' marriages outside the *biraderi*. In fact, the man's wife had made an arrangement many years ago for her own sister's daughter to marry her eldest son in due course. This girl's sister is in Bristol, along with several other less close relatives. The couple themselves were childhood friends and want the marriage to take place, but they cannot do anything without full parental consent. The girl's parents were apprehensive when they heard of her potential father-in-law's 'girl-friend' in Britain, and the relatives in Bristol think that the boy's father opposes the match because the girl's family could not command a large enough dowry to satisfy his ambitions. All the relatives think that the match between these cousins should proceed.

These then are the counts on which this man is condemned by his relatives, in Bristol and Pakistan: he has become rather too *modern* in his ambitions for his children and in having a 'girl-friend', and he has burdened his relatives with responsibilities for his wife and children which he should have undertaken himself.[11] Since he is not always in

Bristol, his relatives do not have to meet him much; his wife on the other hand takes an active part in the social activities of her relatives with her children. The other members of the *biraderi* feel sorry for her and feel an obligation to look after her.

The other case is somewhat different, since the husband and wife both live in Bristol, and they are both cut off from contacts with their relatives. The success of the ostracism can be gauged from the fact that I did not even know of their existence until the middle of the fieldwork period in Pakistan, although I had previously asked about kin in Bristol.[12] I returned to Bristol with some goods for this man's wife, but none of their relatives would take me to meet him and hints were made that there had been a rift between him and his relatives. It transpired that the difficulties with his kin had a lengthy history, and it was felt that it was all very well for him to be ambitious for his own children, but that this did not necessitate doing his other relatives down. In the mid 1950s, the man's mother arranged his marriage with a girl in the *biraderi*, but he broke the engagement, and when his mother later tried to arrange his marriage no one in the *biraderi* would give him a bride: he was forced to marry an outsider. The significance of this will become clear later, but at that point contacts were still retained: indeed, this man housed several of his relatives in Bristol and I have seen photographs of family outings and parties in Britain at which he and his wife are present. Contacts were eventually cut when the relatives discovered that he had been cheating his sister's husband; as one relative commented, it is the duty of a brother to care for his sister and respect her husband, but he had not done so and had tried to make good by cheating the very people whose welfare should have particularly concerned him.

It appears that the brother-in-law (who cannot write English well) asked the man to bank the money which he was saving and other sums which were the rents he was collecting on behalf of another relative. Instead of banking the cash, the man gambled (unsuccessfully) with it, and could not provide the sum when his sister's husband wanted to buy a house. He refused to re-mortgage his own house in order to repay the debt, and only repaid the sums collected in rent because his relative (a man married to his brother's daughter) threatened legal action. Relatives wrote to his mother in Pakistan, who offered to make good the sum, but no one had a record of the amount of money involved, and the debt is still outstanding. This man's wife complained to me that he had prevented her from visiting Pakistan to see her dying mother; a relative commented that this was very wrong, but that the man was probably 'ashamed' and did not want his wife to be pressurized by his kin in Pakistan. In addition, he has called off a proposed match between his own daughter and the son of his recently deceased brother. This has wide repercussions among the *biraderi* members in Bristol, since his brother's daughter, his brother's wife's sister and brother's wife's sister's daughter are in Bristol, and the others in the *biraderi* can all trace connections to him. These misdemeanours are compounded by the man because he is regarded as careless about ensuring that his family eats only *halaal* meat, he is thought not to teach his children Urdu properly, and (while he sends the children to the mosque school) a British woman teaches his children to read the Bible. His wife says that she does not want her children to think they are being 'held back' (as she considers their relatives are holding back their children), and she allows them to take school lunches and visit school friends, and the girls go alone to the public library. The man thinks his relatives may throw him out for being too *modern*, but he says he does not want to arrange his children's marriages, or insist that his sons live in his house after they marry. He considers that his relatives are 'old-fashioned': they idealize Pakistan, and they have made no effort to change their ways since coming to Britain.

After his cheating was exposed, he excused himself from a birthday party for a relative's son on the false grounds that his daughter was ill, and then shortly afterwards failed to attend the *chehlum* (memorial service) for a relative's mother who had died in Lahore, although his wife and a daughter did attend. Both these events were important, since the *chehlum* prayers are intended to ensure that the soul of the deceased reaches heaven, and the birthday party was for a youngest son (the mother had been sterilized after the birth) and was the occasion for new clothes, complete redecoration of the house and a large feast for all relatives. Since 1971, contacts between this man and his relatives in Bristol have ceased.

The crucial difference between this case and the one discussed above relates to the position of the wives of the miscreants: in the first case, the wife was closely related in her own right to the other members of the *biraderi* in Bristol, while in the second the wife was an outsider, or as one man put it, 'nothing to us in her own right — she is only a relative through her husband'; her own relatives have married one another and not into the *biraderi* in question. As can be seen, in the event of a dispute this difference has important implications. In both cases, the men are seen to be at fault: they have not fulfilled some very basic kinship obligations, and have burdened their relatives with responsibilities, in the first case to care for a wife and children inexperienced with life in Britain, and in the other with helping a sister's husband with paperwork he was unable to deal with. In the first case, however, the wife has been able to keep up her contacts with her relatives even though they want to have very little to do with her husband. In the second case, there is very little leverage that the wife can use against being ostracized by her husband's kin, for there are no people with interests in both camps who could be intermediaries, and she has no weight herself; she has been effectively cut off and there is nothing she can do to alter the situation. She is now very isolated in Bristol.

These two cases indicate something of the expectations which kin hold of one another. Migration does not entitle a man to mistreat his relatives. He should continue to care for the people who are his prime responsibility, and should lend a hand wherever there is a need. In both these cases, the relatives stress the active co-operation which usually goes on amongst themselves which they compare with the wilfulness of these two men. While relatives are the preferred contacts, this does not mean that the relative who fails in his duties, goes back on marriage arrangements or cheats his kin will be able to escape punishment. As can be seen, the practice of marrying close kin provides the opportunity to erect a united front, either to put substantial pressure on deviants to conform or, if that fails, to cut them off.

Generally, though, as we have seen, the migrants prefer to mix with their own kin, or as a very poor second best with 'made kin', and I now want to turn to those people with whom the informants do not mix, and examine why those who have no kin (and the woman who has been cut off by her husband's kin) are so isolated in Bristol. All the men make contacts with others at work, and so there is the possibility for the networks of their families to be enlarged. However, this has not been the case, except in a few cases where kin have been 'made'. Generally relationships at work are single-stranded and fleeting: they die when the man changes work and are not brought into the home. The same can be said of the children's ties made at school. There are two sides to this question, that kinship relationships are the most highly valued of all relationships and that contacts with non-kin are dangerous and may result in unsuitable contacts.

The notion of *izzet* (which was discussed in more detail in 1.4.5) is a crucial influence on the choice of friends and spouses. It can be enhanced by judicious social investments, but it is also fragile. A person will hesitate to become involved with any doubtful characters, lest his kin fail him in times of need or refuse to marry their children to his be-cause they consider that his associates reflect badly on their own *izzet*. The scrupulous observance of kinship obligations bolsters *izzet*, just as failing in those obligations damages *izzet*. Among the families in ques-tion, the dominant idiom of social contact in Pakistan is kinship, and they generally say that it is only possible to know beyond any doubt of the respectability of one's kin: outsiders may conceal their faults, and families who let their women visit friends rather than kin are con-demned because of the potential dangers. Rashid argues that one of the reasons his family makes a practice of making marriages between close kin is that adequate information can be gained only from within the *biraderi*: his family is large and he does not see any point or necessity in looking outside the *biraderi* when he comes to marry his children. The same sort of principle operates in the choice of friends: kin are (or ought to be) more reliable than mere friends, and in any case are more amenable to pressure, so close friends are generally sought from inside the *biraderi*. Indeed, kin have the first claims on their relatives as friends.

In the cluster of relatives discussed above the expectations that kin will maintain close contacts in effect precludes contacts outside, but in any case there is a feeling general among the Muslim informants that it is only 'natural' to be cautious about making contacts with strangers, and outsiders are kept at a distance. They are not interested in establish-ing new contacts with other Pakistanis through clubs or the mosques, and the men respond to new contacts established at work by trying to keep them single-stranded. Just as boundaries are erected between my informants and people of other nationalities, so too do they erect boundaries in relation to other Pakistanis.

People from the villages in Pakistan are a particular instance of this. None of my informants could (or would) introduce me to any Pakistanis from rural backgrounds, although they often knew of such people. There is a widespread assumption that village people are *jungli* (wild, uncouth), and that they are given to gossiping and revel in creating dis-putes and squabbles. Tahira, for instance, asserts that many Pakistani women in Bristol just gossip and stir up trouble for one another and she has nothing to do with them as they will tell all their friends what she has been saying the moment she is out of earshot. Her daughter says they only visit the two families from Sialkot as the other women *larai-jagra karti heyn* (fight and squabble) and they avoid contact with these *larai karniwali* (gossips). The woman ostracized by her husband's kin is very isolated because she does not want to get involved with village women, who she claims only gossip and cause trouble.

Specific knowledge of problems in other families reinforces their inclinations not to mix with outsiders. Parvez disapproves of the way in which Yasmin's daughter visited people who were not related (in response to such criticisms, the girl began to be kept at home), while Yasmin does not want to have much to do with Zafar and his family (as it was rumoured that Zafar's eldest daughter had become rather friendly with Parvez's son at a summer school) or with Parvez because of his wife's gossiping. Rashid and Iqbal worked at one time at the same place as Kalim, and for a time Iqbal lived very near to his house, but visits were not exchanged, and since Kalim left his job there has been hardly any contact: Rashid says there is something wrong in Kalim's family, and he does not want to harm the *izzet* of his own family. Thus, on the basis of generalized stereotypes and information about particular families, contacts with outsiders are curtailed: those with kin in Bristol mix almost exclusively with their relatives and those without prefer isolation to mixing with people who gossip and do not meet their demanding standards. The dominant feature of the networks of the Muslim informants is the tendency for kin to mix with one another (or failing real kin, 'made' kin), and for the clusters so formed to have little contact with each other.

Two further points elaborate the separation between these clusters: the networks of the men and the women are quite different in structure, and the families are hardly involved in activities which might widen their range of contacts in Bristol. I have already indicated that the men are involved in links at work which are normally single-stranded and transient. The women, however, are incapsulated inside the small clusters of which they are part and they meet fewer people than the men: Tahira says that her husband knows a lot of men whom he met before she arrived, but she does not know their wives at all. Yasmin's husband has extensive contacts through his involvement in the Pakistan Association and the film club, but she knows few people and rarely visits. Usually the relationships of the children at school are also single-stranded. Zafar's children meet Tariq's children, and the children in the kin cluster also play together, but outside school hours unrelated children do not normally meet. After leaving the Language Centre, the girls depended on me to convey information about one another, and some weeks after one girl had returned to Pakistan and another had moved to London, only the girls who attended the same secondary school had any

131

idea of the departures. Shahida's daughter commented that she would like to visit Tariq's home, but could not since she would have to be taken there by her brother, who could not be allowed to meet Tariq's daughters. In general, the men and children have more links than the women, but these extra links do not become multiplex.

My informants are also very little involved in activities which might lead them into contact with other Pakistanis. It is my impression that the men used the mosque as a social club before their wives arrived, but that questions of *purdah* have meant that the men have curtailed their contacts with men who are not relatives now that their families have joined them. Several of the women have never been to either of the mosques in Bristol, and the men only attend festivals; the children have rather more contact, but several parents no longer send their daughters to learn to read the Koran. Mumtaza says that as her daughters have never been in Pakistan they are unable to distinguish between good and bad Urdu and she has stopped sending them to the mosque school as the boys swear a lot and speak bad Punjabi; Yasmin no longer sends her eldest daughter, for the boys tease her. Again, attendance at the film clubs is irregular, and they tend to go as households: but even when they go to the cinema, this is not the site for striking up new social contacts. Contacts could also be extended by the women if they attended the English and sewing classes organized in St Pauls, but none of them goes any more; a few used to go, but they say that they learnt no English and the other women who attended spent their time gossiping in Punjabi.

5.2.2 The networks beyond Bristol

While the ties in Bristol are those which have day-to-day interactional relevance to the Muslim families, all of them have relationships outside Bristol which are (or ought to be) 'intense', even though interaction may be limited to brief visits elsewhere in Britain during holiday weekends, or more extended visits to Pakistan. In practice, there is no discontinuity between the ties in Bristol and beyond. The temptation to view migrants within very close geographical bounds may necessitate ignoring very important ties (of various types) which migrants retain with their place of origin. In Chapter 4, I indicated the importance of the resilience of evaluations which the migrants carry over into their new homes. Now I want to examine the ways in which the migrants may remain part of the social system in Pakistan despite the geographical distance involved. Kinship ties are not (or ought not to be) severed with kin at home, and the obligations entailed in them are not put into cold storage. Some families which look isolated in Bristol take on a different face when Pakistan is brought back into view, and those families with relatives in Bristol can also be seen in a different light.

In considering how geographical dispersal affects social relationships, it will again be seen that kinship plays a central part. The kinship bias is even more conspicuous than in Bristol, where fictive kinship was in evidence: outside Bristol, whether elsewhere in Britain or in Pakistan, ties are only with kin.

All the Muslim families have relatives living elsewhere in Britain. Contacts are kept up through letters and the exchange of visits when possible. Tariq and Tahira (who are first cousins to each other) have first cousins in London, whom they visit occasionally. Tahira stayed with them for a while with her daughter when she was buying items for the daughter's dowry. Zafar and Yusuf also have relatives in London whom they describe as 'cousin-brothers', a term which implies that kin who are a little distant in terms of genealogy (e.g. they may be second cousins) regard one another as closer kin. Mahmud has a real brother in Newcastle but he sees very little of him. Iqbal used to live in London with his sister, and they are still on good terms and visit one another often; the entire cluster of kin in Bristol attended the wedding of Iqbal's niece. Some of the families also have kin in other cities in Britain whom they no longer meet: usually, this is because of some misdemeanour, as in the case of a man who married an English woman and stopped supporting his wife and children in Pakistan.

Contacts with kin in Pakistan cannot be as frequent as with those in Britain, but, nonetheless, mutual aid between the migrants and their relatives at home takes many forms. Kin at home also have expectations about how their migrant kin will behave (and they may employ sanctions against them), and contacts should be kept up through letters and visits; and on the other side, the migrants are given help by their kin.

5.2.2.1 The duties of the migrants

At the most general level, the migrants should ensure that their behaviour in Britain does nothing to harm the *izzet* of their *biraderi*: they should be careful not to make contacts with people of bad reputation, they should observe religious injunctions, such as not drinking alcohol and eating only *halaal* meat, and they should educate their children in the ways and language of Pakistan and Islam. They should, in other words, remain Pakistani in outlook and behaviour.

There are also several more specific obligations which the migrants should fulfil for their relatives in Pakistan over and above not misbehaving in Britain. For as long as the migrant's wife and children are still in Pakistan, the migrant should send money for their keep. My informants usually enabled their families to live better than before: Saleem refused to let his sons work, but insisted that they attend college; Tariq was able to build a new house in Sialkot where his wife and widowed sister lived with their children, and he still sends money for his sister[13] and also to enable his son to establish a workshop (which he has not done, much to his father's annoyance); Rashid was able to send his second son to an English-medium school and he also sent money for his mother; Bashir took a television set and electric sewing-machine for his wife as well as sending sums of money regularly for her use. The migrant who fails to support the relatives who are his prime responsibility is breaking one of the most important rules for migrant behaviour, and while my informants in Bristol fulfilled their obligations properly, they and their relatives could all talk of men who had failed to do so.

It is also expected that the migrants will help relatives to come to Britain. The married migrant is expected to take his wife and children to Britain when he can afford to, but in addition other relatives expect help. Several young men in the *biraderis* known to me were in the process of completing paperwork connected with coming to Britain, and relatives in Britain were helping to get work vouchers for them and explaining how to go about the organization of their journey. Saleem's brother sent a message with me to remind Saleem to help his son to go to Britain, Ruxsana's brother was hoping that Rashid would help him, and Imtiaz had a long holiday in Pakistan in order to help her brother with the paperwork. Tariq was also trying to arrange for his son to come to Britain. The son was in Abu Dhabi when his mother came to Britain and could find no work when he went back to Pakistan. In addition, Tariq wants his son to help him support the family, since he considers it wrong that his son should be kept by the earnings of his sisters in Bristol.

The migrant who is unmarried at the time of migration or the migrant who already has children of marriageable age also has the obligation to consider the claims of his kin. Javed and Iqbal both married kin after they came to Britain, Javed marrying Jamila (his father's sister's son's daughter and also his father's brother's daughter's daughter),

and Iqbal marrying Imtiaz (his mother's sister's daughter's daughter).
Recently, Imtiaz's sister has been married to Iqbal's sister's son in
London. In all these cases, the men went to Pakistan for the marriage,
and stayed until all the papers had been arranged to allow their wives
into Britain. Other men have claims on their children. The two families
who returned to Pakistan during the period of fieldwork did so in order
to marry adolescent daughters to sons of relatives. It does not always
work out as simply as this, however, and there is some sign of problems.
Yasmin had to cope with the claims of Yusuf's five sisters, who each
had a son of the right age (i.e. slightly older than her daughter). They
wanted the girl to be sent back to Pakistan to be married, but the girl
did not want to go. Now she has been married to a cousin of one of
Yusuf's sisters' husbands in Bristol, who, although in the same *biraderi*,
could be considered to have less claim on the girl than her father's sisters. Both the men discussed in 5.2.1 had called off matches arranged
between their children and those of close relatives, and the angry response of their kin in Pakistan and Bristol is indicative of the importance of arranging marriages inside the *biraderi*. It is interesting that both
men claim that they do not believe in marriage between close kin, but it
is hard to assess how much this is the case, and how much it is rhetoric
in response to their relatives' anger over their breaking other obligations
to their kin. As we saw, one man married a woman from outside when
his kin would not let him marry one of their daughters because he had
previously broken an engagement. In the other case, where the man did
not want to marry his son to his wife's sister's daughter, this girl's
parents were themselves doubtful about pressing for the match because
they feared the young man might become like his father and want an
English 'girl-friend'. Rashid's brother would like his daughter to marry
Rashid's eldest son, but he is hesitating, because of the work the young
man is doing in Britain. He arrived in Britain when he was twelve and
never caught up at school. Now he is in unskilled work and Rashid's
brother is unhappy about this: either Rashid's son will return to
Pakistan one day, maybe to establish some sort of business, but would
be unable to give his wife the status an educated man could give, or else
if he decides that he cannot afford to return, he will remain in unskilled
work in Britain and his wife would have to face being parted from her
family permanently.

There would seem to be some strains, though even within Pakistan it
is clear from my informants that there is competition among kin for the
hands of relatives' daughters. But in the migration situation, additional

factors crop up. People in Pakistan have less chance to marry outside the *biraderi* than their migrant relatives: upward social mobility achieved through migration enables fathers to provide larger dowries for their daughters and command better brides for their sons. The possibility that migrants will escape the expectations of their kin is a very real one, as they could often marry above their erstwhile equals in the *biraderi*. Migration should not make a man too 'good' for his relatives, nor should he let his relationships with his kin degenerate to such a sorry state that proposed matches are called off. On the other hand, while my informants in Pakistan usually expected migrant kin to continue arranging marriages with relatives, there is also some evidence of sources of anxiety and doubt, either through fear for the morals of the migrant in Britain, or worries that the migrant might be unable to meet the requirements of an *England-returned* if he returns to Pakistan, or concern that the migrant may not be able to marry a girl who has been in Britain for some years, for many people in Pakistan will assume that she has been corrupted by the experience and will be unwilling to take her as a daughter-in-law. I have no specific examples of informants who found it difficult, to marry their daughters, but there was an awareness of the possibility of problems in years to come, and several informants planned the avoiding action of returning to Pakistan before their daughters might be deemed irrevocably damaged. While marriages between kin are still expected, several factors in the migration situation complicate the issue and raise problems on both sides.

The improved financial state of the migrants means that they are expected to visit Pakistan. Not surprisingly, few relatives have come from Pakistan simply for a holiday: Mahmud's father is the only one to come at his own expense, and recently Saleem and Bashir have paid for their mother and mother-in-law respectively to visit Britain and go on *haj* to Mecca. Otherwise, the traffic has all been in the other direction. Several of the men have been back to Pakistan, as we have seen, sometimes to visit their wives, sometimes to arrange for their families to come to Britain. In addition, several of the women have been back to Pakistan for holidays. Rashid thinks it is very important that the women should be allowed to go to Pakistan. Ruxsana went in 1971, and was very happy to be going, as she said she had never spent a day before coming to Britain in which she had not seen her mother or sisters, and leaving them had been a great wrench to her. She went at the same time as Imtiaz, and the parents and siblings of both women were excited at the prospect of seeing the two, who were bringing their children born in

Britain to show the families. Ruxsana's sister lamented that Ruxsana would have to go back to Britain again, and even wanted to prevent her return journey. Such visits are very important to the relatives left at home. Zebunnisa's brothers wanted her to visit them again with the children, and Tariq's sister desperately wanted Tahira to return permanently to live in the same house, as she was so lonely (though Tariq said he had hardly recovered financially from bringing his wife and children to Britain and could not afford to send them all back again).

The migrants also consider that it is important to go back to Pakistan at times of crisis. Rashid, for instance, went to Pakistan when he knew that his mother was seriously ill in 1963; when she died in 1971 after an accident, Rashid's brother decided to send a letter rather than inform him by telephone, as he felt he had no right to involve Rashid in the expense of attending the funeral.[14] Mumtaza was very upset that she had not been informed of their mother's death, as she had not been back to Pakistan at all. Rashid respected his brother's decision, and sent some £50 to be used for erecting a fine grave-stone for his mother. The case of Iqbal also indicates the sort of situation in which the migrants are prepared to inconvenience themselves in order to go to Pakistan. His marriage was first arranged with a relative in Pakistan, but it was called off when Iqbal wanted the marriage to be conducted by telephone; shortly afterwards his mother became ill and he rushed home. His mother died before he arrived, and after he attended the funeral his father arranged for him to be married to Imtiaz. In 1971, the marriage of Iqbal's younger brother was arranged to coincide with Imtiaz's visit, and she attended the ceremony, but Iqbal's brother died of typhoid within three weeks of the marriage and Imtiaz also had to go to the funeral. Iqbal was annoyed that he had not been sent for: although he had just bought a new house and could hardly afford to go to Pakistan himself, he felt that this was the sort of occasion when he should have given support to his relatives.

In addition, the migrants and their relatives in Pakistan consider that it is proper that the migrants will return home permanently one day. Only two of the families have yet done so, but the others are all considering doing so, either when daughters reach adolescence, or when the migrant himself retires.

When a migrant visits Pakistan, he is expected to go laden with presents. Taking of presents is one of the major ways in which the migrants maintain their links with relatives at home. Before leaving Britain, the migrant contacts his relatives and arranges to collect any presents which they might wish to send, and generally the returning migrant is loaded with cases filled with presents. The most popular presents are electrical goods, which are expensive or unobtainable in Pakistan: several families have sent tape-recorders and sewing-machines, and one of the most frequently given items is the electric coffee grinder which women in Pakistan like as it enables them to grind spices quickly themselves (and so avoid having to use ready-ground spices, which are reputed to be adulterated). Cardigans or pullovers made of wool or synthetic materials and nylon shirts are also commonly requested by relatives in Pakistan. Most families send family photographs to their relatives, so that they can keep in touch with the children and have some mementos of family parties in Britain. Rashid even sends his brother unexposed colour films, which the brother uses and then returns to Britain to be developed.

These, then, are some of the obligations which face the migrants. Some are very general and concern the preservation of the respectability and *izzet* of the family, and others are more specific obligations to maintain relationships of gift-giving and mutual aid: in other words, the relationships are expected to be intense even though they are no longer face-to-face. This is not always easy for the migrants, if their relatives in Pakistan hold rather unrealistic ideas of the savings which can be made in Britain. Yasmin, for instance, was hesitant about letting me visit her kin in Pakistan: she feared they would expect me to take expensive presents from her, and at that time she was not able to live up to their expectations. In general, my informants try to ensure that the relationships with their kin at home persist, but most of them could tell me of relatives or other people known to them who had let their families in Pakistan down. Should the migrant fail to live up to the expectations of his kin, they may operate sanctions against him: they may refuse to associate with him, or reject any offers of marriage which he might make, and those in Pakistan may refuse to look after his property there. In fact, for most of my informants, fulfilling their obligations to their kin in Pakistan (and Britain too) is seen as 'natural', but these feelings are reinforced by the sanctions which may be raised against them. One reason why relatives still in Pakistan are able to operate sanctions against those who do not conform is that most migrants fulfil one final obligation to their kin at home: that is, they keep open the communication channels between Britain and Pakistan, through the regular exchange of letters, supplemented by personal communications from migrants on holiday in Pakistan. Most of my informants were in regular contact with kin in Pakistan, and as well as telling relatives there about the progress of the children in school, discussing financial matters and sending other news, they would also give details about any relative in Britain who had misbehaved. Since it is the custom among the families I knew for close kin to marry, it is not surprising that the contents of every letter spread like wildfire. There is a lot of talk in Pakistan about the ways in which migrants in Britain were failing in their duties: relatives of the two men discussed in 5.2.1 knew about their actions, and other cases were brought to my notice. Any prospective migrant would have a clear idea of what his relatives would expect of him, through the invidious comparisons made between the deviants and their kin who do their duty. They, and kin in Pakistan on holiday from Britain, may convey personal messages and letters for deviants from relatives who believe that this is a way of adding more force to their persuasion. Kin in Britain are expected not only to inform people in Pakistan about the misdemeanours of others, but also to co-operate in the exercise of sanctions against them.

5.2.2.2 The duties of the kin who remain in Pakistan

While the migrants should perform certain duties for their kin at home, they themselves rely on relatives still in Pakistan to execute certain tasks for them in their absence.

For the men already married when they went to Britain, the first requirement was that their kin would care for their wives and children. In Chapter 2 (2.5.6) we saw that the migrant's father or brothers generally took on this responsibility, though with the expectation that the migrant would send money for their support. Their duties would not normally extend beyond giving the woman a place to live and taking the place of her husband in any dealings she might have with people outside the family, such as the school authorities. Several women were helped by their fathers-in-law, brothers-in-law or brothers when they were trying to obtain their passports and permits to come to Britain, and these are duties usually undertaken in good grace by the migrants' kin; but the migrant who stops sending money to his wife and tries to cut off contacts with her is considered to have over-stepped the mark.

Even after the wife and children have left Pakistan, the kin who remain there generally perform some duties for them. In several families, migrants send some money to help their brothers to care for relatives. Yusuf (whose brother is married to Yasmin's sister) sends money to help his brother care for Yasmin's widowed mother and unmarried

139

sister. In addition, the Muslim families all have some property in
Pakistan, and they expect their kin there to act as guardians of it. Several of the houses I visited in Pakistan had locked rooms in which the
migrants' household goods were being stored: Imtiaz's dowry has never
been used, as she came direct to Britain after her marriage, and all her
furniture, bedding, china and ornaments are packed up in a room of her
parents' home. Another man is living in his brother's house in order to
keep a close watch on it, and Tariq's widowed sister and his son are
living in his new house in Sialkot (though Tariq is rather concerned that
the son is not looking after the property conscientiously enough). Migrants with separate homes or with land also expect that their kin will
collect and bank the rents: Rashid has three houses in Lahore and his
brother collects the rents each month, and Mahmud's brother oversees
some land which he owns near Lyallpur.

When a relative spends a holiday in Pakistan, his kin are also expected
to provide him with hospitality while he is there. They should house and
feed him, and receive the people who come to see their guest. In some
cases, the migrant has returned to be married, and for the duration of
the stay his relatives organize their lives round him: they arrange the
wedding, and also entertain him and his bride as they make their visits
to their kin all over Pakistan before departing for Britain. In other cases,
migrants have indicated their intention to return for a holiday, and relatives have settled the date for a proposed wedding to coincide with their
stay: Imtiaz was to attend Iqbal's brother's wedding, and Mumtaza was
able to be at her brother's daughter's wedding. Zebunnisa's brothers
were anxious that she return for a holiday, since two of them were due
to be married, and they wanted her to be present.

It is also expected that the returned migrant will come back to
Britain laden with presents from his relatives in Pakistan. Generally,
they send traditional Pakistani handicrafts or clothing. Several houses in
Bristol have ornaments, embroidered cushions and painted camelskin
table lamps which were sent to them from Pakistan. Several women in
Pakistan embroidered handkerchiefs and dresses for their female relatives in Britain, and embroidered or 'mirror-work' waistcoats, dresses or
handbags and Kashmir shawls are also popular presents. Jewellery is also
sent, often to mark a special occasion, as when Mumtaza's brother sent
gold earrings for two of her daughters who had just completed their first
reading of the Koran. In terms of the exchange of gifts, the relationships
between the migrants and their kin in Pakistan are clearly unequal.
However, this is not a source of problems to my informants: the mi-

grants do not, for instance, complain that their kin are ungenerous. The inequalities in the wealth of the migrants and their kin and their access to certain valued objects encourages them to try to live up to the image of the *England-returned* to whom money is no problem. In addition, the non-migrating kin in their positions as custodians of the migrants' property are performing invaluable services for their kin, and the migrants are well aware that it is in their interests to maintain the gift exchange.

Finally, the kin in Pakistan are also expected to make every effort to keep in constant contact through the exchange of letters with their kin in Britain. They are expected to report on the progress of their children at school, on plans for marriages in the *biraderi*, on the state of the migrants' property and on any other general or family news which helps the migrants to keep in touch with their homes. Some migrants felt that their kin at home did not write often enough, and would ask relatives returning on holiday to remind their kin in Pakistan of their obligations: some of them are so anxious for news that they expect all their letters to be answered by return.

5.3 The migrants' economic ties with Pakistan

In the previous section we have seen that the migrants are expected to retain important social links with their kin still in Pakistan and that while they are in Britain it is considered proper for them to mix largely with their kin and avoid contacts with strangers who might in some way be dangerous. The migrants also have important economic links with Pakistan, through property which they owned before migration, or new houses or land which they have bought using money earned in Britain.

As in the cases discussed by Manners and Philpott,[15] remittances from nationals overseas are a very important element in the economy of Pakistan. During the 1960s, private transfer payments were the third highest earner of foreign exchange for united Pakistan, after jute and cotton (raw and manufactured). They also formed an increasing portion of these earnings, being about 5 per cent in 1965–6 and about 10.5 per cent in 1968–9.[16] Many families in Pakistan receive substantial sums of money from their kin abroad: Dahya's reports on the way families in Pakistan invest the remittances in a new home, land, equipment or a business for the family are indicative of the significance of remittances.[17] The scale of remittances is very hard to assess, as there are several extra-legal means of conveying investments to Pakistan. A recent report said that £33 million was sent to Pakistan through banks and post offices in

Britain in March and April 1974, an increased sum thought to be largely due to bank nationalization and devaluation of the rupee.[18] Lomas's figures indicate that there were in Britain over 83,000 Pakistani-born males over the age of fifteen in 1971, which gives an average sum of nearly £400 remitted in those two months by each Pakistani man. In fact this figure must be an under-estimate since Lomas's figures include an indeterminate number of Bangladeshis.[19]

For the Muslim informants in Bristol, the sending of money to Pakistan is also important, but in a rather different way from Dahya's informants. Many of his informants were unmarried men who were sending money back for the use of their fathers and brothers, generally to invest in the family agricultural enterprises or, for example, to set up a transport business. Others were married but had not brought their wives to Britain, and they were sending money for their support in Pakistan. For my own informants, it is rather different: while their wives were in Pakistan, they used to send money for their support, but now very few of the informants are sending money for the day-to-day subsistence needs of relatives. Rashid sent money for his mother until 1971 when she died, and Tariq sends money for his son and widowed sister. However, most money which is sent is intended for the use of the migrants and their wives and children only.

The Muslim informants in Bristol are all living in their own houses, and most of them have already completely paid for their homes. They are usually able to live well within their incomes, and for all of them the question arises of what they should do with their spare cash. All of them have followed the same pattern of investment: to send money to Pakistan in order to buy land or have a house built. There are no other suitable alternatives in Pakistan, since there is so little industrial investment, and conversion of trading and other profits into land or housing is the most common and secure way of saving. Some of the migrants intend to set up a business in Pakistan with the capital they save. Yasmin is trying to persuade Yusuf to have a house built in Karachi, although they share a house in Jhelum with his brother, as she wants to settle in a place which is sophisticated. Mahmud has already bought some agricultural land near Lyallpur and his brother collects the rent for him, and he also has some property in Lahore. Rashid has bought a house in Lahore, and Ruxsana took more money to be invested when she was on holiday in Pakistan. Imtiaz was also intending to invest there: Iqbal sold their house in Bristol and from the cash raised he put down a deposit for his new house and gave Imtiaz £1,000 to invest in Pakistan.

142

She did not in fact do so, because of the political situation at the end of 1971. They intend to buy a plot of land in Lahore and have a house built there, and she left the money in Pakistan to be used when the situation improved. Tariq had already sent enough money to build a new house before his wife and children arrived in Britain. In those cases in which properties in Pakistan are being rented out, the incomes are banked in Pakistan.

There are several points to be noted here. Firstly, the migrants are trading on the differentials between the buying power of sterling and the rupee equivalent of that sterling. They can be said to be 'entre-preneurs'[20] in this, in that they have perceived discrepancies in evalu-ation in the world economic system, and are trying to 'construct bridging transactions'.[21] Several of them complained of the impossi-bility of achieving mobility in Pakistan, and their migration can be seen as a means of circumventing blocked mobility: before migration they were unable to save, but now their savings from work in Britain can (they hope) permit them to buy land or housing in Pakistan and ulti-mately to return there.

In addition, their intentions to invest in Pakistan tie in with some points raised in Chapter 3 in relation to their life-styles in Bristol. Sev-eral informants were quite explicit that although they could sell their house in Bristol and move to a more expensive one, they preferred to send surplus income back to Pakistan and invest in housing there. Along the same lines, Mumtaza said that she had bought cheap second-hand furniture in Bristol since they would not get a proper return on expens-ive new furniture when the time comes for them to sell up their goods in Britain: it was more sensible not to spend much money in the first place and then they would not lose out so much. In other words, there is a general feeling that it is appropriate for them not to live as expens-ively as they could in Bristol, in order that they may send their savings to Pakistan.

Furthermore, it must be borne in mind that the investment of savings in Pakistan is virtually final: it is generally very difficult in Pakistan to convert rupees into foreign currency because of Government restric-tions, and while there are certain illegal routes for exchange, my inform-ants consider that their investments in Pakistan will ultimately be for their use there. At various stages so far, I have indicated that the Muslim families intend to return to Pakistan. Their relatives in Pakistan expect that they will go back, and the migrants themselves often articulate their plans and intentions. Several informants have voiced concern about how their children will settle when they return to Pakistan, and Mumtaza for one sees herself on a knife-edge, between avoiding making her children different at school (and making their education suffer) and retaining a Pakistani home life (so that the girls will not feel out of place when they go to Pakistan). For the adults, though, Pakistan is the Muslim homeland, the place where the culture and religion are their own, and it is an important element in their patriotism that they assume that they will return there one day. Their having created securities which can be used only in Pakistan indicates the strength of these intentions.

5.4 The rhetoric of 'the return'

In this chapter, I have been considering the networks of the migrants in Bristol. In Bristol itself, they prefer durable, intense and multiplex relationships to be conducted amongst kin, or, in the absence of real kin, amongst 'made' kin. Strangers are avoided, and there is little effort to extend social contacts in Bristol: the men and children meet people at work and school (but these links are not brought into the home), and in their leisure hours they are (as the women are all the time) enclosed or incapsulated in dense clusters, which are separated from one another and within which the relationships which are most important to the migrants are conducted. In addition, very important ties are retained outside Bristol, with kin only, elsewhere in Britain or in Pakistan: all the migrants in Bristol have more links outside than within Bristol, and it is expected that these links with their kin will be durable and intense even if they do not involve much face-to-face interaction at the moment. The *biraderi* is able to straddle great distances and even to operate social control over migrants who try to avoid their obligations. The situation might be characterized in terms of *biraderis* in Pakistan which have satellites in Britain, outposts from the base-camp. The migrants and their kin in Pakistan alike consider that the stay in Britain is no more than an interlude. Indeed, the cash investments in Pakistan made by the migrants suggest the force of these assumptions, and I have indicated at several points in this and the previous chapter how intentions to return to Pakistan influence life-styles and attitudes among the migrants now. In a great many ways, they are looking back over their shoulders towards Pakistan.

Given the weak base in Bristol and the social and economic importance of links with Pakistan and intentions to return there, I would argue that any analysis of these migrants which remains geographically bounded within Britain will of necessity ignore vital facets of the situation. Values carried over from Pakistan influence patterns of interaction in Bristol; links with kin at home contain obligations and necessitate a constant orientation in the direction of Pakistan on the part of the migrants; and their investment patterns and intentions to return have an impact on the life-styles they choose (within the limits set by their earning power, of course) for themselves in Bristol. While the involvement of the migrants in the British work force indicates their lowly position in Britain, an actor-oriented perspective brings out other elements: their attitude to their work is instrumental, and they hope that the savings which they make in Britain can enable them to 'construct bridging transactions' to Pakistan and ultimately return 'home' to lead the gracious and leisurely lives of the newly rich.[22]

This, at any rate, is the intention, but it is difficult to assess how much this reflects real hopes and how much it is no more than rhetoric. This reflects a difficulty present in all social research, for my informants are no doubt trying to give me impressions and not lose face in what they tell me. Nevertheless, the direction of their ambitions is interesting, for it emphasizes their lack of attachment to Britain; what they have not done very often is voice problems and ambiguities which are obvious to the outsider. Their plans are optimistic: their intention to return implies anticipation that they will be able to play the role of *England-returned* successfully in Pakistan. In order not to lose face, they will need to be wealthy and generous, they will live in fine homes, educate their children so that they can have professional work in Pakistan, and themselves live respectable lives, supported maybe by rents from their properties or from the incomes from business.

But their optimism conceals some likely problems. For one thing, there would be an ambiguity in their position in Pakistan. If they wish to be *ashraf*, their claims might be held in doubt because of their having been to Britain, while if they want to be *modern* they may find that their education is insufficient to prevent their being treated as parvenus. Only if they achieve their ambitions for their children and manage to enrol them at medical college or university is it likely that their claims to being *modern* would be taken seriously by *modern* people outside their *biraderi*. Maybe the best they can hope for themselves is to be outstanding among their own kin, and put themselves into positions of greater influence through manipulation of their power over their tenants. A more serious problem is just how realistic they are being in assuming that they will ever accumulate 'enough' savings for them to go back without loss of face. Inflation is even more rapid in Pakistan than in Britain, and building costs, the price of land and living expenses are rising all the time. In addition, the material conditions of life in Britain are very different from those in Pakistan, and items considered luxuries before migration may have achieved the status of necessities after several years in Britain: electrical goods such as refrigerators they now take for granted, but in Pakistan such items are expensive and difficult to have repaired. Their wants have expanded since coming to Britain. Furthermore, where their ambitions entail the granting of Government permits, they may find that they are thwarted by being outside accepted corruption channels or by having to pay larger bribes because of being *England-returned*.[23] Conditions in Pakistan may also change in such a way that the person who returns for a holiday has his dreams broken by what he finds, though Dahya considers that the myth of return is generally retained as the migrant would otherwise be renouncing his membership of his kin group.[24] My own informants were surprised that expenses were so great in Britain: they had simply translated reports of their potential earnings in Britain into rupees and believed that the 'astronomical' sums involved would enable them to save enough for their return in a very short time. On arrival in Britain, they found that their savings were much smaller than anticipated.

All these factors will make it more difficult for the migrants to return to Pakistan quickly, and the longer they stay in Britain the more problems arise with respect to their children. Children are the point at which the ethnic boundary is the most vulnerable: the adult migrants are well-socialized Pakistanis who have strong loyalties to their homeland, but the children are likely to develop other loyalties and be unwilling to return to a country they hardly know. Several informants were clearly worried about the prospects of their children not settling in Pakistan. Indeed, even some of the women said they were glad to be back to the comforts of Britain after holidays in Pakistan, and a woman I met in Lahore had had her holiday made miserable by her children's pestering her to take them 'home' to Britain.

It is not possible to predict how many of the Muslim families will manage to achieve their ambitions and become respected *England-returned* in Pakistan. There are obvious difficulties and constraints, but nevertheless, the rhetoric of 'the return' is important, for the myth of going back to Pakistan encourages the migrants to keep themselves and their children 'Pakistani' and resist any changes which would prevent them from being accepted back in their homeland.

6. The Christian informants

6.0 Introduction

So far, I have been primarily concerned with the Muslim informants, though at several points I have hinted that the Christians differ from their compatriots. In this chapter, I want to indicate in more detail the differences between the Muslims and the Christians, and explore the reasons for these differences. Garbett and Kapferer suggest that many of the differences in the behaviour of migrants can be attributed to differing involvements in various sets of relationships.[1] In this chapter, I show how the networks of the Muslims and Christians differ, and then go one step back to consider how such differences have arisen.

6.1 The migration[2]

Most of the Muslim men left Pakistan at a time when rumours of impending immigration restrictions were rife there; only three had previously been in the Middle East. A few men have sponsored relatives since their arrival in Britain. By contrast, only three of the Christian men came directly to Britain. The rest had been outside Pakistan for several years before they came to Britain: as we saw, several had been living in Iran. In other words, most of the Christians had left Pakistan several years before any discussion of immigration control in Britain.

The wives and children of the Christian migrants generally left Pakistan sooner than the Muslims. While Matthew was in Iran his wife and children were living with him, but all three Muslim men who worked outside Pakistan before coming to Britain left their families at home. Apart from Mumtaza and Akhtar (who joined their husbands in Britain within a year), the Muslim families generally joined the men after a longer time-lag than the Christians. In cases where the migrant was unmarried at the time of migration, Muslim and Christian men alike were quickly joined by their wives once they had been married.

There are also differences in the personnel involved in the migration. The Muslim men have brought only their own wives and children, and a few of them have sponsored male relatives. None has brought aged relatives to live in Britain. Among the Christians, a rather different picture emerges. Matthew came with his two brothers, Martha and children, his wife's brother (plus wife and child), her unmarried brother, her widowed mother, and Wahid (who was the widower of Martha's sister). One of Matthew's brothers, Benjamin, has since been joined by his wife and children. In Emmanuel's case, four of his siblings were already in Britain when he arrived; he later went to Pakistan to collect his mother and his younger brother and sister. His father was to follow later, but died before retirement. Emmanuel also tried to persuade his sister Sarah to come with her husband Samuel and two sons, but Samuel was unwilling to leave at that time. Samuel's sister Esther (who later married Emmanuel) told me that her mother-in-law was glad she had been able 'to get her family out', even though she knows very little English and was finding it rather difficult to adjust to life in a strange country. Similarly, Robert brought his parents from Pakistan. His is the only case where no sibling remained in Pakistan to care for parents: Emmanuel has three married sisters in Punjab, and Martha still has siblings in Karachi.

One of the most important contrasts between the Muslim and Christian informants lies in their attitudes towards their migration. The Muslims say they will return to Pakistan, and when talking of difficulties over jobs in Pakistan they talk about nepotism and low pay. The Christians say that they cannot find good jobs in Pakistan because of religious discrimination, and they do not see any point in returning to Pakistan. Several of them have either gone to Canada or are considering going there or to Australia.

Attitudes are also very important when it comes to reasons for moving to Bristol. Some of the Muslims arrived in Bristol by chance, and others were summoned there by relatives: Abdul told his kin that they would stand a better chance of finding jobs in a city in which there are few coloured immigrants. All the Christian men spent some time in Bradford but left before being joined by their families: they were all quite explicit that they did not want to stay in a place with so many Muslim Pakistanis. Robert considers himself lucky because the area where he lives in Bristol has few Pakistanis in it, and he rather pities Matthew who lives where Pakistanis are more concentrated. One Christian woman in Lahore told me that her brothers who had moved to Birmingham reported that it was like a 'second bloody Pakistan'. In general, the Christian informants have made every effort to avoid close contact with Muslim Pakistanis in Britain.

6.2 Ethnic separation and cultural change[3]

In Chapter 4, I indicated that the Muslims have managed to insulate certain sectors of activity and maintain boundaries between themselves and people of other nationalities. For the Christians, it may be said that they *want* the boundaries between themselves and British people to be weak: they are keen to be accepted by British people in a way that the Muslims are not. This does not mean, though, that the Christians have become 'British', for their home life is in many ways hardly distinguishable from that of the Muslims. Like the Muslims, they patronize Indian and Pakistani shops, some of them take Pakistani newspapers, most watch the television programmes for Indians and Pakistanis in Britain and their women wear traditional styles of dress. It is not until we come to domestic affairs, such as kinship, friendship, leisure and religious activities that contrasts appear.

The Muslim informants usually felt that British women who married Pakistani men 'spoil' them, but several of the Christian men have married non-Pakistanis and there has been no such opposition. Martha's brother David married Deborah from Bristol who had been a close friend of Martha's eldest daughter Joanna. Three of Emmanuel's brothers married non-Pakistanis, one a British woman, one a Canadian, and the third a German living in Canada. Matthew's youngest brother, Albert, has set up home in Bristol with his English girl-friend and their son (his wife is still in Pakistan). In the field of friendship too, there is more contact with non-Pakistanis. Joanna prefers to make British friends at college and has had several British boy-friends. She has married a Pakistani Christian, though, for she did not want to marry anyone who would not understand her 'own culture'. Her sister also prefers to make British friends at school, and she exchanges visits with them. Emmanuel's sister Karen is also visited by friends from her school days, and she too had British boy-friends before her marriage. Their brothers also have British friends, but only by dint of a considerable struggle to be accepted.

A major difference in leisure activities hinges on the Christians' attitudes to taking alcoholic drinks. In Pakistan they could not afford to drink, but now (to varying extents) they all drink. Matthew's relatives may even be said to be notorious among the Christians for the quantities they consume: Robert hardly likes to entertain them because they are not satisfied to drink tea. Robert himself and Emmanuel too drink alcohol sometimes at home. Among Matthew's relatives the men go to the local pub, and Joanna sometimes goes with her mother's youngest brother and his British wife. The families occasionally have drinks parties, at Christmas or for birthday celebrations. While the children are not allowed to go to teenage dances, they do go to local cinemas (as well as seeing Indian or Pakistani films sometimes), and Karen once went to a pop concert. There has also been no opposition from their parents to their having boy-friends or girl-friends.

It must not be thought, though, that they spend all their spare time in activities like this, or that all the children will eventually marry British people. Like the Muslims, they are home-based and most of their social contacts are with kin. The contrast between the Muslims and the Christians lies in the willingness of the Christians to countenance contacts with British people in the private spheres, and to occupy some of their leisure time in activities which the Muslims would abhor. Their home-life looks very similar to the Muslims, but the crucial difference is in the existence of close ties with British people.

The Muslims came to Britain with firm and negative ideas about Britain, and their criticisms of Christianity and of British morality are important elements in the boundaries they have erected to protect their private activities. The Christians are in sharp contrast: they are not, of course, critical of Christianity, but in addition they are generally favourable towards British people. They are aware that some British women are prostitutes (Robert even had a lodger who was a prostitute), and they know that illegitimate children are born, but from these cases they do not extrapolate to the rest of the British population in the way the Muslims do. On the whole, they want to be accepted as friends by British neighbours and work-mates. While the Muslims idealize Islam and life in Pakistan, the Christians have hardly a good word to say about Pakistani Muslims, in Britain or in Pakistan.

While the Muslims are always ready to stress the differences between themselves and British people, the Christians treat very much the same differences in a completely different way. In their styles of dress and their dietary habits they are very similar to the Muslims. The women keep their legs covered, with *saris* or trouser-suits, and apart from drinking alcohol they continue to eat Pakistani-style food. In the home all but Karen and her husband and brother speak Punjabi or Urdu. Winifred (whose husband is the Muslim man Wahid previously married to Martha's sister) even spices her speech with *inshallah* (if God wills) and *mashallah* (by the grace of God), which are both Muslim turns of phrase. To the outsider it would be hard to distinguish between the Muslims and the Christians in Bristol.

However, the Christians do not consider that the differences between them and British people ought to be relevant: they are, when all is said and done, Christians. When I asked how they thought of themselves, most said unequivocally that they are British. Ruth does not consider herself Pakistani, except that her parents and siblings still live in Pakistan. Karen also considers that she is hardly Pakistani, though she is to the extent that she does not let her in-laws know that she smokes and she would wear mini-skirts but for the trouble they would make. Joanna wants the best of both worlds: on the one hand she says she and her family are very westernized, for her mother smokes and she herself smokes in front of her parents, and all the members of the family including the women also drink. On the other hand, she also considers that they are very Indian (N.B. not Pakistani) and she wants to be considered Indian as well. She and her brothers are interested in Indian music and dancing and performed some concerts. Their father at one time intended to send Joanna to India for proper tuition. Joanna and her mother usually wear *saris*, and Deborah also wears a *sari*. She is being taught to speak Urdu, and her children, along with Joanna's small brother, are being taught Urdu too: Joanna thinks it is right that they should be taught their 'own' language before they learn English. In general, while the Christians are aware of having come from a different cultural background (and some of them maintain an active interest in this background) they do not consider that this creates an enormous and insurmountable cultural gulf between themselves and British people, for they are rendered fundamentally the same by their Christianity.[4]

The Muslims are also set apart from British people by their lack of certain skills: in particular, their lack of ability to speak English fluently affects them all, especially the women. The contrast here between the Muslims and the Christians is most striking with respect to the women, for the Christian women all attended mission schools before coming to Britain, and learnt some English. Unlike the Muslims, all the younger Christian women know enough English to be able to converse. Several of the women have even been asked to read the lesson in the local church they attend. When this ability is set beside the desire of the Christians to be accepted by British people, the contrast between them and the Muslims is even more striking, and it is reinforced by the 'shared understandings' which the Christians have (or believe themselves to have) with British people. While the Christians remain for the most part interested in 'their own' culture, their interest does not prevent them from being interested in British culture at the same time. They see Indian films, listen to the film music and eat Pakistani-style food, and the women wear traditional dress; in addition, they are quite prepared to eat British food, the children are interested in 'pop' stars and their music, and on several occasions I compared notes with Karen and Joanna on the novels we were reading at the time. These are subjects which do not interest the Muslims: the Christians have opened up an extra dimension for themselves, and this, at the very least, facilitates contacts with British people.

In addition, the Christians' ties with Pakistan are much weaker than those of the Muslims: the Christians write less often, do not send money to relatives, and seldom visit Pakistan. The constraints which their kin have over them are weak: indeed, few of the kin in Pakistan thought they had any rights over their migrant kin. In addition, the Christians do not own property in Pakistan and they do not plan to return: their incomes in Britain are not eaten into by their desire to invest in Pakistan, and any change in their ways since arriving in Britain does not pose the great threat to them that it does to the Muslims.

It is not the case, though, that the Christians have completely discarded their old ways, while the Muslims have clung tenaciously to theirs, for as we have seen the domestic styles of the Muslims and the Christians are very similar. However, while the Muslims resist many changes, the Christians not only consider that people inevitably change when they move to a new country, but they also make some adjustments willingly.

The Christians often criticize the Muslims for their refusal to change their ways. Winifred felt that Muslim Pakistanis should make more effort to learn English and should be more willing to change their ways when they come to a new country. Karen felt very much the same. She, in fact, knew of one of the Muslim families which returned to Pakistan, and she was very critical of the parents. The girl aged twelve who was being taken back to be married, had been in Britain since she was six, and Karen was angry that the girl's parents expected the girl to accept an arranged marriage at such an early age. They should never have brought the girl to Britain if they were not prepared to alter their ways: Muslim parents in general, she feels, treat their children badly by letting them see another country but refusing to let them have love-marriages. People inevitably change, and just as she is different from her sister

153

Sarah still in Pakistan, so the members of her family in Canada will be different from her — that is just a fact of life, which the Muslims cannot accept. But the Christians are not negative about such changes: while they do not like manual work or co-education any more than the Muslims do, they make other changes in their behaviour which are not forced on them. Particularly in their leisure activities, the Christians are prepared to accept British patterns of behaviour: these are the very areas which the Muslims strive so strenuously to insulate. A consequence of the Christians' willingness to mix with British people is that their adjustments can take on a British tone. For the Muslims, who are thinking of going back to Pakistan and who do not want to mix with British people, their social isolation from British people means that they do not have the information on which to base accurate imitation of British people, even if they wanted to. The voluntary changes of the Muslims are best seen within a perspective which includes Pakistan, while the orientation of the Christians could be more satisfactorily called 'anglicization'.[5]

Nevertheless, to the outsider, the domestic styles of the Muslims and the Christians are very similar: the point is that the Christians' pride in 'their own' culture does not result in denigration of British people and their behaviour, and they tend to underplay the differences between themselves and British people. They would like to achieve full acceptance by British people and they would like the boundaries between them to be broken down. This brings up again the question referred to in Chapter 4, since it is at this juncture that the question of power becomes very important.[6] For the Muslims, who are not interested in being accepted by British people, this question does not arise, but for the Christians, it is very important. They want to define themselves as Christians (and only secondarily as Indians or Pakistanis); for them this is the crucial ethnic marker, and as far as they are concerned, it marks them off very clearly from Muslim Indians or Pakistanis. However, they often find that this definition of themselves is not accepted by British people, who do not see 'Christian' as a relevant ethnic marker in this context: several of the Christians complained that British people refuse to accept their claims to common allegiance, and insist on their being fundamentally different because they are 'Pakistani'. For British people, 'Pakistani' is often the crucial ethnic marker, and they sometimes exclude these Pakistanis who consider that their common religious allegiance self-evidently ought to make them acceptable to British people. They define their basic identity in one way, but many British people define it in another and are in a position to impose their definition on the situation and exclude the Christians, whom they see as Pakistanis. However, as will be seen, this exclusion is not total and the Christians all have some British friends with whom they exchange visits.

6.3 The networks of the Christians[7]

When the social networks of the Muslims and the Christians are compared, several differences are very striking. The Christians mix more with people who are not kin, including British people, and the ties which they retain with kin in Pakistan are very weak.

6.3.1 The mixing of the Christians in Bristol with one another

At first, the Christians lived in only two houses in Bristol; Matthew lived in one house with his own wife and children, his mother-in-law, Martha's married brother (plus wife and child), her unmarried brother David, his own two brothers, Benjamin and Albert, and Wahid; and Emmanuel and Robert lived in another house. Gradually, relatives joined them, and the households split up, though most social activities were conducted amongst these individuals, often in terms of fictive kinship. Robert and Emmanuel considered themselves brothers, and when Winifred first met Ruth and discovered that they were the same age and had been trained as teachers, they regarded each other as sisters. The families met regularly at the Y.M.C.A., and also exchanged visits to one another's homes.

Now however, several factors have led to a considerable decline in contacts among these informants. Karen has virtually no contact with the other Christian Pakistanis in Bristol, though this is a fairly recent development. First of all, her brother Emmanuel broke off his ties with Robert shortly before he went to Canada: Robert's sister and two daughters were visiting Robert from Tehran, but Ruth argued with her and she moved to Emmanuel's house. Her mother died soon afterwards and she would not go to the funeral because of the family argument. Robert was angry with Emmanuel (who he thought had persuaded his sister not to attend the funeral), and Emmanuel felt he had been wrongly burdened with responsibility for Robert's sister and nieces. Karen tried to cut down her contact with Ruth after this. Shortly after Emmanuel went to Canada, there was further trouble between Ruth and Karen: Benjamin's son-in-law had asked Kalim to get him a job at Avonmouth (although Benjamin himself was also working there at the time), and when he had an accident at work he began to blame Kalim. The story was passed from Benjamin to Robert, and Ruth began to chide Esther about Kalim's activities: since then, Karen has had no voluntary contact with Robert and Ruth, and Esther has joined Emmanuel in Canada. Although Karen never visits Ruth, Ruth and Robert (and Robert's father too) have visited her complaining about one another; since she has moved, she has been less bothered by this. Kalim does not want to see Robert any more as he thinks he only brings them trouble.

Karen also used to have much more contact with Matthew's family, especially Joanna. Karen's marriage was arranged with Winifred's brother, but only a few days before the wedding she eloped with Kalim, whom she had known at school. She says that she did not love Winifred's brother, but she is rather afraid to meet Winifred as she knows that she involved her in a lot of expense. Matthew and his family still disapprove of Karen's action: he had previously tried to stop Joanna meeting Karen as he felt Karen had too many boy-friends (including a West Indian at one point), but now none of them wants contact with Karen. For her part, Karen wants to cut down contacts with Matthew and his family. She feels they are inhospitable, and yet they were quite prepared for her to spend a whole evening cooking for them (after she had just come out of hospital after a miscarriage) while they were in the sitting-room drinking with her brother. She has had several miscarriages, and she feels that they are very insensitive about her gynaecological problems: the final blow fell when Karen was visited in hospital (where she had a septic uterine cyst removed) by Matthew's son and his wife (who was pregnant) and asked by them when she was thinking of having children. Karen is also annoyed as she considers that Matthew's sons are leading her brother Luke astray. His regular drinking sessions with them are costly and often he does not go to work afterwards. Karen feels she has no control over him, and is very keen that he should go to Canada where her brothers would be able to take him in hand.

Robert, too, has much less contact with Matthew and his family, and again the drifting apart is mutual. Robert on his part feels he is not earning enough to be able to provide the freely flowing drinks which Matthew and his family expect from their hosts. In addition, Matthew is angry with Robert, for offering to bring Albert's wife Abigail to Britain when he went to collect his own parents.[8] Robert says he was told to mind his own business, and he considers that Matthew does not want his brothers to be joined by their wives as he wants to keep control over them and have them contribute to his finances. Karen reports on a dispute between Matthew and Benjamin (which she learnt of via Ruth and Winifred) which ties in with this supposition: Benjamin moved to another house when his wife and children arrived from Karachi, and when he was made redundant Matthew took him to court and claimed that Benjamin owed money lent by Matthew to help him buy a house: according to Karen the sum claimed amounted to Benjamin's redundancy payment, and the claim was made when Matthew was faced with Joanna's wedding festivities. How much all these rumours and comments are justified it is difficult to assess, but it can be seen that there is quite a lot of hard feeling among the Christians.

It is Martha and her two brothers who keep up most contact. Her bedridden mother lives in her house and her brothers live not far away. David's English wife spends her days with Martha, and helps with the housework. She leaves her children with Martha when she goes to her part-time job, and she and David spend most evenings in Matthew's home. Martha's other brother moved to another house only in 1970: he had a stroke and cannot go out much, but his wife and daughter are frequent visitors at Matthew's home. Winifred and Ruth are still friendly, but they do not see much of one another, as they live in different parts of the city. While Ruth has little contact with Matthew and his relatives, Winifred still sees Martha nearly every day.

In the early days, the network of the Christians in Bristol was dense and based on real and fictive kinship, but gradually the links have loosened, and not just along the lines of fictive kinship. The centrifugal tendencies contrast with the situation described in Chapter 5, in which the Muslims try to create dense networks based on real or, failing that, fictive kinship.

6.3.2 The mixing of the Christians with Muslim Pakistanis in Bristol

The Christian Pakistanis have very little contact with Muslims in Bristol. Some of the men work with Muslims, but the ties are not brought into their homes and the women have little contact with Muslim people. Muslims are generally considered unsuitable contacts, and this can be seen as boundary-maintenance on the part of the Christians.

Robert knows a few Muslims whom he considers 'passable' as friends (as they are prepared to drink alcohol) but most are too strict. Joanna says that her father 'hates' Muslims and cannot bear to let one inside his house: he did not mind if she had British boy-friends, but would have been furious if she had been friendly with a Muslim. Her brothers' drinking companions are all British, except Karen's brother Luke; they are used to 'laughing, drinking and good conversation', and Muslims are too strait-laced. Most of the Muslims in Bristol have too much land in Pakistan, she says, but no education, they are very 'ancient', but have no appreciation of Indian culture. When she dances, they think she is no better than a *murassi* (street musician), and Joseph thinks the Muslims in Bristol are not sophisticated enough to understand the art in what she does.

There are, however, some contacts with Muslim Pakistanis. Through his involvement with the film club, Robert has met Kalim's father and also Yusuf. Kalim's father began the club, and when Robert's club in Cardiff failed, brought Robert into the organization in Bristol. The important point, though, is that Robert only sees these men in connection with film club business and Ruth does not know the wives of the other two men.

In addition, two of the Christian women have married Muslim men, but in both cases these men are rather unusual, in that they have no contacts with other Muslims and can scarcely be described as practising Muslims themselves. Winifred's marriage to Wahid was arranged by Martha: Wahid had made a love-marriage with Martha's sister (who died in childbirth), and he was incorporated into Martha's family. He moved to Karachi from Mysore with them at the time of Partition. Winifred is the sister of Abigail, the wife of Matthew's youngest brother Albert. She says that Wahid does not want to go back to India or Pakistan as he enjoys drinking too much, and he has no relatives in Britain. Their major social contacts are with Matthew and Martha and their kin. Winifred had slight contact with a Muslim woman who lived in the same street (but who has now returned to Pakistan): these two women seemed to be brought together by their attitude to *dehati* types (peasants). Winifred is accused of being snobbish by village women as she speaks Urdu at home (Wahid does not understand Punjabi), and Winifred herself thinks poorly of village people who come to Britain and make a lot of money, but who still use bad language and allow their wives to stir up trouble by gossiping. Winifred spends most of her free time with Martha.

Karen's husband Kalim also comes from a Muslim family. Her family was not happy about this, though they like Kalim himself, but Kalim's family have never accepted Karen (except for Kalim's step-mother, who herself is cut off by Kalim's father's brothers in Bristol). Neither Kalim nor Karen has much contact with his relatives, and Kalim is not interested in keeping in touch as he feels his relatives just make trouble for people. Kalim's father was married against his will to the woman who became Kalim's mother, and he divorced her and married Kalim's step-mother when he came to Britain. His brothers opposed the second marriage and brought Kalim's mother to Bristol; Karen thinks they are jealous of Kalim's father's success and want to be an embarrassment to him. Kalim's mother sometimes visited him, but was never civil to Karen, and tried to use the occasions when Karen had a miscarriage to reclaim Kalim's allegiance. Kalim's step-mother on the other hand is ostracized by Kalim's father's brothers, and used to visit Karen to pour out her woes. This was one further factor which impelled Kalim to move to a rather less central house, and after the move they had little contact with his father, mother or step-mother. Like Wahid, Kalim can hardly be described as 'Muslim': he drinks with his in-laws, he cannot read the Koran, and Karen teases him that he does not know the compulsory prayers and did not know when *Ramzan* was starting until a work-mate told him. Since he left work to begin his own business, he has had practically no contact with other Muslim Pakistanis. Most of the contacts which the Christians have in Bristol with other Pakistanis are in fact with Christians and not Muslims.

6.3.3 Contacts with British people

While the Christians do not do a great deal of visiting, it is significant that they all number some British people among those with whom they exchange visits. Many of the contacts with British people were made at church. Martha and Winifred are both active in the local Methodist church and British women from the church visit them sometimes; Ruth attends a Pentecostalist church, where she has also made some West Indian friends. She knows the parents of children friendly with her own, and all the Christians who attended school in Britain for a time still know British people from their school days.

In addition, several of the men have married British women (and two of Emmanuel's brothers married women they met in Canada): Emmanuel's eldest brother and Martha's brother David both married British women, and Albert (Matthew's youngest brother) had set up house with a British woman, by whom he has a son. Although Albert has effectively abandoned his wife in Pakistan, he is not condemned by his relatives. Even Winifred (Abigail's sister) considers that Abigail brought the situation on herself by stipulating that she would only come to Britain if Albert collected her himself. The general feeling is that Abigail has behaved stupidly.

In fact the Christians are very home-centred and most of their contacts are with one another; marriage to British people is not the pattern, for Joanna, her brother, Benjamin's daughter and Karen all married Pakistanis. However, the important point is that they have contacts with British people which are not limited to the work or school spheres. The Christians are all competent (though to varying degrees) in English, and this enables them to make contacts with British people. They are also not hostile to British people. As was indicated in 6.3.1, the contacts among the Christian Pakistanis themselves have declined, and this is connected with their competence in English. In comparison with the Muslims, they do not need to invest so much in their links with one another, for the Christians who withdraw from contacts with other Christian Pakistanis need not be isolated. Karen wants to keep her contacts with Pakistanis to a minimum as they gossip too much, and Joanna also prefers British to Pakistani people as friends at college; but they would not be so sanguine about cutting their ties with Pakistani people if they were not both fluent in English and had not already achieved acceptance at school and college.[9] The declining contacts among the Christians contrast them with the Muslims, and are connected in part with their greater facility at English and lack of hostility towards British people.

6.3.4 Ties with kin outside Bristol

Another factor which is also connected with the contact between British people and the Christian informants is the nature of their networks outside Bristol. Only Winifred has a real relative in Britain: her brother, who lives in London. Karen and Robert have no links in Britain outside Bristol, while Matthew has some Pakistani Christian friends in London. In addition, their ties with their kin in Pakistan are weak, and they write rarely to them.

The kin of the Muslims expect that the migrants will keep in touch, and also remain 'Pakistani'. On the Christian side, only Abigail considered that her migrant relatives had a duty towards her; she is bitter that Albert did not take her to Britain and no longer sends money. She and her mother and two daughters are supported by her brother, but she considers that Albert should support her, and compares herself with other people in Lyallpur who have been sent expensive presents by their kin in Britain. Otherwise, the kin remaining in Pakistan do not expect anything from their migrant kin. The widow of Matthew's eldest brother lives in a *kutcha* house in Lahore, supported by her son. While their neighbours receive money from migrant kin, they say that they do not expect their kin to send anything, and she was overwhelmed to receive a *sari* from Martha. The family in Bristol had no idea of the conditions under which she was living, and her son had only the vaguest idea about the identities of his cousins in Bristol. Sarah (the sister of Karen and Emmanuel) also does not expect any help from her relatives. She has little contact with Karen, and asked me detailed questions about Kalim's character. She does not expect Karen to write, and thinks it is probably better that they have little contact as they will only remind themselves of the past. Sarah would like Karen to have a holiday in Pakistan before going to Canada, but does not think Karen is very interested and she shrugged her shoulders, saying it did not matter that much.[10] Karen has lost contact with everyone in Pakistan except her sisters, and rarely writes to Sarah as she fears disapproval over her marriage to Kalim. She used to write to friends but stopped when she was inundated with requests for presents: people in Pakistan have quite the wrong idea about the cost of living in Britain, she says. Similarly, Robert has few ties in Pakistan. He only has a cousin in Quetta, and they exchange letters occasionally. Ruth's family live in Wazirabad, and Ruth used to send money to enable her sister to study to First Arts. Ruth wants her sister to come to Britain and become a nurse, as she is lonely in Bristol, especially since Esther joined Emmanuel in Canada. Robert's father sometimes sends small sums of money to his brother (a retired pastor in Sheikhupura). Otherwise, no other money is sent to Pakistan, and none of the Christians is investing savings in Pakistan.

They also put very little emphasis on going to Pakistan for holidays. Matthew and his family had a short holiday while they lived in Tehran, and the shock at seeing the poverty there was one reason they gave for moving to Britain. They have never been back. Matthew's brother's wife, Beatrice, is the only one to have gone for a holiday from Britain. In all the other cases, the returned migrants have fetched other relatives: Emmanuel collected his mother and Karen and Luke, and Robert first collected his wife and then his parents. There are no other plans for holidays in Pakistan and none of them plans to return to Pakistan permanently.

Furthermore, the Christians have important ties with kin outside

Britain who are not in Pakistan. One of Martha's brothers remained in Tehran after the others came to Britain, and they maintain active links with him: he has been to visit them twice and sends Persian and Indian records for Martha's children. Robert also lived in Tehran for a while with his sister, and she has been to Bristol, and her two daughters attended a fee-paying school in Bristol for a while. However, since Ruth and his sister argued, there has been no contact.[11] As we have seen, Karen also has extensive ties outside Britain, this time to Canada. All her brothers are already there, except Luke, who has the necessary papers arranged. Karen is keen to join her siblings and mother there. She sees it as one way of escaping from Kalim's relatives, but she does not want to force the issue. Her brothers are willing to include Kalim in their business. Karen attended a brother's wedding in Canada, and returned to Bristol full of enthusiasm for the friendliness of Canadian people; she would like Kalim to see for himself, but does not want to be left 'to the mercies' of her in-laws and is content to wait until Kalim makes the decision and her brothers sponsor them. Robert also wants to leave Britain, but Karen says that Emmanuel considers that their relationship is over and is unlikely to sponsor Robert; Robert thinks he might go to Australia. Joanna has also thought of going to Canada, and Winifred thinks her brother may take her mother and sister (Abigail) to Canada after his marriage. The existence of these ties outside Britain and Pakistan, and the stress put on them by the Christians, is an important point of contrast between them and the Muslims.

6.4 Summary of the contrasts between the Muslims and the Christians

The Christians generally left Pakistan earlier than the Muslims, and several spent some time in Iran. Most of them arrived in Britain shortly before the Commonwealth Immigrants Act (1962) was enforced, and they were quickly joined by their wives. Several have also brought aged relatives to Britain. They believe that Christians cannot find good jobs in Pakistan, and they have chosen to live in Bristol because there are relatively few Muslim Pakistanis there. They look on British people in a favourable light and maintain strong boundaries between themselves and Muslims. They have not, though, completely discarded their old ways; rather they do not consider the differences between themselves and British people to be very significant, and they are not averse to changing their habits. Contacts among the Christians have declined, but they all have some contacts with British (and even West Indian) people. They do not have much contact with their kin in Pakistan, they do not invest savings there, and they do not intend to return. Several have important ties with kin outside Pakistan, and a number are planning to move on from Britain.

6.5 The reasons behind the differences between the Muslim and Christian informants

In this and the previous two chapters I have indicated a number of differences between the Muslim and Christian informants, particularly in the structures of their networks, their attitudes to Britain and their intentions for the future. Why is it that migrants from such similar backgrounds react in such different ways to their migration and their situation in Bristol? In the remaining part of this chapter, I discuss several ways of approaching this puzzle.

6.5.1 The adequacy of the sample

I did not attempt to draw up a random sample of Muslim and Christian Pakistanis in Bristol, so it might be that the differences described above are artefacts of the sampling process. The Christians constituted the entire settlement of Pakistani Christians in Bristol, at least as they knew it, but there are many Muslims who did not fall under my scrutiny. Some are unmarried men, many from rural backgrounds, but there are also some families to whom I did not gain an introduction. While I have no information about Christian Pakistanis elsewhere in Britain, it is clear that the Muslim informants are not typical of their compatriots in some respects. I obviously cannot claim that the differences which I have described above would be replicated throughout the country, though both Saifullah-Khan and Dahya indicate that their Muslim informants often say they will go back home and that they retain important social and economic links with Pakistan, like the Muslim informants in Bristol.[12] One additional problem is that my informants could tell me of a few Muslim Pakistanis who had 'absconded', so it cannot be assumed that all Muslim Pakistanis in Britain retain strong ties back home and want to go back (though it is likely that their kin are annoyed with them, and this would seem to set them apart from the reactions of the Christian informants).

However, for my informants, it is possible to talk about the Muslims as a whole and the Christians as a whole. While this divide may not be replicated throughout Britain, it is significant that there is a divide, that it falls between the Muslims and the Christians, and that the Christians themselves are very much aware of such a split. The question is, what is at the root of this divide?

6.5.2 The length of the time the informants have spent outside Pakistan

The Christian women and children have generally been in Britain longer than the Muslims, and the differences suggested above may be due to this. Since the Christians came to Britain before many other Pakistanis were here, they may have been forced to strike up contacts with British people in order to have company, and they have also had more time in which to accumulate the social skills needed for interacting with British people. Time might also be a crucial element in their drifting away from their kin in Pakistan.

An explanation along these lines is simple-minded, and does not cover all the cases. A few of the Muslim women have been in Britain longer than the Christian women. Kalim's step-mother arrived in the mid 1950s, but she cannot converse in English, and her contacts are restricted to her husband, her children and Kalim and Karen. Mumtaza arrived in 1961: she speaks little English, mixes only with people in her own *biraderi* and plans to return one day to Pakistan. The Christian women all arrived after these two, they all speak passable English, they all have British friends and they do not plan to return to Pakistan. Time spent in Britain does not appear to have any clear relationship with assimilation and the development of the idea that Britain is the new homeland. This is precisely the point made by Philip Mayer in his discussion of urbanization: he did not find that the time spent in East London could be directly correlated with full 'urbanization', in the cultural and structural senses.[13]

Mayer argues that the networks and aspirations of the migrants have to be taken into account, and this is a useful way to approach the different responses made by the Muslim and Christian women. If length of time in Britain is considered crucial, then the Muslim women who have been in Britain for ten years or so become awkward cases. However, consideration of aspirations reveals that there is a divide between the Christians as a whole and the Muslims as a whole. There is no straightforward relationship between length of time in Britain and the extent to which migrants have become assimilated: migrants may resist assimilation. On the other hand, the migrant who is bent on assimilating may make adaptations rapidly. Moreover, the Christian men all spent time in Bradford and moved to Bristol because they heard there were few Muslim Pakistanis there: one cannot argue, therefore, that the Christians were *forced* to be 'assimilating' because of an absence of compatriots, for they *chose* to move to a city with few Pakistanis. The interesting question is why they should want to live in a place with few Muslims.

Similar points can be made about the acquisition of social skills. It might be that the Muslims will be able to maintain links with British people better after they have been in Britain longer, but here again we are faced with the problem of the Muslim women who have been in Britain for longer than the Christian women. Part of the answer no doubt does relate to the different education of the women, for most of the Christian women knew some English before they arrived in Britain, so they obviously had a head-start over the Muslims. However, this cannot be the whole story. The Christian women can all speak English, but they are more relaxed when speaking Punjabi or Urdu, and this requires an explanation of why they are prepared to restrict their contacts with Muslim Pakistanis (with whom they can easily communicate) and why they are keen to develop links with British people. Is it the case that they feel they have shared understandings with British people which they do not have with their Muslim compatriots? This seems a more fruitful line to pursue.

Again, why have the Muslims tended to retain stronger links with their kin in Pakistan than the Christians have? This issue is complicated as several male informants spent time outside Pakistan before coming to Britain, and it might be that length of time spent outside Pakistan is more significant than length of time spent in Britain.[14]

Three of the Muslim men (but none of their wives) spent several years in the Middle East before moving to Britain. Two of these men are the ones discussed in 5.2.1. They came to Britain in 1960 and 1961 and their wives followed later. The wives have kept up their links with Pakistan, but the two men have not. It could be that the cutting off of their ties with Pakistan is the result of the long time they have spent outside Pakistan. On the other hand, bad relations at home might have encouraged an early migration, though as far as I could establish the migration was simply economic in motivation. It is not very clear how to interpret this. The third case seems to indicate that time spent outside Pakistan is not necessarily important; the man spent several years in Kuwait, and then a few years running a drapery business in Lahore. His partner absconded with the profits and my informant came to Britain in search of him; he stayed in London with his son for a while, and after he was joined by his wife and children moved to Bristol and set up a café. This did not flourish and he moved back to London and talked of returning to Pakistan, as he was so disappointed with his life in Britain. By then he had not been to Pakistan for ten years, but he still retained strong ties with his brother and his two married daughters, and could countenance returning to Lahore. The case of Emmanuel contrasts with this. He came to Britain direct from Pakistan in 1960, and he and his siblings have very tenuous links with Pakistan.[15]

A particularly interesting point in this context relates to the position of the respective kin of these men on the issue of the maintenance of ties with Pakistan. In 5.2.1, I indicated that the kin of the two miscreant Muslims consider that they should have kept their links with their kin alive. The first man's kin consider that he should have contributed to his mother's keep and visited her when he collected his family from Lahore, and they also think that his son should marry the man's niece. The second man was also heartily criticized by his kin for the way he had treated various relatives. Neither of these men has been living in Pakistan for more than about three of the years since Pakistan was created in 1947, and yet their kin there (and their migrant kin) consider that they should keep their links alive. By contrast, as we saw in 6.3.4, the kin of the Christian migrants (apart from Abigail) do not consider that they have any claim on them, and this includes the kin of Emmanuel, who left Pakistan so much later than these Muslim men.

These cases are too few to enable the drawing of firm conclusions, but the differing approaches of the kin of the migrants suggest that it may be useful to return to the aspirations of the migrants (and their kin). The relatives of the Muslims, including the kin of the men who have tried to escape their responsibilities, expect that their migrant kin will go back to Pakistan; they also expect that their kin will remain 'Pakistani' even when they are living outside Pakistan. The kin of the Christians, on the other hand, do not entertain such assumptions and expectations. A divide again appears, this time more clearly between the kin of the Muslim and Christian migrants than between the migrants themselves, and I do not find it satisfying to argue that the length of time spent in Britain or outside Pakistan can explain this divide.

It is possible that the factors which I have been discussing have combined with one another, and that the differences I am pointing to are illusory and insubstantial. But there are several reasons why I am loath to accept that the differences are mere artefacts, not least because the

Christians themselves sharply differentiate between themselves and Muslim Pakistanis. I still suspect that there is something about being Muslim or Christian *per se* which is connected with the contrasts between the Muslim and Christian informants.

6.5.3 The tenets of Islam and Christianity

Maybe, then, the roots of the contrasts can be traced back to the tenets of the two religions of which the informants are adherents. Do the premises and demands of the two religions result in differences in life-styles and attitudes among their followers?

This is a very complex question. There *are* many similarities in the fundamental tenets of Islam and Christianity: both are in principle monotheistic and egalitarian (a particular contrast with Hinduism), and many scriptures are shared. The major difference hinges on whether Christ is the Son of God, which Islam denies. But having said this, it is very difficult to discern what this means for the present argument. The relationship between the fundamental tenets of a religion and the form it takes on the ground is not necessarily clear: theological debates and social, economic and political factors may mean that one religion takes on various forms at different times and in different places. Islam arrived in north India in the eighth century A.D. and has taken on many cloaks since then.[16] Christianity arrived in the mid nineteenth century, in a land ruled by Britain. How can the impact of the varying forms of these two religions on their adherents be assessed?

This impasse may be avoided by directing attention to the present life-styles of the adherents in Pakistan. Are there any differences which could be attributed to the 'fundamental tenets' of the two religions? From the outside, the impression obtained is that the life-styles of Muslims and Christians in Pakistan are very similar. Muslims in India have long retained an aloofness from India, yet their 'Islam' has a distinctively Indian flavour.[17] Much the same seems to have occurred with Christianity in India. The question of caste is a good example of this, for both religions are supposedly egalitarian and yet reports often point to 'caste' organization among Muslims and Christians in the Indian subcontinent.[18] Leaving aside actors' self-perception for the moment, Islam and Christianity seem to have been laid rather loosely onto regional Indian life-styles.[19] Variations in life-style appear to relate more closely to wealth than religion in Pakistan: for Muslims and Christians of comparable incomes, the homes, diets and dress are largely the same. The same food is eaten, and meats are ranked in the same way; pork is practically unobtainable, and only the most wealthy (including some Muslims) can afford to drink alcohol. While Christian women do not wear the *burqa*, their dress at home is the same as that of Muslim women, and their attitudes to modesty are much the same: Christian women do wear the *duppatta* and they carefully cover their hair and bodies in public. Only a few rather daring women in Karachi do not cover their legs with *shalwar* or a *sari*. For Muslims and Christians alike, most marriages are arranged. Moreover, the life-styles of my informants in Bristol are not strikingly different.

There are of course some differences, though it is not clear how they might influence responses to migration. A larger proportion of Christian women work in Pakistan, partly because of the disadvantaged position of Christians as a whole in Pakistan, but also because teaching and nursing are 'service' occupations which appeal more to the Christians than to the Muslims. Of course, there are also differences in the 'religious' sphere, in the forms of worship and prayer and in the festivals celebrated. However, I find it very difficult to see how these *in themselves* might result in different attitudes to migration. In view of the 'Indian flavour' of the life-styles of Muslims and Christians in Pakistan it seems most plausible to suggest that the basic tenets of the religions have had little influence on the life-styles of the adherents, and if this is the case, then the problem of interpreting the differences delineated above between the Muslim and Christian informants in Bristol still remains.

6.5.4 The pattern of marriage relationships

I have already indicated that the Muslim informants say that it is the custom in their families to marry within the *biraderi*.[20] The material on the Christians is less clear-cut, and I have been unable to locate any ethnographic material on north Indian Christians and the patterning of their marriage relationships. Given their fairly recent conversion, and the position from which the converts came, it might be expected that their marriage patterns would still resemble those described of low-caste Hindus: they might insist on *gotra* exogamy, though permit sister exchange marriages, for instance.[21] It is very hard to judge, though there was one case of 'sister exchange' (Emmanuel married Esther and his sister Sarah married Esther's brother Samuel). Otherwise no pattern emerges. There are a couple of attempts to reinforce marriage links by creating new ones: Wahid (the widower of Martha's sister) is now married to Winifred, who is the sister of the wife of Matthew's youngest brother. In addition, the marriage was arranged between Karen and Winifred's brother, but it did not take place. There are no marriages between cousins, however, and none of the Christians talked of any preferences for marriages between kin. On the basis of this rather limited information, it appears that the marriage patterns of the Christians are less involuted than those of the Muslims, though there does seem to be some desire for links between people to be reinforced through marriage.

Might it be the case, then, that the contrasts between the Muslim and Christian informants can be attributed to differences in the ways they arrange their marriages? Marriages between close kin make it much easier to control relatives and put pressure on them if they do not conform. The more open-ended marriage networks of the Christians may make it easier for a man to succeed in not conforming, and this might be connected with the weaker ties which the Christians retain with their kin in Pakistan.

However, this line of argument fails to account for several aspects of the situation. While I grant that it might be easier for the Christians to extract themselves from obligations to their kin in Pakistan, this does not explain why they would want to do this. The material on Sikhs in Britain (whose marriage networks might be more comparable to those of the Christians than to those of the Muslims) indicates that they retain strong ties back home, make investments there and visit their families in East Punjab and in this respect are very similar to the Muslim informants.[22] It is difficult to argue in the face of this that marriage patterns are related to the ties which migrants retain with their homes. Furthermore, why do the Christian migrants' relatives who remain in Pakistan not expect their migrant kin to send them presents or visit them? Again, as we have seen, the Christians have not in fact cut themselves off from all their kin: most of them have strong ties with kin outside Britain, but who are not in Pakistan. Moreover, how can the patterning of marriages among the Christians explain why they are quite willing to accept British people as friends and even marriage partners? (In this too, Sikhs in Britain appear to resemble the Muslim informants.) Finally, why do the Christians not make investments in Pakistan, and why do they not want to go back there permanently? These are important contrasts between the Muslim and the Christian informants, and I fail to see how they could be explained in terms of different marriage patterns: at most it could be said that the lack of marriages between close kin makes it easier for the Christians not to keep up their ties with Pakistan.

6.5.5 The differential positions of Christians and Muslims in Pakistan

There is still enough in the data to make the pursuit of this puzzle worth while, especially since the actors themselves perceive differences, and there are some clear differences in the networks of the Muslim and Christian informants. What is at the root of their 'differential involvement in various sets of relationships'?[23] What is it about Islam and Christianity which could give rise to these differences? It is not, I would argue, that the differences can be located in the different tenets of the two religions; rather the contrast between the Muslim and Christian informants is intimately connected with the different meanings which are attached to adherence to these religions in Pakistan. The behaviour and attitudes of the migrants, their networks and their plans to return to Pakistan (or not) can be connected to the differential positions of Muslims and Christians in Pakistan.

In Pakistan, adherence to Islam is closely tied up with patriotism: it is the 'Muslim homeland', the country many of my informants can remember struggling to come into existence. Islam is the dominant faith, and its significance is constantly stressed in Pakistan. Political parties often take on an 'Islamic' slant: even Pakistan Peoples Party appealed to the electorate on the basis of 'Islamic socialism'. National holidays tie in with Islamic festivals. Christians feel uncomfortable in Pakistan. They often regret the passing of the British era, and those who have left say they are glad to have done so. A consideration of some issues on which the Muslim and Christian informants consistently differ can expand these points: the Partition of India, relationships with India, Kashmir and what is now Bangladesh, religion in Pakistan, opinions about migration and plans for the future are all issues on which there is a stark divide between the Muslim and Christian informants.

Muslims in India have long considered themselves different from Hindus and fears of being overwhelmed by Hindu power were used in the movement which demanded the creation of Pakistan.[24] Pakistan was to become the Indian Muslims' haven. With the solitary exception of Abdul, all the Muslim informants consider that Partition was both inevitable and desirable. Life in independent India would have been difficult; and Muslims living in India now face the continual threat of anti-Muslim riots, they say. Pakistan may be a poor country, but that is not the fault of the Government: Britain never wanted Pakistan to be created (and the boundaries established ensured that Pakistan would be weak) and involvement of the big powers has hampered Pakistan (for

170

aid given to India has enabled her to come out well in conflicts between India and Pakistan).[25] Abdul argues that Britain always tried 'divide and rule' tactics in her colonies (he referred to Nigeria in this context) and Partition would not have been necessary if politicians had not aroused religious feelings. In this, he contrasts with the other Muslims, who consider that Partition was a natural and proper development, but like them he considers that the boundaries drawn up in 1947 never gave Pakistan a chance, and when I pushed him, he would not agree that Jinnah was to blame for Partition: 'Jinnah was the Quaid-e-azam' (the Great Leader).

To a man, the Christians regret Partition, and some even regret the granting of independence at all. Esther's brother (Karen's sister's husband) Samuel saw much of the bloodshed when he was in Lahore in 1947. Partition also split families up: two of his sisters live in India, but their letters are censored, and since the 1965 war they have not been able to visit Pakistan. He is afraid to write to his sister in Jammu (as the area is so touchy) because he might be considered a spy and lose his job. He works in a Government Department, but considers he is lucky to have been in his job since before Partition: Christians in Pakistan have no prospects now. He considers the fact that no other Christians have been appointed in his office since Partition clear evidence of discrimination. Christian countries should fulfil their responsibilities to their Pakistani brethren and resettle a number of them each year. He thinks he might move on to Canada and join Sarah's brothers: he has a good job himself, but worries about his sons. Life was so much better before the British departed: Christians could celebrate Christmas and Easter properly, but now very few are in a position to take time off work for such activities. Similar nostalgic sentiments were voiced by the other Christians, and they all looked on Britain in a favourable light. It is almost as if the Christians see Britain (and not Pakistan) as their homeland.

Contrasts also appear on some central political issues in Pakistan: while the Muslims tend to take the 'Government line', the Christians are critical and even cynical. According to the Muslims, India has been stirring up trouble for years, India wrongly took Kashmir and meddled in Pakistan's internal affairs in East Pakistan in 1971, and the Bengalis' demands for secession were treachery. During the fieldwork in Pakistan, conversation kept coming back to the trouble brewing in Bengal. As early as March 1971 many felt that war with India was inevitable — and it would be India's fault if war broke out. Abdul's brother did not agree, but he felt that Mrs Gandhi was merely making political mileage out of

171

the situation to help her through the elections to be held in April 1971: as usual, India was just out to make trouble for Pakistan, and in this he was like the other Muslim informants. The Kashmir dispute was a case in point: if the U.N. had acted with justice, he argued, the dispute would long ago have been settled in Pakistan's favour. In Bristol, Yusuf made similar points just before war did break out: Mrs Gandhi was out to make trouble, she had no intention of talking to Yahya Khan, and she had no right to interfere in Pakistan's internal problems. He received my comment that India was necessarily involved because of the refugees from East Pakistan with the retort that India had been throwing Muslims out for years and was now creating a fuss about accepting the Hindus leaving East Pakistan. It was widely believed that the 'miscreants' in East Pakistan were all Hindus: the Muslims in Bristol and Pakistan would not accept that the Muslims in East Pakistan would break faith with Jinnah's dream of a united Muslim homeland. This was a commonly expressed view in the press in Pakistan, as was the view that the number of 'miscreants' was very small. The Muslim informants considered that the action of the Pakistan army in East Pakistan was a legitimate attempt to keep a small number of trouble-makers under control. Informants who had been in Britain during the crisis came to the same conclusions: India was meddling and wanted to cause trouble for Pakistan, and it was the Hindus in East Pakistan who were pressing for secession and confronting the forces of law and order. In Javed's opinion, Yahya Khan had played the game very cleverly by agreeing to talk to Mujib and thus giving himself time to move men and arms into East Pakistan, but now that the East was lost Javed considered that the Pakistani forces in East Pakistan would fight to the death rather than surrender to the Indian troops: troops captured in the 1965 war reported on the bad treatment meted out to them in India. The situation in the West was more hopeful: when India attacked in 1965 (India claims that Pakistan made the first move), Pakistan was not ready, but stores of arms had been accumulated and they could now face India with confidence.

On the other hand, the Christians argue that Pakistan is partly (if not completely) responsible for the conflicts with India; Pakistan has no particular right to Kashmir; newspapers in Pakistan were lying about the crisis in East Pakistan and were wrongly trying to make out that secession was being demanded by a small number of trouble-makers. Pronouncements on 'Muslim brotherhood' are viewed cynically: they are just empty words.

In early 1971 the Christians also considered that war was likely.

172

Sarah was adamant that if war did break out it would be Pakistan's fault. At this time, conflict seemed very likely to erupt. At the end of January 1971 an Indian plane on an internal flight was hijacked to Lahore by two 'Kashmiri freedom fighters'.[26] They were granted political asylum, and, after the crew and passengers were returned to India, they blew the plane up. The Pakistan High Commission in Delhi was attacked by demonstrators and India banned the overflight of Pakistani planes.[27] The press and the Muslim informants were unanimous: India had provoked a dangerous situation by banning overflights. But the Christians took a different view: Sarah considered that Pakistan had no business interfering in Kashmir (an internal question for India), and the hijackers should have been sent to India for punishment instead of being given heroes' welcomes in Lahore. India had made investments in Kashmir, and it was reasonable that she should want to keep Kashmir. (The Muslims' line on this is that India has been moving non-Muslims into Kashmir in order to make her claims more respectable, and the Indians only want Kashmir because of Nehru's sentimental attachment to the place and so that they can manipulate Pakistan's destiny by controlling vital irrigation headwaters.) For all the protestations over Muslim brotherhood, Sarah considered that the Pakistanis care only about their Kashmiri brothers, not their Bengali ones.[28] Like the other Christian informants in Pakistan, she was very cynical about press reports from East Pakistan, and she even listened to All India Radio in order to hear both sides of the story.

After the war, I talked to her sister Karen in Bristol. Karen had a letter from Sarah praising Pakistan and saying that India would have been beaten but for Yahya Khan's incompetence. Karen considered that Sarah had not written 'from the heart' because she was frightened to be frank: Christians in Pakistan had suffered after the 1965 war, she said, and it was only prudent to pretend to be patriotic. Life in India is fine for Muslims (contrary to what the Muslims in Pakistan say), for Hindus are not as worried about religious differences: the fact that not all of them have moved to Pakistan is evidence enough for Karen that their life in India cannot be unbearable. But Christians have no security in Pakistan, and she is fearful for the safety of her sisters still there. Emmanuel offered to help Samuel to leave in 1964, and Karen very much regrets that Samuel did not take up the offer. Muslims are always talking about *Hamara Pakistan* ('Our Pakistan') and fighting for their own country, they are quick to say *'bhai, bhai'* ('brother, brother') about their Muslim brothers, but just as quick to make havoc of East Pakistan. Bengalis have had nothing but trouble since the cyclone in

1970: the west wing of the country was the only part of the world which did not help in the rescue work, and yet the Pakistan army was on the spot in an instant when there was any breath of trouble.

Differences also appear on the question of religion in Pakistan. I have already commented on the position of the Muslims on Islam and Christianity in 4.1.2.1. The position is reversed for the Christians. Robert considers that Pakistan's major trouble is that there is 'too much religion'. In the whole world, religion has so much power only in Punjab: other countries have forgotten religion, and are all the better for it. *Ramzan* in Pakistan is 'bloody terrible' because it is so difficult to buy anything to eat during the day. Ruth objects to women being veiled in a *burqa*, and Muslims in general are bad people and liable to cheat. They despise Christians and force them to sweep the streets. Her sister in Wazirabad felt the same way, and angrily pointed out to me the home of a family which had just converted to Islam. Sarah is generally scornful about changes which have taken place in Pakistan since Partition: what was the point of changing the name of the Lawrence Gardens to *Bagh-i-Jinnah*, what need was there for a mosque in the garden, and what was wrong with The Mall that it now had to be called *Shahrah-e-Quaid-e-Azam*?[29] Winifred also criticizes Pakistan: religion there divides, but before Partition there were no differences between people of different religions. Esther, too, objects to the dominance of Islam in Pakistan, and complains about the restrictions on the teaching of Christian doctrine in mission schools: Christians have no chance in Pakistan.

One of the most illuminating comments about Muslims comes from Sarah, who asked me why British women were prepared to spoil themselves by marrying a man of such a different religion. Contrast this with the comments from the Muslims discussed in 4.1. Sarah also reported that when the son of her Muslim neighbour came for a holiday from London, he spread stories of how British women are *sasti mylti heyn* (cheaply obtainable): he told of prostitutes offering themselves for £2. Sarah's response is cynical: Emmanuel never told stories like that about Britain, and she considers that the Muslims enjoy telling false tales about a Christian country.

In addition, not only do the motives behind the migration differ for the Muslims and the Christians, but so too do their reactions to it and their plans for their families. For the Muslims, migration was seen as a way of circumventing the problems they had in Pakistan in saving enough to give their families security: in Britain (they believed) they could save and soon return to Pakistan to be in a better position than before they left. Several Muslim informants have been disappointed: they would return to Pakistan any day if they could afford to, they would not still be in Britain if they had managed to save enough money to enable them to live in Pakistan. Several, including Abdul, say they would be expected to live in fine houses and provide large dowries for their daughters and they cannot afford to yet. Yasmin asked if I really thought they would have come so far from home if they had not needed the money: she would dearly love to go back to Pakistan, but they cannot 'afford' to yet. Others were more negative: Tahira considers that her family has seen no financial advantage in coming to Britain. She had no idea that costs would be so high (that it would cost over £4 to take the family to the cinema), and she might have thought twice about coming if she had known. Her husband did not want to return to Pakistan immediately, so she is glad to have united the family, but really her rather damp house in Bristol does not compare with her new *pukka* house in Sialkot, which was built round a courtyard and had mango, pear and apricot trees in the garden. Mumtaza also thinks it has been no advantage to them to come to Britain: Mahmud's family was quite well-to-do (his father was a judge) and if Mahmud had completed his studies he would have got a good job in Pakistan. Now if he went back, he would have difficulty getting any job. In Lahore, they lived in a large house and Mahmud has some land. The housework was shared and Mumtaza had little to do but care for her children, and when she was tired there was always a relative at hand to look after them: what a contrast this is to her present life, where she has to do all the household tasks and most of the time Mahmud is at work and is not at hand to help with the children. She considers that her children's upbringing has been impoverished by coming to Britain, for she cannot give them the attention they would have in Pakistan, but they cannot afford to transport the family to Pakistan and set up a home there until they have saved more. The Muslims, then, are not wholeheartedly in favour of having come to Britain, and even those who do not point to actual disadvantages still yearn for the day when they can 'afford' to go home.

A useful way of putting them into focus is to consider their relatives in Pakistan, whom I often asked if they would like to go to Britain. While many said they would (and lamented the problems of obtaining passports and entry permits), the ones who said they did *not* want to leave Pakistan are more interesting at the moment. The response to my questioning was always pitched in terms of '*mujhey England jana to nahin chahey'* ('I don't need to go to England'). Abdul's brother was puzzled that I had even asked him: why should he want to go to England? After all, his business (an electrical goods shop) was doing well, so he had no reason to leave his home. If he went, he might not find a good job, and he would have forfeited his business for nothing. A similar response came from a man who was married shortly before his wife's mother and younger siblings left for Britain: his business (dealing in sewing-machines) was thriving, so there was no need for him to leave Pakistan. His younger brother, though, was not satisfied with his job (as a clerk in a Government Department) and would like his brother's father-in-law to sponsor him. Rashid's brother Ghulam also felt no need to leave Pakistan: as his wife said, he earns Rs. 300/- per month (which in itself would not be enough) and also has rents amounting to Rs. 200/- per month from various properties. The family can live adequately in the small house which Ghulam built from his savings when the children were small. They have a television set, and all the children are attending school or college: they have just what they need, so why should they go to Britain? In brief, for the Muslims, those who have migrated (or would like to migrate) say they do not have enough financial security in Pakistan, while those who think they are secure enough cannot see any reason for leaving their homes.

The Christians, by contrast, are more positive about their life in Britain. They do not regret leaving Pakistan, and say that even if a Christian were to return to Pakistan with savings from his work abroad, he would face innumerable difficulties.[30] Joanna thinks that her family has come down in the world. Her father left a good job in Pakistan to go to Tehran and then left a job there to move to Britain; they had a good life in Tehran and their house in Bristol is a 'hut' in comparison with their home in Tehran, but there are no regrets. In Tehran, Matthew worried about the security of the family in a Muslim country, but now he is confident for the future. Joanna's husband had unpleasant experiences trying to find work in Pakistan (even after attending college) and came to Britain because he felt his future would be brighter. Karen also stresses that her family came in search of security, which they are glad to have found (and they were not expecting much else); but the Muslims come, she says, expecting to save a lot quickly. When they are here, they are only interested in living as cheaply as they can so that they can return to Pakistan: they buy a chicken and make it last for the whole week for the family. This is what they have to do in order to save.

She thinks that many early reports from migrants in Britain translated earnings in sterling directly into rupees without taking price levels into account, and many did not realize how they would have to struggle in order to save in Britain; but for herself, she is content on the financial front, though she would like to join her family in Canada. Her brother-in-law Samuel in Lahore is a bit ambivalent about leaving Pakistan, because he was told by a Christian friend working in the British Council offices that in Britain *paise zyada, leykyn kherch bhi zyada* (there is more money, but expenses are also greater): Samuel has a reasonably good job in Lahore and does not think he would benefit financially from going to Britain or Canada. On the other hand, though, he is worried about what will happen to his sons: he is buying them a good education at a reputable mission school, but fears that they may not be able to get the jobs they deserve when they leave school, and his mind keeps turning back to leaving Pakistan, in order that his sons may have their chance in life without the problems which would face them in Pakistan.

Several of the Christians even appear to consider that they have more right to be in Britain than Muslim Pakistanis have. Samuel, as we saw, considered that Christian countries have a responsibility to take in Pakistani Christians, but he agreed with Sarah when she argued that strict immigration restrictions were necessary in Britain because otherwise all Pakistanis would go to Britain. The Christians are entitled to preferential treatment because of their religion. Similarly, Joanna set herself apart from 'these immigrants' at the time of one of Enoch Powell's speeches: she did not feel they would have any right to complain if new regulations prevented a man from being joined in Britain by his wife and children: 'these immigrants' could go back to Pakistan if they were so concerned about being with their wives. She did not, however, consider that she and her relatives were 'immigrants' — they are, after all, Christians.

6.6 Migrants and refugees

In terms of the stances of my informants on certain political and religious issues and their responses to migration there are contrasts between the Muslims and the Christians. Perhaps the way to put the contrasts in a nutshell is to describe the Muslims as 'migrants' and the Christians as 'refugees'; these are not words used by my informants, but they do not do an injustice to their positions. As in the previous chapters, the necessity of including Pakistan in the interpretation becomes clear.

The Muslims do not see themselves as 'immigrants' to Britain: they do not intend to stay here permanently. They do not put down roots in Britain, they retain links with Pakistan (or ought to, according to their kin), they change their ways when necessary, and they have property interests in Pakistan. They would not have to come to Britain but for the money, and they would return home if they felt they could afford to. For them, Britain is merely a staging-post: a short spell in Britain will (they hope) help them to short-circuit barriers to their social mobility in Pakistan. They would like to use their savings from Britain to provide them with a style of life which they could not have attained if they had stayed in Pakistan. They want to be more successful at home, and temporary emigration is seen as a means (not always a very happy one) to this end.

The Christians see themselves as refugees: they are escaping from a situation in which they sense hostility against them, in which they feel they have poor chances of getting good jobs, and in which they believe their very physical safety to be in jeopardy, especially during political crises. Money could not buy them safety and security in Pakistan: their future can only be outside Pakistan and they try to put down roots in their new home. In Pakistan, they feel foreign and vulnerable: emigration is the only way to rectify this, and it can only be a permanent exile.

In 6.5, I considered the extent to which the differences between the Muslims and the Christians are real, and how they should be approached. In the face of the issues discussed in 6.5.5, the strength of the other explanations (6.5.1–4) wanes considerably. The Christians consciously stand apart from the Muslims, and for them the separation is real. They see themselves as aliens in Pakistan, while the Muslims see Pakistan as their own Muslim homeland. Once the importance of this is accepted, then the other points raised in this chapter begin to fall into place. Garbett and Kapferer consider that migrants' behaviour can be comprehended by considering the different sets of relationships in which different migrants are involved.[31] Here we can begin to understand why the Muslims' and the Christians' networks should be different in the first place.

The position of the Christians in Pakistan (as they themselves see it) is the most useful way to view the material presented here. The question of time spent outside Pakistan can be seen in this light; in 6.5.2 it was suggested that the length of time might bring about differences in the behaviour of the migrants in Bristol. However, I would prefer to argue that the early departure from Pakistan and the differences in behaviour and plans of the migrants can both be traced to the same root: the differential positions of the Muslims and Christians in Pakistan. The length of time outside Pakistan ceases to be a *cause* of differences in Bristol and becomes merely an *index* of these differences. The differences in the networks can also be seen in the same light: the Christians' greater stress on ties with the British, their weaker ties with Pakistan, their lack of contact with Muslims in Bristol, and their intentions not to return to Pakistan can all be seen as symptoms of their unease in Pakistan. Their political opinions, their lack of patriotic attachment to Pakistan, and their tendency to make much of apparently slight differences between themselves and the Muslims can all be made more comprehensible by shifting the focus back to Pakistan once again.

The foregoing summarizes the intentions and hopes of at least the adult informants. At that level, the contrasts between the 'migrants' and the 'refugees' remain; but at the level of behaviour which can be anticipated, it is likely that the hopes of many of the informants will not materialize.

As I indicated at the end of the last chapter, there is good reason to be cautious in accepting without question 'the rhetoric of the return': while the expectation of going back to Pakistan has an impact on the Muslims' attitudes to their work in Britain, the way their children are educated, and the ways they invest their savings, there are several reasons why many of them may ultimately not return home. Their changing 'needs' and the very steep inflation rate in Pakistan, plus the difficulty they all face in Britain of saving as quickly as they would like, are factors which may put the day when they could 'afford' to return to Pakistan far into the future. The position of their children is crucial. In the early days of the migration from Pakistan, the chain migration of young adult men (intent on staying only a few years in Britain) did not present a severe problem of how to ensure that the allegiances of Pakistanis in Britain remain in Pakistan. However, all the Muslim families are now faced with this problem. Many of the children born in Britain start school knowing little English and having been immersed in a Pakistani family setting, and the older children who have lived in Pakistan for some time also retain strong cultural ties there. These are strengthened by the way in which contacts outside school with British

179

people are discouraged and the children remain largely home-based and in an environment which is clearly Pakistani. As yet, at any rate, none of the Muslim children is in any doubt about being 'Pakistani'. But there is one element in their identity which differs from that of their parents: even those adolescents who have been in Britain only a short while are unwilling to think of going back to Pakistan permanently. While their fathers might be quietistic and willing to accept poor jobs, in order (as several men told me) that they might not find themselves in any trouble, there is little reason to believe that young men who do not want to go back to Pakistan will be willing to accept meekly obstacles put in their way: success in Britain will be more relevant to them than to their parents.

There is no reason to expect the Christian families ever to return to Pakistan, though they may well move to some other country, and as we have seen, their orientation to their migration and to assimilation is radically different at present from the Muslims'. Unlike the Muslims, the Christians are keen to be accepted: they want to assimilate, at least in the structural sense. While British people often claim that they dislike Pakistanis because they 'keep themselves to themselves', it is ironic that my Christian informants often complain of the difficulties they have had in being accepted by British people. It is also important to bear in mind that, while the Christian informants are keen to be accepted by British people, they are nonetheless very 'Pakistani' in many of their ways. As an anthropologist, part of whose professional role entails being an assimilating immigrant, I can fully appreciate how much of a person's language and basic assumptions are taken for granted, how difficult and even stressful at times it is to make radical alterations to behaviour and how necessary it is sometimes to lapse into contexts in which other people speak the same verbal and cultural language. Even with the intention to assimilate, the adjustments which have to be made are difficult to put into operation and are very daunting. Simply from a humanitarian point of view, we should not expect that cultural adaptations can or should be made rapidly, even by people who express willingness to make such changes.

But even if cultural adaptations are made, what might be the outcome? Assimilation is commonly only assessed on the cultural dimension, but, as Barth and Gordon both point out, it is vital to look also at the structural dimension, and consider the way in which social relationships are patterned.[32] Gordon pictures the United States in terms of structural pluralism, in which substantially similar cultures are contained within the different structures. What of Pakistani children in Britain, then, who have been schooled in British schools and brought up in Pakistani homes? The families of my informants have been in Britain for only a few years, but even there the interests of the children are beginning to include football, and culturally they are beginning to look like amalgams of Britain and Punjab. What does this mean for the patterning of social relationships? Working in a context in which the processes can be viewed in a longer time-scale, Ballard reports on the way in which outwardly 'anglicized' young Sikh men may return to their ethnic fold, even wearing the turban again and accepting an arranged marriage.[33] In part, this was because of rejection by British people, in part it was due to a realization of the consequences of refusing to marry as their parents desired. As a result, young men who appear partly 'British' become enclosed in their ethnic group, and tend to consider that they are reorienting their Punjabi culture rather than anglicizing. Structural assimilation is not inevitable, and may even be reversed, while what appears to be cultural assimilation may often be perceived as a revision of 'traditional' ways, to create a new 'tradition' of Punjabi-ness in Britain, which while different from Punjabi culture in Punjab, is definitely not British. In other words, even where cultural changes are occurring, structural separation may continue, and the children of the migrants may still perceive themselves as Punjabis.[34] It is likely that the Muslim informants will follow the same track: even if the children suffer no rejection or disappointments from British people, they are likely to remain proud of their 'Pakistani' identity (although they would fit uneasily into Pakistan itself). Even children who have been in Britain for several years still assume that their parents will choose a spouse for them, and this is not questioned. Thus not only are some informants inclined to assimilate and find it difficult, but there are also those who wish to remain distinct and separate.

At present, as the preceding analysis has argued, it is vital to bring Pakistan into focus when considering the ways in which the informants in Bristol orient to Britain and Pakistan and to their migration. For the adult Muslim and Christian informants alike, their links with Pakistan have a crucial impact on the way they live in Britain. It is on these grounds that I would insist that great care must be taken in selecting the unit for the analysis of this sort of situation and that ethnocentric assumptions that Britain can be such a unit would be erroneous in this case. While it is no doubt technically easier to execute a 'community study', such a study would tend to exclude important factors and an analysis confined within restricted geographical bounds would inevitably be limited. By trying to paint a picture of the world as my informants see it, I have indicated that migration to Britain can be comprehended only when the geographical horizons are widened. As I have stated in the introduction, it is also vital to maintain a long historical perspective, though this was not perceived as important by my informants.

The nature of the links outside Britain is radically different for the two sets of informants, and while these links are critical *now* it is obviously very difficult to make predictions. The Christians are most unlikely to return to Pakistan, but it is not clear that they will remain in Britain or (if they do) how their lives will evolve. For the Muslims, it may well be that many of the links which I have traced with Pakistan will gradually fade, and that the children will become less concerned with their 'Pakistani-ness' in Britain. In other words, my analysis may simply reflect a very specific historical phase. It would be necessary to have more information about the responses of 'British society' to the assimilating moves of the informants' children before it would be possible to suggest likely developments. Ballard indicates that some young Sikh men have become re-enmeshed in their ethnic fold in response to rejection, and several of my Christian informants commented on the difficulties which they had faced in trying to make British friends; and evidence elsewhere indicates that rejection by British people is commonplace. It also suggests that the conscious reassertion of 'Pakistani-ness' is a probable response to such rejection, though the Muslims are more likely to move in this direction than the Christians. In other words, the cultural and structural separation of the Muslims is probably more than a first-generation phenomenon, and it is likely to be with us for many years.

Glossary

ashraf: noble, person of good birth; honourable, refined, urbane; connected with *sherif* and *teshrif*

azad: free, independent

bagh: garden

bazaar: market place, commercial area; from old Persian *aba* (provisions) + *zar* (place)

bazaari: pertaining to the *bazaar*, vulgar, ordinary

behn: sister; often used to address a person who is not a real sister, as in *behnji*

bhai: brother; often used to address a person who is not a real brother

biraderi: brotherhood, fraternity, connection, kindred

burqa: garment which conceals a woman when she leaves her home

chaddar: covering, including shawl, mantle, sheet, table-cloth; *chaddar utarna* means to insult a woman (literally, to lift the *chaddar*)

chappatti: thin round cake of unleavened bread, used to scoop up stews

charpai: a bed with four legs and a wooden frame strung with interwoven rope

chehlum: memorial service, connected with *chahlys* (40): about 40 days after the death, special prayers are said to ensure that the soul goes to heaven and food is distributed in the name of the deceased

choli: close-fitting blouse worn with a *sari*

dahi: yoghourt, curd

dahl: lentils, which are usually eaten as a thick stew

dehati: rustic, peasant, of a village

din: faith, religion (usually only with reference to Islam: *mazhab* is the more general word meaning religion)

duppatta: chiffon length used by women to veil themselves

dyrama: 'drama', a relatively new art form in Urdu

eid: festival, holy day; there are several *eids*, for instance *eid-ul-fitr*, to mark the end of Ramzan, and *eid-ul-azha* or *bakr-eid* (goat *eid*) held during Zulhaj to commemorate Abraham's (Ibrahim's) offering to sacrifice his son Isaac (Ishmael)

England-returned: person who has returned home from Britain; connotes wealth, urbanity, expensive styles of dress and generosity

ghar: house, home

183

gotra: clan

Guru Granth Sahib: the holy book of the Sikhs

hadith: narrative, tradition, especially with reference to the doings and sayings of Mohammed

haj: pilgrimage to Mecca, one of the religious duties of Muslims

haji: person who has performed *haj*, used as a title in front of the personal name

hakim: in common parlance, doctor who practices *Unani* medicine; also ruler, governor

halaal: lawful, legitimate, having religious sanction

hazrat: title for any great man, presence, dignity; 'holiness', 'highness', as in *Hazrat Ibrahim* and *Hazrat Isa*

huqqa: water-pipe or 'hubble-bubble', still a popular form of smoking especially in rural areas

inshallah: God willing

Islam: subjection to God's will

Islamiyat: academic subject, concerned with the doctrine and history of Islam

izzet: honour, prestige; in several regions, pronounced 'ijjat'

jagra: quarrel, squabble

jang: war

jeevan: livelihood, subsistence

juma: collection of people, congregation, assemblage

jungli: uncultivated (of people as well as flora) wild, uncouth, boorish; connected with *jungl*, which means an area which is uninhabited, overgrown or scrubland

Ka'ba: the shrine at Mecca

kalimah: confession of faith; from *kalam* (proposition, speech) + *ullah* (of God)

khaddar: coarsely woven cotton material

khatm-i-nabuwat: end (*khatm*) of the prophethood (*nabuwat*, from *nabu* meaning prophet); it is believed by Muslims that Allah ended the prophethood with Mohammed

kherch: expenses

koh-i-noor: literally mountain (*koh*) of light (*noor*)

Koran: the sacred book of Islam

kurta: dress, shirt

kutcha: unripe, raw, crude, immature, simple, inferior; opposite of *pukka*

Glossary

la ilaha illallah Mohammed rasul allah: the *kalimah*, meaning 'there is no god but Allah (God) and Mohammed is His prophet'

larai: fight; from *larna* (to fight)

madrissah: collegiate mosque, school, college; from Persian *dariss* (to read)

mahr-i-mithl: sum of money handed over by bridegroom to bride, and forfeited by the partner who initiates divorce proceedings; generally not given in Indian sub-continent (though the sum may be named); in Punjab, Muslims usually give a dowry (*jahiz*) along with their daughter

mashallah: by God's grace

mashriq: east

mela: harmonious gathering, as at a festival; from *mylna* (to meet)

merdana: the part of the house reserved for the men, separate from the *zenana*; from *merd* (man)

modern: a borrowed term which connotes sophistication, literacy, and a 'Westernized' style of life

mohalla: environment, surroundings, district

molwi: Muslim religious scholar, 'priest'

murassi: low-caste musician

mushayra: a poetry symposium or competition; connected with *shayr* (poet)

Muslim: a person who has subjected himself to God's will

namaz: prayer, usually only the ritual prayers performed by Muslims, the five daily prayers, the Friday congregational prayers and other special prayers; Christian prayers are called *ibaadat* (worship), and Hindu prayers are called *puja*

paise: money; also one-hundredth of a rupee

pak: holy, pure, clean

pranda: three skeins of black wool which are woven into the plait; they often have 'gold' or 'silver' tassles at the end

pukka: ripe, cooked, mature, sophisticated, solid, substantial; opposite of *kutcha*

Punjab: literally, Five Waters, from *panch* (5) and *aab* (water)

purdah: curtain, veil; often used to connote the syndrome of practices which keep unrelated men and women separate

qemiz: dress, shirt

quaid: leader

Glossary

quaid-e-azam: the Great Leader (used only of Jinnah)

Ramzan: the ninth month of the Islamic calendar, the month of fasting; the Islamic calendar is organized around lunar months of about 29 or 30 days, of which there are 12 in the year, and thus the religious calendar shifts each year in relation to the solar one

rickshaw-wallah: person who drives a *rickshaw*, which is a form of taxi; in Pakistan, most *rickshaws* are 'scooter' *rickshaws*, in other words, three-wheeled scooters with a space for two or three passengers, and a roof and doors to conceal passengers (especially the women)

roza: fasting, especially the abstinence from eating, drinking, smoking, and sexual intercourse between sunrise and sunset during *Ramzan*; the sighting of the *eid* moon signifies the end of *Ramzan* and the time for the *eid-ul-fitr* celebrations

salen: stew, eaten with rice or bread

sari: a garment for women, made of several metres of cloth wrapped round the body

sasti (f), sasta (m): cheap

shahid: martyr

shahrah: royal road, highroad; from *shah* (king) + *rah* (road)

shalwar: loose pyjamas or trousers, worn with *qemiz*

shariat: religious law of God, ordinance, justice

sherif: high-ranking, noble, honourable; connected with *ashraf* and *teshrif*

Shia: one of the branches of Islam, which holds that Ali was rightful successor to Mohammed as he was his son-in-law: only 10% of Muslims in Pakistan are *Shias* (also known as Shiites)

Sunni: major branch of Islam in Pakistan, differing from the *Shias* in their belief that the Caliphate should have been awarded on merit rather than on genealogical closeness to Mohammed

teshrif: honour, dignity

tikka: jewelled pendant which hangs over the forehead; original meaning is 'spot' or 'blemish', but it also means the spot which Indian women paint onto their foreheads, as well as an inoculation or vaccination

ulema: learned men, scholars (singular: *alym*)

Unani: literally, Greek; in practice refers to the system of medicine traditionally associated with Muslims in India

zamindar: landlord; from *zamin* (land, earth) + *dar* (holder)

zat: supposedly endogamous unit of a caste, elsewhere called *jati*

186

Glossary

zenana: the part of the house reserved for the women, from *zan* (woman)

zindagi: life

zukat: the compulsory tithe, which is one of the five pillars of Islam

Notes

Introduction

1 *Koh-i-noor* means 'mountain of light'. It is a famous and much-travelled diamond, which formed part of the booty from the Sikh wars in the mid nineteenth century. The British authorities had the good sense to return it to London for safe-keeping: other invaders had carried it round with them and it had changed hands as political fortunes waxed and waned.

2 B. Ward, L. D'Anjou and R.D. Runnalls (eds.), *The Widening Gap: Development in the 1970s* (New York, 1971), pp. 278–9.

3 P.M. Jeffery, 'Pakistani families and their networks in Bristol and Pakistan', unpublished Ph.D. thesis, University of Bristol, 1973.

4 On Pakistanis see B. Dahya, 'Pakistanis in England', *New Community*, 2(1) (1972–3), 'Pakistanis in Britain: transients or settlers?', *Race*, 14(3) (1973) and 'The nature of Pakistani ethnicity in industrial cities in Britain', in A. Cohen (ed.), *Urban Ethnicity* (London, 1974); and V. Saifullah-Khan, 'Purdah in the British situation', paper presented at the B.S.A. Conference, 1974. On Indians see U. Sharma, *Rampal and His Family* (London, 1971); R. Ballard, 'Family organisation among the Sikhs in England', unpublished manuscript, 1971, and 'Family organisation among the Sikhs in Britain', *New Community*, 2(1) (1972–3); R. Ballard and C.L.M Ballard, 'Incapsulation', draft unpublished manuscript, 1972; J. Pettigrew, 'Some observations on the social system of the Sikh Jats', *New Community*, 1(5) (1972); and M. Thompson, 'The second generation — Punjabi or English?', *New Community*, 3(3) (1974).

Chapter 1. The background: Pakistan

1 For more details see F.A. Khan, *Banbhore: A Preliminary Report on the Recent Archaeological Excavations at Banbhore* (Karachi, 1969); B. Gascoigne, *The Great Moghuls* (London, 1971); V.D. Mahajan and S. Mahajan, *Mughal Rule in India*, 4th edn. (Delhi, 1961); P. Spear, *A History of India*, 2 (Harmondsworth, 1970); and P. Woodruff, *The Men Who Ruled India*, 2 vols. (London, 1971).

2 P. Hardy, *The Muslims of British India* (Cambridge, 1972); M. Mujeeb, *The Indian Muslims* (London, 1967); and A. Tayyeb, *Pakistan: A Political Geography* (Oxford, 1966).

3 R. Levy, *The Social Structure of Islam* (Cambridge, 1965); N.J. Dawood (trans.), *The Koran*, 3rd rev. edn. (Harmondsworth,

1968); S.A.A. Maududi, *Purdah and the Status of Women in Islam*, trans. Al-ash'ari (Lahore, 1972) and *Towards Understanding Islam*, trans. K. Ahmad (Lahore, 1973); M.M. Siddiqi, *Women in Islam* (Lahore, 1969); M.H. Khan, *Purdah and Polygamy* (Peshawar, 1972); E.A.H. Blunt, *The Caste System of Northern India* (Delhi, 1969); Tayyeb, *Pakistan*; A. Ahmad, *An Intellectual History of Islam in India* (Edinburgh, 1969); and Mujeeb, *The Indian Muslims*.

4 There are also small numbers of Wahabis and Ahmadiyyas. In September 1974 the Pakistan National Assembly decided that Ahmadiyyas are not Muslims since they do not believe in the finality of the prophethood of Mohammed (*khatm-i-nabuwat*) and Ahmadiyyas are now accorded minority status in Pakistan. Ahmadiyyas have been active in missionary work among Pakistanis in Britain, so it will be interesting to see what effect this decision has here.

5 M.R. Raza, *Two Pakistani Villages: A Study in Social Stratification* (Lahore, 1969).

6 Attempts through legislation to persuade people to give daughters their inheritance rights (e.g. West Punjab Muslim Personal Law (Shariat) Application Act of 1948) have met with little success. See Z. Eglar, *A Punjabi Village in Pakistan* (New York, 1960). It is not the case, though, that Muslims in other countries always follow Islamic prescriptions to the last detail: the point is that the details being considered here render Indian Muslim practice very similar to the practices of adherents of other religions in the vicinity. Practice in the border regions of Pakistan is rather different: F. Barth, *Political Leadership among Swat Pathans* (London, 1965), and R.N. Pehrson, *The Social Organization of the Marri Baluch* (Chicago, 1966), both describe the giving of bridewealth, among the Swat Pathans and the Marri Baluch respectively. As Barth points out, this is contrary to Hanafi doctrine, since the marriage gift (the *mahr*) should go to the bride and not to her guardian.

7 The Pakistan Government has an arrangement with the Saudi Arabian Government in which the Pakistani pilgrim pays rupees to the Pakistan Government and is issued with a passport valid only for the *haj* period. Then the Saudi Arabian Government takes full care of the pilgrims for the duration of their stay in Saudi Arabia.

8 See for instance Tayyeb, *Pakistan*; Woodruff, *The Men Who Ruled India*; J. Ahmad, *The Final Phase of the Struggle for Pakistan*, 2nd edn (Lahore, 1968); and P. Moon, *Divide and Quit* (London, 1961); and for the earlier period R. Gopal, *Indian Muslims: A Political History (1858—1947)* (Bombay, 1959); Hardy, *Muslims of British India*; and M.A. Karandikar, *Islam in India's Transition to Modernity* (Bombay, 1968). The name 'Pakistan' was first coined in 1933 by some Muslim students in London. According to

Tayyeb, the word's origin lies in the names of the areas to be included in the proposed Muslim state: *P*unjab, *A*fghania (i.e. N.W. Frontier), *K*ashmir, *S*ind and Baluchi*stan*. It should also be pointed out that the word *pak* itself means 'holy' or 'pure'. My informants consider that 'Pakistan' means 'Holy Land' or 'Land of the Pure', an indication of their belief that Pakistan was formed solely for reasons of religion. As I shall indicate below, there are good grounds for supposing that religion was used as a way of generating mass support by politicians, whose motives were mainly secular.

9   For more details of British activity in Bengal and on the opium trade, see, for instance, Spear, *History of India*, 2; E.J. Hobsbawm, *Industry and Empire* (Pelican Economic History of Britain, 3 (Harmondsworth, 1969)); and V.G. Kiernan, *The Lords of Human Kind: European Attitudes towards the Outside World in the Imperial Age* (Harmondsworth, 1972). Some of the success of the British policy in Punjab can be seen from the fact that the Punjab army (in particular the Sikhs) remained loyal to the British in the Sepoy Revolt in 1857. Subsequently, Punjabis were 'rewarded' by being included in the 'martial races' and were recruited in large numbers into the forces. For many, this entailed travel overseas, and this is one factor in the migration of Punjabis to Britain.

10   See Tayyeb, *Pakistan*; Gopal, *Indian Muslims*; and Karandikar, *Islam in India's Transition to Modernity*.

11   'Separate electorates' were supposed to protect the interests of minority groups by ensuring that they always had representation in government. Under a system of separate electorates, people of the various 'communities' would vote separately for candidates from their own community. The number of seats available for the minority groups varied in different schemes which were put forward over the years.

12   Tayyeb, *Pakistan*, pp. 171–2, quotes figures which indicate that refugees made up 49% of Karachi's population, 43% of Lahore city and 71% of Hyderabad in 1951. He estimates that the number of refugees in all Pakistan (East and West) would be around 9 million (not counting those who fled India but never reached their destination).

13   'Punjab' means 'five waters', and refers to the five rivers which flow into the Indus: Jhelum, Chenab, Ravi, Sutlej and Beas.

14   Concern over the control of floodwaters in Pakistan has resulted in the construction of several dams. Among these is the Mangla Dam on the Jhelum, whose building resulted in considerable displacement of population. Many Pakistanis in Britain come from District Mirpur which was one of the areas affected. See, for instance, Dahya, 'Pakistanis in England', 'Pakistanis in Britain' and 'The nature of Pakistani ethnicity'.

15   The elections were initially arranged for the summer of 1970, but were postponed because of a cyclone in East Pakistan. Yahya

Khan refused to postpone them again after a second and much more serious cyclone in November: they were held in December 1970.

16   The voiced reason behind school nationalization was that standards varied radically between schools, and that the rich monopolized the 'best' (and most expensive) schools. Ironically, in the event, schools such as Aitchison College in Lahore have not been taken over, and lack of funds has prevented the improvement of standards in other schools.

17   In the years between 1959 and 1969 the Pakistan Government spent between 46% and 61% of total revenue expenditure on defence services. See Government of Pakistan, *Pakistan Economic Survey, 1969–70* (Islamabad, 1970), Table 23.

18   T. Ali, *Pakistan: Military Rule or People's Power?* (London, 1970); K. Siddiqui, *Conflict, Crisis and War in Pakistan* (London, 1972), takes a similar view.

19   See K.B. Griffin and A.R. Khan (eds.), *Growth and Inequality in Pakistan* (London, 1972), esp. Part 4.

20   During a brief visit to Pakistan in 1974, it seemed that some of the gloom about the dismemberment of Pakistan had been dispelled. East Pakistan had contributed to Pakistan's foreign exchange earnings through the export of jute and it was feared that Pakistan's economy would be wrecked by the secession of Bangladesh. Jute is now seen to be a risky export commodity, and Pakistan has now developed trading links with the Arab Middle East: before 1971 West Pakistan sent a great deal of agricultural produce to East Pakistan, but now they are getting better rates for their produce elsewhere and are hoping to obtain concessional prices for oil in return. However, as I have suggested in the text, it is not clear that any benefits that might accrue (e.g. better prices for agricultural produce, less astronomical rises in the price of fertilizers) will be distributed equally.

21   Hassan Nawaz Gardezi, 'Industrial patterns and urbanization in the United States and the Indo-Pakistan sub-continent', in S.S. Hashmi (ed.), *Pakistan Sociological Studies* (Lahore, 1965), and 'Urbanization in Pakistan', in Gardezi (ed.), *Sociology in Pakistan* (Lahore, 1966).

22   Government of Pakistan, *Evaluation of the First Two Years of the Fourth Five Year Plan (1970–75)* (Islamabad, 1973), p. 67. More than half the civilian labour force finds employment in the agricultural sector.

23   It is obviously hard to calculate income levels in a situation where most of the working population is at least partially dependent on agriculture and can supply food from their own labours. Many families supplement their non-cash incomes with cash from other occupations. The impression that income is unevenly distributed will be supported when I turn to the variations in life-style in Pakistan.

24 Ali, *Pakistan*.
25 There are schemes for the benefit of Government employees. Only 8% of industrial workers are covered by insurance schemes (and in any case they are a very small proportion of the work force).
26 See G. Myrdal, *Asian Drama: An Enquiry into the Poverty of Nations* (Harmondsworth, 1968), Ch. 21. J.N. Sinha, 'Employment magnitudes and prospects in India, Ceylon and Pakistan', in R. Dutta and P.C. Joshi (eds.), *Studies in Asian Social Development, No. 1* (Bombay/New Delhi, 1971), also discusses the way in which the definition of 'labour force' has been changed, making comparisons between the 1951 and 1961 Censuses difficult.
27 Government of Pakistan, *Guidelines for the Third Five Year Plan (1965—70)* (Karachi, 1963) and Sinha, 'Employment magnitudes and prospects'.
28 Government of Pakistan, *Pakistan Economic Survey, 1969—70*.
29 Government of Pakistan, *The Second Five Year Plan (1960—65)* (Karachi, 1960). See also J.B. Edlefson, 'Some implications of world demographic trends with special reference to Pakistan', in S.S. Hashmi (ed.), *Pakistan Sociological Studies*, and Mirza Mohammad Ahmad, 'Composition and trends in labour force of Pakistan', abstract in H.A. Chaudhari et al. (eds.), *Pakistan Social Perspectives* (Lahore, 1968).
30 Government of Pakistan, *Census of Pakistan*, Census Bulletin No. 5: *Economic Characteristics* (Karachi, 1961), Table 3.
31 In the next chapter I shall deal with the backgrounds of my informants in more detail, and it will be seen that they have not come from the most disadvantaged sectors: the men all had jobs before coming to Britain, mostly in clerical work. Nonetheless, the informants point to their low incomes and inability to guarantee the security of their families. In terms of their ambitions for their children and the pattern of their investments in Pakistan they are more typical of Pakistan as a whole.
32 My informants have had more schooling than many of their compatriots: all have received some education in Pakistan, though generally not beyond Matric., and the women have tended to have less schooling than their husbands. For a more detailed analysis of the overall picture see A. Rauf, *West Pakistan: Rural Education and Development* (Honolulu, 1970), and Myrdal, *Asian Drama*, esp. Chs. 31, 32 and 33.
33 It should be remembered that boys drop out too, so the decline in attendance by girls is even more precipitous than these figures show.
34 There is little evidence on how financial factors operate, but see Zafar Masud and Hassan Nawaz Gardezi, 'Patterns of school attendance in a metropolitan city', abstract in Chaudhari et al. (eds.), *Pakistan Social Perspectives*. They found that 83% of the children in the sample of families had never been to school; that

boys are more likely to be admitted to school early if their families' incomes are relatively high and if their fathers have had some
education; that families with relatively high income and with
fathers who had had some education sent proportionately more
of their children to school than other families; and that girls are
more likely to be admitted to school (if at all) later than their
brothers. See also Myrdal, *Asian Drama*, esp. Figs. 33–6 where he
is looking at drop-out figures. While 65% of 'current school-age
cohorts' graduate from Grade I, the figure for Grade II is 40%;
15% of the cohort completes primary education, and about 5%
graduate from Grade X.

35   Rauf, *West Pakistan*. The 1,717 urban secondary schools cater for
only about 20% of the population. See below, section 1.3.3.

36   Rauf, *West Pakistan*, p. 60. The table is adapted from the 1961
Census of Pakistan, Census Bulletin No. 4, 'Literacy and Education', pp. xiii and xiv. Myrdal considers that literacy figures for
Pakistan are likely to be inflated as there is no evidence that the
enumerators did more than accept respondents' claims to literacy,
and the reading tests were probably not used in all cases.

37   Myrdal, *Asian Drama*, pp. 1798–800.

38   See Tayyeb, *Pakistan*, p. 116.

39   Sociaal Wetenschappelijk Instituut, *Azam Basti (Karachi): Socio-
logical Enquiry and Recommendations for Development Work*
(Amsterdam, 1969). This is a study of a slum area in Karachi, in
which there is ethnic, educational and occupational heterogeneity.
There was little inter-mixing of the various groupings and ties
were kept up with home areas when possible. See also J.D.
Lybarger, 'Urbanization in Pakistan', and M. Sabihuddin Baqai,
'A study of patterns of social cohesion among labour migrants of
Karachi mill area', both abstracts in Chaudhari et al. (eds.),
Pakistan Social Perspectives; and S.M. Tanzeem Wasti, 'The prob-
lem of socio-economic adjustment of labourers in Landhi area,
Karachi', abstract in S.S. Hashmi (ed.), *Pakistan Sociological
Studies*.

40   The parallels between internal migration and migration to places
such as Britain are very considerable: the impetus behind them is
often the same, though obviously internal migration is the only
option for the very poor. Apart from the distances involved, there
are similarities: residential clustering, mixing with kin or people
from the same area, retention of ties with the place of origin, and
economic motives behind the migration are all relevant for
Pakistani migrants in Britain. Again, my informants in Bristol are
rather different from the average, as they have long roots in urban
centres (even those who were refugees from India). The fact that
they have brought their wives with them also sets them apart from
most Pakistani migrants.

41   See Government of Pakistan, *The Second Five Year Plan (1960–
65)*, p. 324, where it is stated that 70% of homes in West Pakistan

193

are built of mud. *Kutcha* in this context refers to homes made of sun-baked mud bricks, and contrasts with *pukka* houses, which are made of kiln-baked bricks. *Pukka* houses are more solid, while *kutcha* homes suffer in the monsoon and have to be completely rebuilt every few years.

42　Dahya ('Pakistanis in England', 'Pakistanis in Britain' and 'The nature of Pakistani ethnicity') reports that Pakistani migrants in Bradford often send money to their relatives in Pakistan to enable them to replace the *kutcha* family home with a *pukka* one.

43　Government of Pakistan, *The Second Five Year Plan (1960–65)*, Ch. 12.

44　See A.D. Bhatti, 'Urban–rural housing conditions in Pakistan', and M.K.H. Khan, Saleem Saeed and M. Rafiq, 'Housing conditions of households of different income groups in the central part of the city of Lahore', both abstracts in Chaudhari et al. (eds.), *Pakistan Social Perspectives.*

45　The Government tries to conserve stocks by preventing the slaughter of animals on two days each week. Muslims are not allowed to eat pork, and other meats have to be killed in the required or permitted (*halaal*) way. The Koran indicates which meat is acceptable for Muslims: 'You are forbidden the flesh of animals that die a natural death, blood, and pig's meat; also any flesh dedicated to any other than Allah. You are forbidden the flesh of strangled animals and of those beaten or gored to death; of those killed by a fall or mangled by beasts of prey (unless you make it clean by giving the death-stroke yourselves); also of animals sacrificed to idols.' See Dawood (trans.), *The Koran*, The Table.

46　Maududi, *Purdah*. Siddiqi, *Women in Islam*, takes a similar view.

47　It must be emphasized that the creation of a secluded realm for women in the *zenana* does not necessarily entail loneliness and isolation, as many households have several women. My impression is that women living in *purdah* often lead happy and active social lives, though their mixing is exclusively with other women and close male kin.

48　Saifullah-Khan, 'Purdah in the British situation'.

49　There is little information about which women in Pakistan wear the *burqa*. According to Salma Mussert Faridi, women in a new suburb of Lahore are more likely to favour *purdah* observance and the wearing of the *burqa* outside the home if they are of low socio-economic status. However, she quotes other findings which suggest that the poor cannot afford to observe full *purdah*, as many women have to work outside the home and the *burqa* is too expensive. Women of the middle ranks generally observe *purdah* and go out veiled, while women of wealthy families do not wear the *burqa* so much. See S.M. Faridi, 'Purdah observance among the females of Wahdat Colony, Lahore', unpublished M.A. thesis, University of Punjab, Lahore, 1967. Economic factors surely play

their part, but as I shall argue below other points should be taken
into account.

50   It would be incorrect to leave the impression that Muslim theological thought on the question of *purdah* is monolithic: several
writers consider that 'pure' Islam does not require the stringent
separation of men and women and that Pakistanis should return
to the pristine religion. A recent book on the subject is an explicit
attack on the views of Maududi, and lays the responsibility for the
downfall of Muslim nations on 'purdah and polygamy' (M.H.
Khan, *Purdah and Polygamy*). My impression, however, is that
families who do not require their women to remain in *purdah* generally justify their position by claiming to be *modern* rather than
in terms of reformed Islam. Hence, although this is a matter of
debate in theological circles, I do not consider that it has great
impact on the man in the street.

51   Use of the word *modern* is merely following the usage of people
in Pakistan. People who consider themselves *modern* value 'modernity' highly and believe that they have escaped from the 'stasis'
of (inferior) 'tradition' into the 'dynamism' of (superior) 'modernity'. In no way do I wish to imply that I concur with these
connotations: such a usage should not conceal the ways in which
'tradition' may be flexible ('the modernity of tradition'), nor indicate approval of the 'colonization of the mind' from which the
modern suffer.

52   For instance, the highest-ranking Muslims are called *ashraf*, and
they include *Syed* (*Said* or *Sayyed*, who are supposed to be the
descendants of the Holy Prophet through his daughter), the
Qureshi (or *Quaraishi*, who are supposed to be descendants of the
Prophet's clan) and also *Farooqi*, *Siddiqi* and *Zaidi*, among others.
The lowest-ranking Muslims include *Derzi* (tailor), *Dhobi* (washer-
man), *Mochi* (leatherworker), *Nai* (barber), *Teli* (oil-man) and the
sweepers, who all rank low in the Hindu system.

53   See Z. Khan, 'Caste and the Muslim peasantry in India and
Pakistan', *Man in India*, 48(2) (1968), for an amplification of this
point.

54   I shall not be touching on the question of caste occupations and
the economic interrelationships between caste groups. I shall be
concentrating on the significance of caste in the context of kinship, marriage and friendship patterns.

55   L. Dumont, *Homo Hierarchicus: The Caste System and Its Implications* (London, 1972), p. 98.

56   Other writers use different definitions of *biraderi*: for Rose,
biraderi is 'a clearly defined patrilineage group, known as a
baradari [sic] or brotherhood, which comprises a number of extended families within a clan' (E.J.B. Rose et al., *Colour and
Citizenship: A Report on British Race Relations* (Oxford, 1969),
p. 442); for Eglar, 'a *biraderi* is a patrilineage. All the men who

can trace their relationship to a common ancestor, no matter how remote, belong to the same *biraderi* . . . *Biraderi* refers to both the whole group of those who belong to a patrilineage and to any individual member of a patrilineage', and the word may be used in an 'extended way' to include people who are not kin (Eglar, *A Punjabi Village*, pp. 75—6). It is true enough that the *biraderis* of my informants have names which suggest the existence of an apical ancestor, but they do not focus on the vertical links; rather, they concentrate on the horizontal links between siblings and affines.

57 Blunt, *Caste System*, p. 10.

58 There are several references to marriages between close kin among Muslims in the Indian sub-continent. Blunt, *Caste System*, p. 196, talks of the marriage circle: 'Both among Sunnis and Shias, it is the custom to select a wife, whenever possible, from a relatively small circle of relations, including not only a man's own family, but families with which his own has in the past intermarried.' For other references to close kin marriage see, for instance, I. Ahmad, 'Endogamy and status mobility among the Siddique Sheikhs of Allahabad, Uttar Pradesh', in I. Ahmad (ed.), *Caste and Social Stratification among the Muslims* (Delhi, 1973); H. Alavi, 'Kinship in West Punjab villages', *Contributions to Indian Sociology*, N.S., No. VI (1972); G. Ansari, *Muslim Caste in Uttar Pradesh* (Lucknow, 1960); V. Das, 'The structure of marriage preferences: an account from Pakistani fiction', *Man*, 8(1) (1973); Eglar, *A Punjabi Village*; C. Vreede-de Stuers, 'Mariage préférentiel chez les musulmans de l'Inde du Nord', *Revue sud-est asiatique* (1962), 'Terminologie de parenté chez les musulmans *ashraf* de l'Inde du Nord', *Anthropologica*, No. 5 (1965), and *Parda: A Study of Muslim Women's Life in Northern India* (Assen, 1968); and Census of India, Vol. XV: *Punjab and Delhi*, Part 1, report by L. Middleton and S.M. Jacob (Lahore, 1921), pp. 258—61. However, it is clear that some Muslims do not like to marry their close kin, but the ramifications of marriage choices have not been sufficiently delineated to enable us to specify who does or does not marry kin and why. Prior to migration, my informants say that their families usually arranged marriages between kin. This preference for close kin marriage is often contrasted in the literature with different preferences among Hindus and Sikhs in the same area: for them rules of *gotra* exogamy proscribe certain marriages (the 4-*gotra* rule forbids marriage with any person from the same clan as his four grandparents, and thus prevents marriages between first cousins, for instance). M. Lyon, 'Ethnic minority problems: an overview of some recent research', *New Community*, 2(4) (Autumn 1973), suggests that these differences may give rise to different types of immigrant community organization in Britain among Muslims and Sikhs. This may be the case, if one contrasts the centripetal preferences of the Muslims with the centrifugal

ones of the Sikhs. However, evidence from the Indian context suggests that the anticipated spraying-out of affinal links (supposedly implicit in the Hindu and Sikh proscriptions) may be slight, and it might be the case that marriage patterns on the ground are not as distinguishable as the different preferences might lead one to anticipate. See for instance A. Mayer, *Caste and Kinship in Central India: A Village and Its Region* (London, 1960), and D. Pocock, *Kanbi and Patidar: A Study of the Patidar Community of Gujarat* (Oxford, 1972).

59 The phrase *huqqa pani band karna* means 'to ostracize'. Literally it means to close (refuse to share) the water pipe (*huqqa*) and to refuse to drink water with the offender.

60 M.N. Srinivas, *Caste in Modern India, and Other Essays* (London, 1962), and *Social Change in Modern India* (Berkeley, Calif., 1969).

61 Vreede-de Stuers, 'Mariage préférentiel chez les musulmans'. S.C. Misra, *Muslim Communities in Gujarat: Preliminary Studies in Their History and Social Organization* (London, 1964), discusses what he called 'Islamization' among several Muslim castes in Gujarat.

62 In addition to marking themselves off from one another, both types of people hold negative stereotypes of poor people, especially from the villages, who are thought of as rustics who are uncouth or *jungli*; for the *modern*, they are 'primitive', unsophisticated and stupid; for the 'noble', they are given to religious heterodoxy and are devoid of the proprieties of family life. These are the people from whom *izzet* needs especially to be protected.

63 The situation is of course a great deal more complex than this brief discussion can adequately indicate, for the cultural traits which mark off different reference groups are themselves an ever-shifting sea: when a group is mimicked by another group which it dislikes, new modes of behaviour tend to be elaborated (either in the back-stage or in the realm of publicly flaunted symbols) so that the original demarcation persists.

64 S. Neill, *The Story of the Christian Church in India and Pakistan* (Grand Rapids, Mich., 1970), R.D. Paul, *The Cross over India* (London, 1952); and J.H. Beaglehole, 'The Indian Christians: a study of a minority', *Modern Asian Studies*, I(1) (1967).

65 P. Thomas, *Churches in India* (New Delhi, 1964).

66 J.W. Pickett, *Christian Mass Movements in India: A Study with Recommendations* (New York, 1933).

67 Neill, *Christian Church in India and Pakistan*, and Pickett, *Christian Mass Movements*.

68 Chuhras were a depressed caste of sweepers, leatherworkers, hide-sellers and agricultural labourers, who were poor and illiterate.

69 M.W. Inniger, 'Mass movements and individual conversion in Pakistan', *Practical Anthropology* (May—June 1963).

70 F.V. Moore, *Christians in India* (New Delhi, 1964).

71   Punjab Government, *Punjab District Gazetteers*, XII, Part B:
      Lahore District (Lahore, 1936). The 1901 literacy rate was very
      high compared with other religious communities.
72   Neill, *Christian Church in India and Pakistan*, p. 81.
73   Chuhras, for instance, were not included in Census schedules as
      agriculturalists and so could not buy land in the old-settled parts
      of Punjab, but they could buy land in the Canal Colonies. See
      Pickett, *Christian Mass Movements*, p. 111.
74   'Social distance in relation to differential attachment'.
75   India became a secular democratic republic. In the discussion
      above on the history of Pakistan, I have pointed to some of the
      other factors behind the demands for a 'Muslim state'. Beaglehole,
      'The Indian Christians', discusses the position of Christians in in-
      dependent India.
76   Neill, *Christian Church in India and Pakistan*.
77   Government of Pakistan, *Census of Pakistan* (1961).
78   *Ibid.* Vol. I, II—58/9, Table 5, and Vol. III, IV—90, Table 19.
79   *Ibid.* Vol. III, IV—90, Table 19.
80   Figures derived from *ibid.* Vol. III, IV—90, Table 19.
81   *Ibid.* Vol. IV, pp. 178ff, Table 2.
82   *Ibid.* Vol. II, V—29.
83   Tayyeb, *Pakistan*.
84   Dahya, 'Pakistanis in Britain', tells of a Muslim in Bradford who
      refused to do the sweeping his British foreman instructed him to
      do on the grounds that sweeping was work for Christians — an in-
      dication of the way in which Christians are perceived by Muslim
      Pakistanis.
85   Neill, *Under Three Flags*, p. 97.
86   It should be pointed out that Government denials are not devoid
      of international political significance, for they often form part of
      claims that while India treats its minorities (particularly Muslims)
      badly, Pakistan's treatment of her own minorities is always ex-
      emplary. S.A.A. Maududi, *Rights of Non-Muslims in Islamic State*,
      trans. K. Ahmad (Lahore, 1967), discusses the position of non-
      Muslims in an Islamic state, which should be guaranteed by the
      Shariah.
87   The British High Commissioner denied that the book had been
      published in Britain. *The Pakistan Times*, 22 Jan. 1971, reported
      that the book was first published in Turkey in the sixteenth cen-
      tury and reprinted in the U.S. in 1965, and then in Britain in
      1969 with the addition of some 'nude pictures'.
88   Letter to *Pakistan Times*, 12 Jan. 1971, from E. Khanna.

Chapter 2. Migrants' backgrounds and their migration

1   G.K. Garbett and B. Kapferer, 'Theoretical orientations in the
      study of labour migration', *New Atlantis*, 2(1) (1970), p. 195.
2   See for instance Dahya, 'Pakistanis in England', and Saifullah-

Khan, 'Purdah in the British situation', who are both dealing with
Pakistanis in Britain; S.B. Philpott, 'Remittance obligations, social
networks and choice among Montserratian migrants in Britain',
Man, 3(3) (1968), and *West Indian Migration: The Montserrat
Case* (London, 1973), dealing with Montserratians in Britain; and
P. Mayer, 'Migrancy and the study of African towns', *American
Anthropologist*, 64 (1962), and *Townsmen or Tribesmen: Con-
servatism and the Process of Urbanization in a South African City*,
2nd edn. (Cape Town, 1971), dealing with rural–urban migration
in southern Africa.

3   G.B.G. Lomas, *Census 1971: The Coloured Population of Great
Britain, Preliminary Report* (London, 1973), Table 1.4. Her
figures are all based on a 1% sample, and have been multiplied by
100 to gain an estimate of total numbers. It should be pointed
out that there is a problem with the designation 'Pakistani' in the
census material. Instructions on the household and personal forms
for the 1971 Census asked people to indicate their own and
parents' country of birth by the name by which it is now known.
In the previous chapter, I described the creation of Pakistan in
1947, through the Partition of India, which was accompanied by
massive exchanges in population between the two countries so
formed, particularly in the Punjab, which is a major source of
Indian and Pakistani migrants to Britain. It is not clear how this
has affected the answers given on the census forms. We do not
know, firstly, if people who consider themselves to be Pakistani
but were born in places now in India consistently recorded themselves and their parents as being 'Indians' (and vice versa) and,
secondly, if people of these two refugee stocks are equally represented in Britain and cancel one another out. The literature available does not cover this problem. Of my informants in Bristol
born before Partition, somewhat under a quarter were born in
places now in India (and some are married to people born in
places in Pakistan), but I have found no mention of the extent to
which refugees in 1947 tended to emigrate later on. Since the
'nationality' questions were included in the Census in 1971 to
establish the size and nature of the coloured population of Britain,
it is lamentable that this matter was not (apparently) considered.
The figures for Pakistanis also include people who would now be
called Bangladeshis, since Bangladesh did not become independent
until late 1971.

4   S. Allen, *New Minorities, Old Conflicts* (New York, 1971); Dahya,
'Pakistanis in England', 'Pakistanis in Britain' and 'The nature of
Pakistani ethnicity'; F. Hashmi, *The Pakistani Family in Britain*,
2nd edn (London, 1967); I. Morrish, *The Background of Immigrant Children* (London, 1971); R. Oakley (ed.), *New Backgrounds: The Immigrant Child at Home and at School* (Oxford,
1968); S. Patterson, *Immigration and Race Relations in Britain
1960–67* (Oxford, 1969); J. Rex and R. Moore, *Race, Com-

munity and Conflict: A Study of Sparkbrook (Oxford, 1969);
Rose et al., *Colour and Citizenship*; Saifullah-Khan, 'Purdah in the
British situation'.

5   The situation for India and Bangladesh is quite similar:
Bangladeshis come mainly from Sylhet, while Indians come from
a small triangle in Punjab and some areas in Gujarat.

6   Urdu is the national language of Pakistan, but very few people
speak it. Urdu grew up in the region of Lucknow and Delhi, where
it is still widely used. People in Pakistan who use Urdu regularly
are either people who moved to Pakistan after Partition, or who
have been formally taught Urdu in school.

7   Rose et al., *Colour and Citizenship*, p. 61. Allen, *New Minorities*,
and S. Patterson, *Dark Strangers: A Study of West Indians in
London* (Harmondsworth, 1965), even go so far as to say that all
Pakistanis are Muslims. I shall discuss the Christians among my informants in the final chapter.

8   Dahya, 'The nature of Pakistani ethnicity'.

9   Lomas, *Census 1971*, p. 32 and Table 1.5. See also D. Eversley
and F. Sukdeo, *The Dependants of the Coloured Commonwealth
Population of England and Wales* (London, 1969). These figures,
of course, include East as well as West Pakistan.

10 Lomas, *Census 1971*, Table 1.4.

11 *Ibid*. Table 3.2.

12 See Eversley and Sukdeo, *Dependants of the Coloured Commonwealth Population*, and the following Home Office statistics for
the Commonwealth Immigrants Acts 1962 and 1968 (Control of
Immigration), to be found in the following Parliamentary Papers:
1967–8 Cmnd. 3594, 1968–9 Cmnd. 4029, 1969–70 Cmnd.
4327, 1970–1 Cmnd. 4620, 1971–2 Cmnd. 4951, 1972–3 Cmnd.
5285, and also 1973–4 Cmnd. 5603 (which covers the 1972 Act).

13 Lomas, *Census 1971*, Tables 3.4 and 3.5.

14 *Ibid*. Table A.4(d).

15 See the Home Office statistics referred to in note 12 above.

16 Dahya, 'Pakistanis in England', 'Pakistanis in Britain' and 'The
nature of Pakistani ethnicity'; Eversley and Sukdeo, *Dependants
of the Coloured Commonwealth Population*; Oakley (ed.), *New
Backgrounds*; Rose et al., *Colour and Citizenship*.

17 See Dahya, 'Pakistanis in England' and 'The nature of Pakistani
ethnicity'. Pettigrew, 'Social system of the Sikh Jats', makes the
same point about Indian migrants in Britain.

18 Dahya, 'Pakistanis in England'.

19 Dahya, 'The nature of Pakistani ethnicity'. Thompson, 'The second generation', comments on sponsorship among Indian migrants.

20 Eversley and Sukdeo, *Dependants of the Coloured Commonwealth
Population*.

21 Rose et al., *Colour and Citizenship*, p. 83. Only 17,000 Pakistanis
entered Britain between 1955 and 1960.

22 Eversley and Sukdeo, *Dependants of the Coloured Commonwealth*

Population, p. 14, Table 7. This rapid increase in the entry of Pakistani dependants contrasts with the entry of dependants from other New Commonwealth countries: in some cases, they showed a decline in numbers coming in, while in others, the increases were much smaller than for Pakistanis. This difference is due in part to the relatively late arrival of Pakistani dependants.

23 Lomas, *Census 1971*, p. 32 and Table 1.5.

24 N. Deakin, *Colour, Citizenship and British Society* (London, 1970), p. 54.

25 See the Home Office statistics referred to in note 12 and Lomas, *Census 1971*. These two sets of statistics are not directly comparable as the former are based on passport holders (and some Pakistani women may have British passports) and the latter are based on origin (with the problems referred to in note 3 above). Furthermore, although some factors are recorded in the statistics, the following are some critical unknowns: the number of women and girls who entered Britain between the 1961 Census and the beginning of collection of statistics in 1962; how many of these would be over 15 in 1971; how many of the dependant children entering were girls (almost certainly considerably less than half, but we do not know); how many of these girls were over 15 in 1971; and how many of the girls under 16 at the time of first entry are later recorded as women in the embarkation and re-entry figures. All in all, it is not possible to assess how many Pakistani females leave Britain for good.

26 A *hakim* practises the *Unani* ('Greek') system of medicine.

27 In 1.3.3 above, I pointed out that only about 20% of the population of Pakistan is regarded as urban.

28 Many city residents in Pakistan are newcomers, either because they fled from India in 1947 or because they are labour migrants. See 1.3.3.

29 Here again, my informants are set apart from the general pattern in Pakistan, and also from most migrants in Britain. See 1.3.2.

30 My informants are unusual in the type of work they were in in Pakistan. See 1.3.1.

31 As I indicated in 1.3.1, unemployment is common in Pakistan, and my informants are fortunate in being by no means destitute in Pakistan. Indeed, if they had been, they could not have afforded to come to Britain; in many cases, they financed their own migration, from savings or mortgaging property, unlike many migrants who relied on kin in Pakistan or Britain to lend money for fares. See 2.5.3 below.

32 It must not be thought that all Pakistani women in Bristol or Britain come from urban educated backgrounds: some certainly come from rural areas and have little or no schooling, but it is not possible to assess the relative numbers. My informants were unwilling or unable to introduce me to women from rural backgrounds. See Ch. 5.

33 See Dahya, 'Pakistanis in England' and 'The nature of Pakistani ethnicity'.

34 I shall look at the question of remittances in more detail in 5.3.

35 There are two types of passport in Pakistan, one valid only for going on *haj*, and the international passport. All my informants hold the latter type of passport, though they claimed that some people circumvented the problems of obtaining passports by using a *haj* passport and then converting it into a full international passport in Saudi Arabia.

36 During 1971 a bus service began to operate between Rawalpindi and Bradford, the single fare being £40.

37 Since I completed fieldwork, Imtiaz's brother has arrived in Bristol: he was sponsored by Iqbal's employer.

38 Since most of the Muslim informants were married to relatives, this distinction is hard to draw, but by 'own relatives' I mean people who were genealogically closer to the wife than to the husband.

39 See Lomas, *Census 1971*, Tables 1.4, 3.4 and 3.5. Pakistani women are outnumbered by men by about 3 : 1. See also 2.1 above.

40 At the time of fieldwork, a Pakistani national who sent £1 to Pakistan would get about Rs. 20/- for it (or even more through various other routes): £5 or £10 per month would be enough to live on in Pakistan. These differentials in the cost of living would have been important considerations at the time the dependants were brought to Britain, though since that time the rate of inflation in Pakistan has been faster than that in Britain. Dahya, 'Pakistanis in England', quotes informants who say they have not brought their wives to Britain for economic reasons, while some mentioned the problem of *purdah* and others that there was no point in bringing their wives to Britain, as their own stay in Britain is going to be temporary.

41 Albert is an exception to this: he has not brought his wife and children to Britain.

42 Such experiences are evidently not uncommon. See M. Akram and S. Leigh, *Where Do You Keep Your String Beds? A Study of Entry Clearance Procedures in Pakistan* (London, 1974).

43 Garbett and Kapferer, 'Study of labour migration', p. 195.

Chapter 3. Pakistanis in Bristol

1 A. Richmond et al., *Migration and Race Relations in an English City: A Study in Bristol* (Oxford, 1973), Chs. 3 and 4.

2 Office of Population Censuses and Surveys, *Census 1971. England and Wales. County Report (Gloucestershire)* (London, 1973), Table 14, 'Population by sex, marital condition, area of enumeration, country of birth and whether resident in the United King-

dom or not' (sheet for Bristol County Borough). The problems referred to in Ch. 2, note 3 are also relevant here.

3   Richmond et al., *Migration and Race Relations*, p. 76.

4   General Register Office, *Sample Census 1966: Great Britain, Commonwealth Immigrant Tables* (London, 1969), Tables 1 and 2.

5   I am grateful to Miss W. Hickson, H.M. Inspector of Schools in Bristol, for this figure.

6   I shall comment on these advantages below.

7   I am grateful to Miss Hickson for giving me permission to attend the Language Centre, and to Mrs Jones and Mr Wadham who helped me while I was there. I deal with Hannah More Language Centre in more detail below in 3.4.

8   I was advised to learn Urdu, as Punjabi is less standardized than Urdu. All my informants know Urdu, though they normally speak Punjabi in the home.

9   Punjabis consider that a daughter should be given to her husband, along with gifts which should continue over a lifetime, and that reciprocation tends to smack of selling the daughter. Thus, the girl's parents and brothers should lavishly entertain her (and her husband) but they should not go to her marital home and take food. It was therefore appropriate for me to visit my informants' homes but not for them to come to my home very often.

10   These figures all refer to incomes in 1972.

11   This tallies with the findings of Richmond et al., *Migration and Race Relations*.

12   At one time a Shia Persian student was the treasurer of the mosque, but the Pakistani Sunnis eventually resented his influence and he was voted out of office.

13   I am grateful to Miss W. Hickson, Inspector of Schools, for these figures and other information in this section. These figures relate to the number of 'immigrant' children in Bristol schools: 'immigrant' in this case was defined by the Department of Education and Science (as it then was) as a child who himself came to Britain, or whose parents came to Britain (though he might have been born here) less than ten years before the figures were collected. Miss Hickson told me that most of the Indian and Pakistani children in Bristol came after 1964 and so would be counted in these figures. After ten years in Britain, the child would no longer be considered to be 'immigrant'.

14   Richmond et al., *Migration and Race Relations*, Ch. 6.

15   *Ibid.* p. 126.

16   A report on discrimination during the mid 1960s found that coloured people often faced discrimination when looking for housing, from landlords, estate agents, building societies and other agencies concerned with allocating housing. However, it also pointed out that Indians and Pakistanis often bought their homes

through ethnic networks, and that they tended to report very little discrimination against them, because of the way in which they did not expose themselves to situations in which white people could discriminate against them. My own informants did not consider that they had suffered discrimination, but it should be pointed out that especially after the Race Relations Act of 1968, discrimination may be concealed, so that victims are unaware of it. See W.W. Daniel, *Racial Discrimination in England* (Harmondsworth, 1968).

17   Dahya, 'The nature of Pakistani ethnicity'. As will be seen in Ch. 6, these points do not apply to the Christian informants, for they do not send money to Pakistan, and they rarely visit Pakistan; moreover, they are not keen to work overtime or on shift-work, while they spend some of their income on British leisure pursuits, such as drinking in pubs.

Chapter 4. Ethnic separation and cultural change

1   M.M. Gordon, *Assimilation in American Life* (New York, 1964).
2   A.M. Greeley, *Why Can't They Be like Us?* (Old Bethpage, N.Y., 1969).
3   Patterson, *Immigration and Race Relations*, and Allen, *New Minorities*.
4   Barth's introduction to F. Barth (ed.), *Ethnic Groups and Boundaries: The Social Organization of Culture Difference* (London, 1969).
5   *Ibid.* p. 15.
6   *Ibid.* p. 16.
7   M. Rischin, *The Promised City: New York's Jews 1870–1914* (Cambridge, Mass., 1967).
8   The word 'incapsulated' is used by Mayer in his discussion of urbanization, and is closely allied to Barth's term 'insulation'. See P. Mayer, *Townsmen or Tribesmen*, and Barth (ed.), *Ethnic Groups and Boundaries*.
9   Gordon, *Assimilation in American Life* makes exactly this point with reference to 'inter-ethnic' marriage in the United States where he considers that it is usual for one partner to convert to the ethnicity of the other. In Britain, the racial dimension may put some couples into a limbo position, with the wife unaccepted by her in-laws as she does not want to 'become Pakistani', and the husband unacceptable to his in-laws because of his 'race' even if he is culturally very 'anglicized'.
10   Informants in Bristol usually keep the curtains at least partly closed and are particularly concerned that people in the street should not see them eating.
11   Islam does not require that Muslims worship in congregations in the mosque: the prayers can just as well be said at home. In

Pakistan very few women, for instance, go to the mosque (where there is usually a secluded but very small portion allocated for the use of women), and while prayers should be said daily, it is only at the *juma* prayers and on festivals that large congregations of men attend. So this lack of involvement in the mosque activities is not in itself a commentary on the laxity of my informants' religious commitment: the fact that only a few of them even say the prayers during *Ramzan* might be more significant, but as I shall point out below (4.2.1), their working conditions in Britain make it difficult for them to be conscientious Muslims.

12   Indian films are considered superior to Pakistani ones, and usually both clubs show Indian films. During the 1971 war, pressure was put on the men who run the Pakistani club (three of my informants) to show only Pakistani films to indicate their patriotism: however, they soon stopped showing Pakistani films as their takings fell dramatically when Pakistani filmgoers began to go exclusively to the Indian club!

13   One other factor involved here will be considered in the next chapter: on the more positive side, my informants prefer to mix with their kin, and the lack of kinship links with Indians curtails their mixing with them. However, they are not inclined to make marriage ties with Sikhs, because of the religious and political questions referred to already.

14   That is, unless they are interested in having access to prostitutes, which some Pakistani men are. Ease of access to such women, of course, ties in well with their belief in the general moral laxity of people in Britain.

15   Sons are particularly important in Pakistan for it is they and not daughters who care for aged parents: it is shameful to take anything from a married daughter's household. Moreover, since Pakistan has only the most rudimentary elements of a welfare state, very few people receive any sort of pension and there are no homes for old people, so the man without sons is to be pitied.

16   In Chapter 1 I pointed out that Muslims share many of the scriptures of Jews and Christians. See 1.1.

17   While the complexion should be fair, it is important that the hair be dark and the eyes brown. Several informants claimed that people with green or gray eyes are widely believed to be untrustworthy. It is not uncommon, in fact, for people to have light eyes, especially in the northern parts of Pakistan bordering Kashmir and Afghanistan.

18   Similar notions are evident with respect to people from south India. These ideas pre-date the British period in India, and are connected with the myths of the invasion of India by fair-skinned Aryans who displaced dark indigenes to the southern part of India and the hill tracts. People from the lowest castes are often thought to be dark-skinned, and thus it is hard to marry a girl who

has the misfortune not to be fair, for her pedigree is in doubt. The British presence in India probably did nothing to counteract these views.

19 Many schools in Pakistan teach pupils to count in English, as Urdu counting is complicated.

20 My position altered radically after I had learnt Urdu and been in Pakistan, as they felt that I had learnt how to play the same game and had matters of interest in common with them.

21 It remains to be seen if their plans ever materialize.

22 R. Desai, *Indian Immigrants in Britain* (Oxford, 1963), pp. 68, 87.

23 See *Guardian*, 28 Jan. 1975.

24 P. Mayer, *Townsmen or Tribesmen*, pp. 4–7.

25 Richmond found that 40% of his respondents were dissatisfied with their work in Bristol. See Richmond et al., *Migration and Race Relations*, p. 96.

26 Patterson, *Dark Strangers*, p. 331.

27 Patterson, *Immigration and Race Relations*, pp. 108–9.

28 Dahya, 'Pakistanis in England', 'Pakistanis in Britain' and 'The nature of Pakistani ethnicity'.

29 It will be obvious that these ideas are very ambitious, and informants often talk of wanting to go back home but being unable to 'afford' to yet. In Ch. 5, I shall consider this aspect of the situation more fully, but it is important to bear in mind that even pipe-dreams can influence present behaviour.

30 Saifullah-Khan, 'Purdah in the British situation'.

31 E. Krausz, 'Factors of social mobility in British minority groups', *British Journal of Sociology*, XXIII(3) (1972).

Chapter 5. The networks of the Muslim informants

1 P. Mayer, 'Migrancy and the study of African towns' and *Townsmen or Tribesmen*; Philpott, 'Remittance obligations, social networks and choice' and *West Indian Migration*; R. Manners, 'Remittances and the unit of analysis in anthropological research', *South Western Journal of Anthropology*, 21(3) (Autumn 1965); Garbett and Kapferer, 'Study of labour migration'.

2 J. Barnes, 'Class and committees in a Norwegian island parish', *Human Relations*, No. 7 (1954).

3 E. Bott, *Family and Social Network* (London, 1971).

4 J. Barnes, 'Graph theory and social networks: a technical comment on connectedness and connectivity', *Sociology*, 3 (1969). He comments that connectedness has been used in several ways, for instance to describe the existence of a link, or the length of the shortest distance between two points, or the directional properties of links, and that the term would be better abandoned.

5 J. Barnes, 'Networks and political process', in J.C. Mitchell (ed.), *Social Networks in Urban Situations: Analyses of Personal Relationships in Central African Towns* (Manchester, 1969). He uses

the term 'clique' to refer to a set of people who are all linked (or 'adjacent') to one another.

6 J.C. Mitchell, 'The concept and use of social networks', in Mitchell (ed.), *Social Networks in Urban Situations*.

7 Bott, *Family and Social Network*.

8 I discussed *biraderi* in more detail in Ch. 1 (1.4.5).

9 This is something he would not have done in Pakistan, as Mumtaza is his sister and it would be considered disgraceful for him to depend on her husband for a home, but in Britain he was prepared to do this in order that his wife and sister might have company.

10 Parveen's unhappiness in Britain was, I am sure, not unconnected with the existence of her husband's 'girl-friend' as is her invention of Yusuf's 'girl-friend'.

11 To be fair to this man, his relatives are also ambitious for their own children, for they hope that they will have professional training; but they argue that their ambitions do not entail harming other relatives.

12 The existence of this man came up in a casual chat about family-planning – an indication of how important information can come up by chance in a relationship conducted over time.

13 His sister married a man who was not a relative, who came alone from India at the time of Partition, and so Tariq has had to take responsibility for her since her husband's death. He died in an accident while employed by a company in the Persian Gulf.

14 Muslims are required to bury the dead as soon as possible, preferably on the day of the death: the burial of Rashid's mother could have been delayed to enable him to attend, but when Rashid was informed by letter, he knew that the funeral would already have taken place.

15 Manners, 'Remittances', and Philpott, 'Remittance obligations, social networks and choice' and *West Indian Migration*.

16 Government of Pakistan, *Pakistan Economic Survey, 1969–70*, Tables 49 and 63. Private transfer payments include remittances from migrants overseas and other transfers such as pensions paid by foreign governments to individuals previously in their employ in the Indian sub-continent. Remittances of course arrive from many countries, since there are Pakistani migrants in the Middle East as well as Europe. Other sums are remitted through extra-legal routes which give better exchange rates.

17 Dahya, 'Pakistanis in England', 'Pakistanis in Britain' and 'The nature of Pakistani ethnicity'.

18 *Pakistan Bulletin*, XXVI(13) (1 July 1974) (publication of the Information Division, Embassy of Pakistan, London).

19 Lomas, *Census 1971*, Table 3.2.

20 F. Barth, *Models of Social Organization* (London, 1966) and 'Economic spheres in Darfur', in Raymond Firth (ed.), *Themes in Economic Anthropology* (London, 1970).

21 Barth, 'Economic spheres in Darfur', p. 171.

22   Richmond found that migrants from India and Pakistan were least likely to accept that they would not return home one day. See Richmond et al., *Migration and Race Relations*, p. 204.

23   Dr Roger Ballard has told me that some of his Indian informants are now disillusioned about their chances of being successful in India, as they found difficulties such as these when they tried to begin businesses in Punjab.

24   Dahya, 'Pakistanis in England'.

Chapter 6. The Christian informants

1   Garbett and Kapferer, 'Study of labour migration'.

2   Cf. Ch. 2.

3   Cf. Ch. 4.

4   This is a good example of the point made by Barth that objective cultural differences and similarities cannot help the observer to predict how actors interact: 'objectively' the Christians are very similar to the Muslims, and very different from British people, but to them the sharing of Christianity with British people creates a basic similarity, while Islam makes Muslims fundamentally different. See 4.1 above.

5   As will be clear from 4.1, I am unhappy about using the term 'anglicization', since it is difficult to specify what it might consist of, but the contrast can be made between the *orientations* of the Muslims and the Christians.

6   See 4.1 above.

7   Cf. Ch. 5.

8   See 6.2 above.

9   Contrast this with the isolation of the man (and his wife) cut off by his kin in Bristol: see 5.2.1.

10   Contrast this with the comments of the relatives of the first man discussed in 5.2.1. Sarah was, however, angry for her Anglo-Indian neighbour whose husband had lent some money to help her brothers to go to Britain: the brothers no longer write and made no effort to repay their debt. Sarah says she feels differently as her family did not borrow any money from Samuel to help them leave Pakistan.

11   See 6.3.1 above.

12   Dahya, 'Pakistanis in England', 'Pakistanis in Britain' and 'The nature of Pakistani ethnicity', and Saifullah-Khan, 'Purdah in the British situation'.

13   P. Mayer, *Townsmen or Tribesmen*, Ch. 1. See also 4.2.2 above.

14   Since these informants were not in English-speaking countries and did not meet British people there, the length of time outside Pakistan but in the Middle East would not be so relevant to the question of assimilation in Britain and learning English, but it might have relevance for ties retained with Pakistan.

15   See 6.3.4 above.

16   See A. Ahmad, *Islamic Modernism in India and Pakistan, 1857–1964* (Oxford, 1967), for details of the various forms Islam has taken since 1857.

17   See 1.1.

18   See Z. Khan, 'Caste and Muslim peasantry', Raza, *Two Pakistani Villages*, and U. Guha, 'Caste among rural Bengali Muslims', *Man in India*, 45(2) (1965), and the papers in I. Ahmad (ed.), *Caste and Social Stratification*, for comments on caste among Muslims, and J.D.S. Paul, *A Survey of the Indian Christian Community* (Palamcottah, 1932), and R.D. Paul, *The Cross over India*, for comments on caste among Christians.

19   This is of course an outsider's view; the actors can distinguish themselves, as can be seen from the material in the earlier part of this chapter.

20   See 1.4.5 above and note 58 for Ch. 1.

21   See note 58 for Ch. 1.

22   See for instance R. Ballard, 'Family organisation among the Sikhs in England' and 'Family organisation among the Sikhs in Britain'; R. Ballard and C.L.M. Ballard, 'Incapsulation'; Pettigrew, 'Social system of the Sikh Jats'; Thompson, 'The second generation'.

23   Garbett and Kapferer, 'Study of labour migration'.

24   As I commented in 1.2, the religious basis of Pakistan has to be interpreted with care, but nevertheless the masses were appealed to on the basis of religious differences.

25   These are points made by my informants, but arguments along the same lines are often made by public figures in Pakistan; see, for instance, Z.A. Bhutto, *The Myth of Independence* (Lahore, 1969).

26   See *Pakistan Times* for 31 Jan. 1971 and for several days following.

27   This dispute festered for some time: a report in *Pakistan Times* (21 April 1971) claimed that the hijackers were Indian agents. The Indian plan was to provoke a situation in which India could look justified in banning the overflights of Pakistani planes: this ban would 'disrupt communications within Pakistan' and would strengthen 'separatist tendencies'. Thus Indian complicity in the Bangladesh crisis was considered to be beyond doubt.

28   It is hard not to have some sympathy with this view: many Punjabi Muslims seem to look down on Bengalis. I was often told how Bengalis eat their food and given an extravagant demonstration of how Bengalis roll up their sleeves and eat in such a messy way with their hands that the juices run right up their arms. Other Punjabis watching would be convulsed in mirth and would provide further unflattering accounts of Bengalis.

29   Lawrence was a Governor of the Punjab, who planted exotic trees which he had collected in an extensive garden. Now it is called 'Jinnah's Garden', and the road on which it is situated has become the 'royal road of the Great Leader' (i.e. Jinnah) instead of being The Mall.

30   In 1.5.2, I pointed to the difficulty of assessing the claims of the
      Christians that they are discriminated against because of their
      religion in Pakistan. However, the existence or not of special
      problems for Christians in Pakistan is not as relevant here as the
      way the Christians perceive their position in Pakistan, for their
      interpretation has important consequences for their behaviour
      and their attitudes towards their migration to Britain.
31   Garbett and Kapferer, 'Study of labour migration'.
32   See Barth (ed.), *Ethnic Groups and Boundaries*, and Gordon,
      Assimilation in American Life.
33   See R. Ballard, 'Family organisation among the Sikhs in England'
      and 'Family organisation among the Sikhs in Britain', and R.
      Ballard and C.L.M. Ballard, 'Incapsulation'.
34   Here again, Barth is relevant, for he stresses that the cultures
      which are contained within ethnic groups may change, and yet
      the separate groups may remain: while 'Punjabi' culture in Britain
      is not identical to that in Punjab itself, and will probably become
      more different as more children grow up in Britain, this is not
      necessarily relevant to 'assimilation' in the structural sense, for
      the actors may consider themselves to be Punjabi and not British,
      and be treated as 'outsiders' by British people.

Bibliography

Pakistani and Indian naming practices are not consistent: I have references from different sources to Zillurkhan, Zillur Khan and Khan, Zillur, but these are all the same person. I have treated the last name as a surname and included any other names given in the sources: in this case, Khan is treated as the surname.

Ahmad, Aziz (1967). *Islamic Modernism in India and Pakistan, 1857–1964*. Oxford: University Press, for Royal Institute of International Affairs, London.

——— (1969). *An Intellectual History of Islam in India*. Islamic Surveys No. 7. Edinburgh: University Press.

Ahmad, Imtiaz (1973). 'Endogamy and status mobility among the Siddique Sheikhs of Allahabad, Uttar Pradesh', in Imtiaz Ahmad (ed.) (1973).

Ahmad, Imtiaz (ed.) (1973). *Caste and Social Stratification among the Muslims*. Delhi: Manohar Book Service.

Ahmad, Jamil-ud-din (1968). *The Final Phase of the Struggle for Pakistan*, 2nd edn. Anarkali, Lahore: Publishers United, Ltd.

Ahmad, Mustaq (1969). 'Social distance in relation to differential attachment: study of Muslims attitude towards Christians'. Unpublished M.A. thesis, University of Punjab, Lahore.

Akram, Mohammed, and Sarah Leigh (1974). *Where Do You Keep Your String Beds? A Study of Entry Clearance Procedures in Pakistan*. London: Runnymede Trust.

Alavi, Hamza (1972). 'Kinship in West Punjab villages', *Contributions to Indian Sociology*, N.S., No. VI.

Ali, Tariq (1970). *Pakistan: Military Rule or People's Power?* London: Jonathan Cape.

Allen, Sheila (1971). *New Minorities, Old Conflicts*. New York: Random House.

Ansari, Ghaus (1960). *Muslim Caste in Uttar Pradesh*. Lucknow: Eastern Anthropologist.

Ballard, Roger (1971). 'Family organisation among the Sikhs in England'. Unpublished manuscript.

——— (1972–3). 'Family organisation among the Sikhs in Britain', *New Community*, Vol. 2, No. 1.

Ballard, Roger, and C.L.M. Ballard (1972). 'Incapsulation'. Draft unpublished manuscript for S.S.R.C. Research Unit on Ethnic Relations.

Barnes, John (1954). 'Class and committees in a Norwegian island parish', *Human Relations*, No. 7.

211

Bibliography

(1969a). 'Networks and political process', in J. Clyde Mitchell (ed.) (1969).

(1969b). 'Graph theory and social networks: a technical comment on connectedness and connectivity', *Sociology*, Vol. 3.

Barth, Fredrik (1965). *Political Leadership among Swat Pathans.* L.S.E. Monographs in Social Anthropology, 19. London: Athlone Press.

(1966). *Models of Social Organization.* Royal Anthropological Institute, Occasional Papers, No. 23. London.

(1970). 'Economic spheres in Darfur', in A.S.A. Monographs, 6, *Themes in Economic Anthropology*, ed. Raymond Firth. London: Tavistock Publications.

Barth, Fredrik (ed.) (1969). *Ethnic Groups and Boundaries: The Social Organization of Culture Difference.* London: Allen and Unwin.

Beaglehole, J.H. (1967). 'The Indian Christians: a study of a minority', *Modern Asian Studies*, Vol. I, Part 1.

Bhutto, Zulfikar Ali (1969). *The Myth of Independence.* Lahore: Oxford University Press.

Blunt, E.A.H. (1969). *The Caste System of Northern India.* Delhi: S. Chand and Co.

Bott, Elizabeth (1971). *Family and Social Network.* London: Tavistock Publications.

Census of India (1921). Vol. XV: *Punjab and Delhi*, Part 1, report by L. Middleton and S.M. Jacob. Lahore.

Chaudhari, Haider Ali et al. (eds.) (1968). *Pakistan Social Perspectives.* Collected papers of the Pakistan Sociological Association's II, III and IV conferences. Lahore: Pakistan Sociological Association, Department of Sociology, University of Punjab.

Dahya, Badr (1972–3). 'Pakistanis in England', *New Community*, Vol. 2, No. 1.

(1973). 'Pakistanis in Britain: transients or settlers?', *Race*, Vol. 14, No. 3.

(1974). 'The nature of Pakistani ethnicity in industrial cities in Britain', in A.S.A. Monographs, 12, *Urban Ethnicity*, ed. Abner Cohen. London: Tavistock Publications.

Daniel, William W. (1968). *Racial Discrimination in England.* (Based on P.E.P. report.) Harmondsworth: Penguin Books.

Das, Veena (1973). 'The structure of marriage preferences: an account from Pakistani fiction', *Man*, Vol. 8, No. 1.

Dawood, N.J. (trans.) (1968). *The Koran*, 3rd rev. edn. Harmondsworth: Penguin Books.

Deakin, Nicholas (1970). *Colour, Citizenship and British Society.* (Based on E.J.B. Rose et al. (1969).) London: Panther Books.

Desai, Rashmi (1963). *Indian Immigrants in Britain.* Oxford: University Press, for Institute of Race Relations, London.

Dumont, Louis (1972). *Homo Hierarchicus: The Caste System and Its Implications.* London: Paladin.

Dutta, Ratna, and P.C. Joshi (eds.) (1971). *Studies in Asian Social*

Development, No. 1. Asian Research Centre, Institute of Economic Growth. Bombay/New Delhi: Tata McGraw-Hill.

Eglar, Zekiye (1960). *A Punjabi Village in Pakistan.* New York: Columbia University Press.

Eversley, David, and Fred Sukdeo (1969). *The Dependants of the Coloured Commonwealth Population of England and Wales.* Institute of Race Relations Special Series. London.

Faridi, Salma Mussert (1967). 'Purdah observance among the females of Wahdat Colony, Lahore'. Unpublished M.A. thesis, University of Punjab, Lahore.

Garbett, G. Kingsley, and Bruce Kapferer (1970). 'Theoretical orientations in the study of labour migration', *New Atlantis*, Vol. 2, No. 1.

Gardezi, Hassan Nawaz (ed.) (1966). *Sociology in Pakistan.* A Tenth Anniversary Publication. Lahore: Department of Sociology, University of Punjab (New Campus).

Gascoigne, Bamber (1971). *The Great Moghuls.* London: Jonathan Cape.

General Register Office (1969). *Sample Census 1966: Great Britain, Commonwealth Immigrant Tables.* London: H.M.S.O., Tables 1 and 2.

Gopal, Ram (1959). *Indian Muslims: A Political History (1858–1947).* Bombay: Asia Publishing House.

Gordon, Milton M. (1964). *Assimilation in American Life.* New York: Oxford University Press.

Government of Pakistan (1960). *The Second Five Year Plan (1960–65).* Karachi: Planning Commission.

　(1961). *Census of Pakistan,* Vol. I: *Population,* Vol. III: *West Pakistan Tables and Report,* Vol. IV: *Non-agricultural Labour Force,* Census Bulletin No. 5: *Economic Characteristics.* Karachi: Ministry of Home and Kashmir Affairs (Home Division).

　(1963). *Guidelines for the Third Five Year Plan (1965–70).* Karachi: Planning Commission.

　(1970). *Pakistan Economic Survey, 1969–70.* Islamabad: Economic Adviser's Wing, Ministry of Finance.

　(1973). *Evaluation of the First Two Years of the Fourth Five Year Plan (1970–75).* Islamabad: Planning Commission.

Greeley, Andrew M. (1969). *Why Can't They Be like Us?* Pamphlet Series, No. 12. Old Bethpage, N.Y.: Institute of Human Relations Press.

Griffin, Keith B. and A.R. Khan (eds.) (1972). *Growth and Inequality in Pakistan.* London: Macmillan.

Guha, Uma (1965). 'Caste among rural Bengali Muslims', *Man in India,* Vol. 45, No. 2.

Hardy, P. (1972). *The Muslims of British India.* South Asian Studies Series. Cambridge: University Press.

Hashmi, Farrukh (1967). *The Pakistani Family in Britain,* 2nd edn. London: National Committee for Commonwealth Immigrants.

Bibliography

Hashmi, Sultan S. (ed.) (1965). *Pakistan Sociological Studies*. Papers from the first Annual Conference of the Pakistan Sociological Association, Karachi, April 1964. Lahore: Pakistan Sociological Association, University of Punjab.

Hobsbawm, Eric J. (1969). *Industry and Empire*. Pelican Economic History of Britain, Vol. 3. Harmondsworth: Penguin Books.

Inniger, Merlin W. (1963). 'Mass movements and individual conversion in Pakistan', *Practical Anthropology* (May—June).

Jeffery, Patricia M. (1973). 'Pakistani families and their networks in Bristol and Pakistan'. Unpublished Ph.D. thesis, University of Bristol.

Karandikar, M.A. (1968). *Islam in India's Transition to Modernity*. Bombay: Orient Longman.

Khan, F.A. (1969). *Banbhore: A Preliminary Report on the Recent Archaeological Excavations at Banbhore*. Karachi: Department of Archaeology and Museums, Government of Pakistan.

Khan, Mazhar ul Haq (1972). *Purdah and Polygamy*. Peshawar: Nashiran-e-ilm-o-Taraqiyet.

Khan, Zillur (1968). 'Caste and the Muslim peasantry in India and Pakistan', *Man in India*, Vol. 48, No. 2.

Kiernan, Victor G. (1972). *The Lords of Human Kind: European Attitudes towards the Outside World in the Imperial Age*. Harmondsworth: Penguin Books.

Krausz, Ernest (1972). 'Factors of social mobility in British minority groups', *British Journal of Sociology*, Vol. XXIII, No. 3.

Levy, Reuben (1965). *The Social Structure of Islam*. Cambridge: University Press.

Lomas, G.B. Gillian (1973). *Census 1971: The Coloured Population of Great Britain, Preliminary Report*. London: Runnymede Trust.

Lyon, Michael (1973). 'Ethnic minority problems: an overview of some recent research', *New Community*, Vol. 2, No. 4 (Autumn).

Mahajan, V.D. and Savitri Mahajan (1961). *Mughal Rule in India*, 4th edn. Delhi: S. Chand and Co.

Manners, Robert (1965). 'Remittances and the unit of analysis in anthropological research', *South Western Journal of Anthropology*, Vol. 21, No. 3 (Autumn).

Maududi, S. Abul A'la (1967). *Rights of Non-Muslims in Islamic State*, trans. Khurshid Ahmad. Lahore: Islamic Publications.

  (1972). *Purdah and the Status of Women in Islam*, trans. Al-ash'ari. Lahore: Islamic Publications. (Originally published 1939 in Urdu.)

  (1973). *Towards Understanding Islam*, trans. Khurshid Ahmad. Lahore: Islamic Publications. (Originally published 1939 in Urdu.)

Mayer, Adrian (1960). *Caste and Kinship in Central India: A Village and Its Region*. London: Routledge and Kegan Paul.

Mayer, Philip (1962). 'Migrancy and the study of African towns', *American Anthropologist*, Vol. 64.

  (1971). *Townsmen or Tribesmen: Conservatism and the Process of*

214

Urbanization in a South African City, 2nd edn. Cape Town: Oxford University Press.

Misra, Satish C. (1964). *Muslim Communities in Gujarat: Preliminary Studies in Their History and Social Organization*. London: Asia Publishing House.

Mitchell, J. Clyde (1969). 'The concept and use of social networks', in J. Clyde Mitchell (ed.) (1969).

Mitchell, J. Clyde (ed.) (1969). *Social Networks in Urban Situations: Analyses of Personal Relationships in Central African Towns*. Manchester: University Press, for Institute of Social Research, University of Zambia.

Moon, Penderel (1961). *Divide and Quit*. London: Chatto and Windus.

Moore, F.V. (1964). *Christians in India*. New Delhi: Publications Division, Ministry of Information and Broadcasting, Government of India.

Morrish, Ivor (1971). *The Background of Immigrant Children*. London: Allen and Unwin.

Mujeeb, M. (1967). *The Indian Muslims*. London: Allen and Unwin.

Myrdal, Gunnar (1968). *Asian Drama: An Enquiry into the Poverty of Nations*. Harmondsworth: Penguin Books.

Neill, S. (1954). *Under Three Flags*. New York: Friendship Press.
(1970). *The Story of the Christian Church in India and Pakistan*. Grand Rapids, Mich.: William B. Eerdmans Publishing Co.

Oakley, Robin (ed.) (1968). *New Backgrounds: The Immigrant Child at Home and at School*. Oxford: University Press, for Institute of Race Relations, London.

Office of Population Censuses and Surveys (1973). *Census 1971. England and Wales. County Report (Gloucestershire)*. London: H.M.S.O.

Patterson, Sheila (1965). *Dark Strangers: A Study of West Indians in London*. Harmondsworth: Penguin Books.
(1969). *Immigration and Race Relations in Britain 1960−67*. Oxford: University Press, for Institute of Race Relations, London.

Paul, J.D. Saveriroyan (1932). *A Survey of the Indian Christian Community*. Palamcottah: Palamcottah Printing Press.

Paul, Rajaiah D. (1952). *The Cross over India*. London: S.C.M. Press.

Pehrson, Robert N. (1966). *The Social Organization of the Marri Baluch*, compiled and analysed by Fredrik Barth. Viking Fund Publications in Anthropology, No. 43. Chicago: Aldine Publishing Co.

Pettigrew, Joyce (1972). 'Some observations on the social system of the Sikh Jats', *New Community*, Vol. 1, No. 5.

Philpott, Stuart B. (1968). 'Remittance obligations, social networks and choice among Montserratian migrants in Britain', *Man*, Vol. 3, No. 3.
(1973). *West Indian Migration: The Montserrat Case*. London: Athlone Press.

Pickett, J. Waskom (1933). *Christian Mass Movements in India: A Study with Recommendations*. New York: Abingdon Press.

Bibliography

Pocock, David (1972). *Kanbi and Patidar: A Study of the Patidar Community of Gujarat*. Oxford: Clarendon Press.

Punjab Government (1936). *Punjab District Gazetteers*, Vol. XII, Part B: *Lahore District*. Lahore.

Rauf, Abdur (1970). *West Pakistan: Rural Education and Development*. Honolulu: East—West Center Press, University of Hawaii.

Raza, Muhammed Rafique (1969). *Two Pakistani Villages: A Study in Social Stratification*. Lahore: Punjab University Sociologists Alumni Association, Department of Sociology, University of Punjab.

Rex, John, and Robert Moore (1969). *Race, Community and Conflict: A Study of Sparkbrook*. Oxford: University Press, for Institute of Race Relations, London.

Richmond, Anthony, Michael Lyon, Sylvia Hale and Roy King (1973). *Migration and Race Relations in an English City: A Study in Bristol*. Oxford: University Press, for Institute of Race Relations, London.

Rischin, M. (1967). *The Promised City: New York's Jews 1870—1914*. Cambridge, Mass.: Harvard University Press.

Rose, E.J.B. et al. (1969). *Colour and Citizenship: A Report on British Race Relations*. Oxford: University Press, for Institute of Race Relations, London.

Saifullah-Khan, Verity (1974). 'Purdah in the British situation'. Paper presented at the B.S.A. Conference 1974. (Revised version forthcoming in Explorations in Sociology Series, Vol. VI B: *Dependence and Exploitation: Work and Marriage* (London: Tavistock Publications).)

Sharma, Ursula (1971). *Rampal and His Family*. London: Collins.

Siddiqi, Mohammad Mazheruddin (1969). *Women in Islam*. Lahore: Muhammed Ashraf Darr, for Institute of Islamic Culture, Club Road.

Siddiqui, Kalim (1972). *Conflict, Crisis and War in Pakistan*. London: Macmillan.

Sinha, J.N. (1971). 'Employment magnitudes and prospects in India, Ceylon and Pakistan', in R. Dutta and P.C. Joshi (eds.) (1971).

Sociaal Wetenschappelijk Institut (1969). *Azam Basti (Karachi): Sociological Enquiry and Recommendations for Development Work*. Amsterdam: Vrije Universiteit.

Spear, Percival (1970). *A History of India*, Vol. 2. Harmondsworth: Penguin Books.

Srinivas, M.N. (1962). *Caste in Modern India, and Other Essays*. London: Asia Publishing House.

(1969). *Social Change in Modern India*. Berkeley: University of California Press.

Tayyeb, A. (1966). *Pakistan: A Political Geography*. Oxford: University Press.

Thomas, P. (1964). *Churches in India*. New Delhi: Publications Division, Ministry of Information and Broadcasting, Government of India.

216

Bibliography

Thompson, Marcus (1974). 'The second generation — Punjabi or English?', *New Community*, Vol. 3, No. 3.

Vreede-de Stuers, Cora (1962). 'Mariage préférentiel chez les musulmans de l'Inde du Nord', *Revue sud-est asiatique*.

—— (1965). 'Terminologie de parenté chez les musulmans *ashraf* de l'Inde du Nord', *Anthropologica*, No. 5.

—— (1968). *Parda: A Study of Muslim Women's Life in Northern India*. Assen: Van Gorcum and Co.

Ward, Barbara, Lenore D'Anjou and R.D. Runnalls (eds.) (1971). *The Widening Gap: Development in the 1970s. A Report on the Columbia Conference on International Economic Development, Williamsburg, Virginia, and New York, February 15—21, 1970*. New York: Columbia University Press.

Woodruff, Philip (1971). *The Men Who Ruled India*, 2 Vols. London: Jonathan Cape.

Index

'accommodation', 102–7, 115
actors' perspective, 2, 4, 42, 108, 114–15, 145, 164, 170, 182, 208n4
Ahmad, Mustaq, 40
Ali, Tariq, 18, 19
Allen, Sheila, 83
anglicization, 83, 107–15, 154, 181
'articulation', 85, 90, 93, 103, 115
Ashrafization, 31, 35–8, 107–15, 145, 195n52
assimilation, 5, 82–4, 88, 103, 115, 164–5, 180–1, 210n34

backgrounds of informants, 5–6, 44, 50–62, 192n31 & n32
Ballard, Roger, 182
Barnes, John, 117–18
Barth, Fredrik, 83–8, 92, 94, 100, 102, 103, 107, 115, 180
Bhatti, A.D., 24
biraderi, 31–5, 119–20, 121, 122, 126–8, 133–6, 144, 195n56
Blunt, E.A.H., 32–3
Bott, Elizabeth, 117, 119
boundary maintenance, 82ff, 100, 103, 107–8, 120, 130, 150
Bristol, Pakistani organizations in, 75, 77, 90, 93, 94, 104, 105, 132, 150; Pakistani women in, 69, 78–9, 104, 201n32

Christians, attitudes to Britain, 57, 150, 151–2, 154, 159–60, 162, 165, 171, 174, 176–7, 180; attitudes to migration, 57, 149, 153–4, 174–82; attitudes to Muslims, 57, 74, 77, 149, 151, 153–4, 157–9, 162, 165, 173, 174, 177; attitudes to Pakistan, 40–3, 57, 58, 59, 62, 149, 151, 162, 170–7, 178–9; attitudes to West Indians, 156, 159; plans, 57, 58, 59, 62, 67, 68, 162, 163, 166, 178–80; in Pakistan, 38–43, 198n86
colonialism, 1–4, 12

Dahya, Badr, 46, 48, 63, 81, 108, 109, 141, 142, 145, 163
Deakin, Nicholas, 49, 50
dependants of migrants, *see under* migrants
Desai, Rashmi, 103
diet, in Pakistan, 25, 168, 194n45; of of informants in Bristol, 77, 90–1, 99, 109, 151–3
discrimination, 41–2, 80–1, 89, 115, 149, 154–5, 171, 203n16, 210n30
divorce, 9–11, 31
dowry, 10–11, 27, 34–5, 96, 114, 126, 136, 189n6
dress, in Pakistan, 26–31, 168; of informants in Bristol, 98, 110–13, 151–3
Dumont, Louis, 32, 33

education, in Pakistan, 20–3, 60, 191n16, 192–3nn32–5; of girls in Pakistan, 21, 61–2, 192n32 & n33; of informants' children in Bristol, 76–8, 90, 103, 105, 107, 113, 119, 179–80; attitudes to co-education, 77, 105, 106, 107
employment, in Pakistan, 18–20, 41, 60–1, 191n22 & n23; of women in Pakistan, 20, 28, 61–2, 168; under-employment and unemployment in Pakistan, 19; of informants in Bristol, 73–5, 90, 103–4; of Pakistani women in Bristol, 78, 104; attitudes to work in Bristol, 5, 51, 57, 103–4, 106, 107; relationships at work in Bristol, 74–5, 103, 119, 129, 131
ethnic boundaries, 5, 82ff, 146, 154, 162
ethnic signals, 84–8, 154–5
ethnocentrism, 1–5, 115
Eversley, David and Fred Sukdeo, 48
exchange rates, viii, 65, 143, 202n40

fieldwork, 70–3, 163, 206n20, 207n12

219

Index

DATE DUE

21/11/76			